CW00553783

One Man in His Time

Also by Xan Fielding

The Stronghold: An Account of the Four Seasons in the White Mountains of Crete

Corsair Country: The Diary of a Journey Along the Barbary Coast

Hide and Seek: Special Operations in Enemy-Occupied Crete

The Money-Spinner: A History of the Monte Carlo Casino

Best of Friends: The Brenan-Partridge Letters (ed.)

One Man in His Time

The Life of Lieutenant-Colonel
NLD ('Billy') McLean, DSO

Xan Fielding

MACMILLAN
LONDON

Copyright © Xan Fielding 1990

All rights reserved. No reproduction, copy or transmission
of this publication may be made without written permission.
No paragraph of this publication may be reproduced, copied
or transmitted save with written permission or in
accordance with the provisions of the Copyright Act 1956
(as amended). Any person who does any unauthorised act
in relation to this publication may be liable to criminal
prosecution and civil claims for damages.

First published 1990 by
MACMILLAN LONDON LIMITED
4 Little Essex Street London WC2R 3LF
and Basingstoke

Associated companies in Auckland, Delhi, Dublin, Gaborone,
Hamburg, Harare, Hong Kong, Johannesburg, Kuala Lumpur,
Lagos, Manzini, Melbourne, Mexico City, Nairobi, New York,
Singapore and Tokyo

ISBN 0–333–48047–3

A CIP catalogue record for this book is available from the British Library

Typeset by Macmillan Production Limited,
4 Little Essex Street, London WC2

Printed and bound in Great Britain by
Billing and Sons Limited, Worcester

And one man in his time plays many parts . . .

As You Like It, II. vii. 142

Contents

List of Plates		ix
Preface		xi
1	The Making of the Man	1
2	The Born Leader	11
3	The Student of Intrigue	25
4	The Irregular Warrior	32
5	The Oriental Traveller	53
6	The Neophyte Civilian	69
7	The Parliamentary Candidate	82
8	The Honourable Member	97
9	McLean of the Yemen	130
10	The Scarlet Pimpernel	156
11	The Unofficial Under-Secretary	170
12	The Unrepentant Patriot	196
References		209
Bibliography		215
Index		217

List of Plates

Billy in his mother's arms.

Billy's father.

Billy with his brother Gillian.

Lance-Corporal McLean, adjutant's orderly, Sandhurst.

Lieutenant McLean with his two operational centre sergeants and two Abyssinian patriots.

Major McLean with Albanian partisans.

Lieutenant-Colonel McLean with pony and falcon in Sinkiang.

Billy and Daška marry in Rome.

On honeymoon in Sicily.

The newly-weds with Daška's mother.

The parliamentary candidate.

Taking cover with fellow journalists in a ditch near Algiers.

Entertaining Soviet VIPs in Scotland.

Billy, while in Yemen with the royalist forces.

Prince Abdurrahman bin Yahya, his nephew Iman al-Badr, Billy, and Said.

Ahmed al-Shamy, the Yemeni foreign minister.

With Daška at La Guardia.

Billy towards the end of his life.

Snorkling with his brother-in-law, Vane.

Preface

The brass plate on the entrance to the large house in Zamalek
bore the four capital letters TARA. A passer-by might well have
wondered how the lovely forsaken name of the ancient wooden
strongtown of high kings of Ireland had come to be preserved in
the city of the pharaohs in the middle of the war. The names of the
inmates inscribed below it might well have puzzled him too: Princess
Dnieper-Petrovsk, Lord Pintpot, the Marquess of Whipstock, Lord
Rakehell, Mr Jack Jargon, the Hon. Rupert Sabretache, Sir Eustace
Rapier, Lord Hughe Devildrive. How could he have known that these
concealed the respective identities of a refugee Polish countess, Sophie
Tarnowska, and a number of British officers: Arnold Breene, David
Smiley, Paddy Leigh Fermor, Billy Moss, Rowly Winn, Billy McLean,
and myself? I forget which of us – I know it wasn't I – adopted the name
and invented the pseudo-Regency appellations, but I'm pretty sure it
was Paddy who chose Jack Jargon (Byron's 'gigantic guardsman') as
an alias for Billy Moss, a six-foot-plus captain in the Coldstream. The
rest of the facetiously snobbish *noms de guerre* were probably mutually
bestowed or – suitably, we hoped – self-arrogated.

This hoax reflected our communal mood, which verged, to say
the least, on the romantic. We were all of us young, hale and hearty
– no other cliché could have described us more succinctly. We were
all engaged on clandestine skulduggery. Tara was the pleasure-dome
(Sophie, its chatelaine, our *princesse lointaine*) to which we used to
repair on leave from our various Balkan fastnesses. 'Life at Tara', a
visitor observed, 'was luxurious rather than comfortable. Sometimes
there were lavish dinners. Sometimes there was only bread and cheese.
In principle, there were hot baths for all. But sometimes there were no
baths at all because vodka was being made in one of them . . . Tara's
evening parties were gay (in the literal sense of the word), but more
surprising were its breakfasts. I went there once in the middle of
the morning to find half a dozen young officers in dressing-gowns

breakfasting around Sophie's bed. She reclined on the pillows armed with a cavalry sword and used it to make sure they kept their distance.'

But we were seldom all to be found in Tara's halls at the same time – our work lay in different countries and did not necessarily synchronise – and so it was not until early 1944 that I first met Billy McLean, recently returned from his first mission to enemy-occupied Albania. This would have impressed me more had I not myself just spent two years on similar duties in occupied Crete – his experience was simply something we had in common. What did impress me, though, was his personality. 'O, young Lochinvar is come out of the west' would have sprung to mind if I had thought of it at the time; in fact it occurred to me only in retrospect, but is no less appropriate.

He struck me as a human epitome of cavalry dash and swagger, even though he had long ago exchanged his steed for a parachute. He was tall and slim, fair-haired and debonair, languid to the point of indolence, with conventional good looks that were far above the average and an elegance that stopped just short of foppishness. But, as I soon discovered, this charming and lackadaisical façade concealed a toughness of steel, great powers of physical endurance, and a needle-sharp intelligence. On second thoughts, then, he appeared to me to step straight out of the pages of *Greenmantle* – Sandy Arbuthnot come to life. In the words of the fictional Sir Walter Bullivant, 'He rode through Yemen. . . . He's a blood-brother to every kind of Albanian bandit. And he also used to take a hand in Turkish politics.' At the time of our meeting Billy had already proved himself in Turkey and Albania, and also in Abyssinia; his deeds in the Yemen were still to come.

But although he had many of the attributes of a Buchan hero, he was far from a traditional stereotype. His mental acuity went hand in hand with an almost feminine sensitivity and an unusual degree of intuition. Enver Hoxha, the guerrilla leader who was to become Albania's first postwar dictator, remarked on his 'intelligent blue eyes, with the look of a savage cat about them' and also described them as 'gleaming like those of a fox'. But what I most noticed in them was the sort of expression that maddens schoolmasters and drives senior officers to apoplectic frenzy – a mixture of muted insolence and mockery which he used with great effect. Sometimes his gaze could be disconcerting and direct, boring into one's brain like a lama's third eye, as though to penetrate one's innermost thoughts and passions. At other times, as though trying to conceal his own thoughts or for fear of betraying a secret, he would lower his lids and assume an evasive, rather furtive demeanour, especially when he adopted – half seriously, half in jest – a posture of exaggerated security-consciousness. On such occasions we used to tease him – 'Billy, why can't you even say, "Pass the salt" without looking over your shoulder?' – at which, accomplished swordsman that he was, he would smilingly acknowledge the hit. As a matter of fact he was no more security-minded, and no less, than anyone else in Tara. All of us, with our sense of belonging to an élite, affected to scorn the rules and regulations that applied to lesser military fry, and considered the admonitory maxims posted up in barrack-rooms and messes ('Even walls have ears.' 'Careless talk costs lives.') beneath our notice. Tara's walls, to us, were earless and, provided our talk was amusing, we little cared if it was careless.

Alas, Cairo didn't last for ever. The call of duty and also, for my part at least, a dwindling bank balance (two years' back pay soon dissolved among Middle Eastern fleshpots) despatched us back to our respective commands. In due course all our brother officers likewise dispersed. Tara closed down. And a full year passed before I saw Billy again, this time in Claridge's in London, where each of us had secured a temporary berth. The war in Europe was coming to an end and many of us who had operated in the Balkans now had our eyes fixed on the jungles of the Far East. Our stepping-stone or springboard was a training camp in Ceylon, where Billy and I found ourselves reunited for a while; but soon we went our separate ways again. I arrived sedately at the fabulous court of Cambodia and he, more adventurously, disappeared over the Himalayas.

After the war our paths seldom crossed. We lived in different countries and in different intellectual worlds. News of him would filter through from time to time and occasionally we met. The enduring bond of friendship forged by comradeship-in-arms made these encounters seem less fortuitous and less rare than they really were; it was as though we had seen each other no less recently than the day before instead of after a gap of a decade. Advancing years and grizzling hair did nothing to impair our relationship; to me he was always the Billy I had known at Tara and I hope he still saw me in the same context. Rumours of his postwar activity endowed him in my eyes with an aura of mystery, on which he carefully shed no light. Paddy Leigh Fermor, who saw him as infrequently as did I, has described his reaction to our probing questions: 'Back in London, in discreet corners of club-land, he would enlarge on Central Asian mores and the various Turkish dialects. When one said, "Yes, Billy, but what were you *really* up to?", a wide silent smile would bisect his face, anomalously accompanied by an oddly youthful blush.'

This book, I hope, will provide an answer, however inadequate and incomplete. Billy should have written it himself; when I last saw

him he told me he was going to. If he had, T. E. Lawrence would
have had to look to his laurels. But there, he didn't; and instead I
had the honour and pleasure of being asked by his estate to make
what I could of his monumental archives. He was clearly a compulsive
recorder. Everything he noticed (and he noticed a lot) was duly jotted
down, but seldom *in extenso*; the notes he left are mostly memoranda,
enough to jog his own memory – and to make his biographer's head
spin. He kept diaries, but with tantalising irregularity; I found myself
constantly bemoaning the number of blank pages compared to those
he had filled. He was also an avid collector and preserver of letters,
pamphlets, invitation cards and visiting cards, bills, catalogues and
menus, not to mention secret reports which he kept, with typical
insouciance, in breach of regulations. If all these documents were
tinsel, they would fill the nests of every jackdaw in the world – at
least that is what I sometimes felt as I worked my way, like a mouse
in a grocer's shop, through the ranks of box-files which were put at
my disposal.

On these I have relied almost exclusively; the other sources of
which I have availed myself are acknowledged in the References.
But even this mass of material furnished no more than the bare
bones of my narrative. To flesh it out, I have drawn on further
information provided by some of Billy's relatives and by the friends
and associates who knew him for a longer time and more intimately
than I did. They too are acknowledged in the References, but I
should also like to give special thanks to the following: His Royal
Highness Prince Abdurrahman bin Yahya, the Right Honourable
Julian Amery PC MP MC and Lady Catherine Amery, His High-
ness Prince Asfa-Wossen Asserate, the Honourable Hugh Astor,
Sir Richard Bayliss KCVO and Lady Bayliss, Caroline Cabrera,
Marina Cobbold, His Royal Highness Major-General the Prince
of Condé, Simon Courtauld, Gordon Etherington-Smith CMG, the
Honourable Alan Hare MC, Sir Stephen Hastings MC, Dr David
Hay, Hugh Henderson, Miles Hildyard MBE MC, Vane Ivanović,
Countess Boriska Karolyi, Peter Kemp DSO, Alexander and Doris
Kennedy, Tessa Kennedy, Lord Lovat DSO MC TD JP DL, Patrick
Leigh Fermor DSO OBE, His Majesty King Leka of the Albanians,
Major Colin Mackenzie MBE MC DL, Callum McLean, Katharine
Viscountess Macmillan DBE, Diana Duchess of Newcastle, Brigadier
Patrick Pollock MBE DL, His Excellency Said Ahmed al-Shamy,
Dr Kenneth Sinclair-Lutit, Colonel David Smiley MVO MBE MC,
Ihsan Bey Toptani, Colonel the Honourable John Warrender MC,
Peter Winter.

This list does not include the name – I have purposely kept it apart – of the source to whom I am most indebted. I refer to Billy's widow Daška, to whom I dedicate this book with affection, diffidence and gratitude.

X.F.

1 *The Making of the Man*

Billy McLean could not have had a more romantic pedigree. He was a direct descendant of Gilleoin na Tuaighe, 'Gillean of the Battle-Axe' – namefather of the Macleans, the 'Sons of Gillean' – who lived in Argyll around 1240 and who traced his own ancestry back to the founder of the Kingdom of Lorn (*c.* 490) through Cuduilig, Abbot of Lismore, and Sean Duhhgall of Sgoinne, 'Old Dugald of Scone', sometimes identified with the 'just and venerable man' who in 1125 was appointed Arbiter of Fife by King David I.

Further Celtic names, which for the sake of simplicity I give in their English translation, reverberate down the centuries: Lachlan the Crafty of Duart, Chief of Clan Gillean, who in 1366 kidnapped the Lord of the Isles after boarding his galley in the Sound of Mull and then married the lord's daughter Marie, 'by her own inclination of yielding'; Red Hector of the Battles, who raided Dublin with his fleet and was mortally wounded at the Battle of Harlaw in 1411 by Sir Alexander Irvine of Drum, whom he himself slew in the combat; Lachlan the Big-Bellied, who after the fight at Lochaber in 1429 was taken prisoner by King James I and confined in Tantallan Castle; Neil of the Thumbs, who fought at the Battle of Bloody Bay in 1486, earning his nickname by the multitude of thumbs he lopped off opponents try-ing to board his galley; and his grandson Neil McLean of Ross, whose branch of the clan became known as 'the Race of the Iron Sword'.

Latter-day McLeans were cast in the same warrior mould. Sir Harry Aubrey de Vere ('Kaid') Maclean, though only a distant relative, might have served Billy as a model. Born in 1848, he joined the army and soldiered in Canada, Bermuda and Gibraltar, where he retired at the age of twenty-eight. But his military career was not ended. He accepted an appointment from Sultan Mulay Hassan as drill instructor to the Moroccan army. He learnt to speak Arabic fluently and was very popular with his men, to whom he was always considerate though he could be firm enough on occasion; of powerful physique, he was able

1

to deal summarily with insubordinate individuals. Having won the sultan's confidence, he accompanied the court wherever it went, visiting all the chief towns, including Tafilet, a city then barred to Europeans. In 1892 he was entrusted with the command of a force engaged in suppressing an insurrection of the Anjera tribe. At the same time he acted as Britain's unofficial agent to the sultan's court, and incurred a reputation for Machiavellian intrigue. In 1907 he was kidnapped and held to ransom by the rebel Sherif Raisuli, and endured seven months of hardship and tedium before being released. His detention undermined his health and in 1909 he resigned, and died in Tangier eleven years later.

Among Billy's forebears there were also many merchant adventurers. In 1820 a certain twenty-two-year-old Gillean Maclaine embarked for Java to seek his fortune. He was travelling in the wake of several others of that name (no matter how it was spelt) who since the sixteenth century had established trading posts in the East Indies, competing for supremacy with the Dutch. In those days commerce and the sword went hand in hand; trade followed the pike; and the rivalry of the two great seafaring nations was intense. But by the time our Gillean Maclaine turned up, peace had been established and together with his friend Edward Watson, a year younger than himself, he founded a mercantile house in Batavia which until 1964, the year it was dissolved, still bore their joint names. Billy's grandfather, Neil McLean, the son of a wealthy shipowner and sea captain, served many years in the family firm and so did his own son, Neil Gillean, one of five brothers, affectionately known as 'Neffie'.

When World War I broke out, Neffie went back to England and was commissioned into the Royal Artillery. On leave in London he fell in love with a glamorous young VAD* called Audrey Kearns. They married and in due course produced the first of two sons, born on 28 November 1918 and christened Neil Loudon Desmond – he was not called Billy until much later, but to avoid confusion I shall continue, as I started, to refer to him by this name. Billy's father did not have a distinguished war record – he entered the army as a subaltern and left it in the same rank – but he was highly successful as a businessman; when he resigned from Maclaine Watson & Co., in 1922, at the age of forty-three – a premature retirement due to his wife's unwillingness to live in Java – his personal fortune amounted to £2 million (roughly £80 million in today's terms).

---

* A member of the Voluntary Aid Detachment, responsible for the care of sick and wounded servicemen.

This was just as well, for she turned out to have very expensive tastes.

Audrey's mother had a name that was subsequently known world-wide, being the same as that of the delightful film actress who married Prince Rainier of Monaco. But they were not closely related, if at all. The older Grace Kelly, Billy's grandmother, married an Irishman called Patrick Kearns – a skeleton in the cupboard if ever there was one. At some stage in his life he got into trouble – rumours of murder even are associated with him – and never came back from British Guiana, where he was living at the time of Audrey's birth. A veil of mystery thus shrouds her antecedents.

There could be no greater contrast in character between the extravagant young flapper, seemingly without a thought in her head other than the pursuit of pleasure, and the easygoing, pipe-smoking middle-aged millionaire who indulged her every whim. But they had many inclinations in common. For both of them, sport and society took precedence over intellectual activity or artistic endeavour, though she appreciated painting that was not too avant-garde and developed a liking for antique furniture. They were also both sticklers for conven-tion, and enemies to any eccentricity that was not socially acceptable. She herself, however, affected an exotic mien which bordered on the ostentatious and which she would not have countenanced in others. Her pet dog was, typically, a Borzoi; her car was – what else? – a Rolls; and she often flaunted a hawk on her wrist.

They had a house in London, 7 Cleveland Row, St James's; another in Nottinghamshire, the Manor House at Oxton near Newark-on-Trent, and counterparts in Scotland as well: 12 Randolph Crescent, Edinburgh; and, for grouse-shooting, deer-stalking and salmon-fishing, Glencalvie, a 17,000-acre estate in Ross-shire. It was in these varied surroundings that Billy and his brother Gillian, born two years after him, were brought up.

The boys were familiar with saddle, rod and gun at a very early age, and in time to come adept in the use of all three. Billy hunted for the first time, with the Blackmore Vale, in 1924; and was blooded with the Cottesmore in 1927. His schooling – first at West Hill Park in Hampshire, then at Eton – interrupted his favourite sport, but he continued to hunt in the holidays. This was the one enthusiasm he shared with his mother, an outstanding and intrepid horsewoman, with whom he was otherwise at variance.

No schoolboy likes his parents to be out of the ordinary and his mother's rather obvious glamour embarrassed him. Though she herself may have wished to pass for a latter-day Catherine the Great or an avatar of Empress Elizabeth of Austria, to him she merely seemed to be showing off. He was conscious of her pretentiousness long before he was old enough to be familiar with the word. Once, when he had invited a schoolfriend to Glencalvie, she said she would personally cook them something very special and called it by some grand French name. It turned out to be rice pudding. Another time, having promised to take him and a friend out to lunch on a half-holiday, she kept them waiting till four in the afternoon, when she arrived in her Barker-bodied Phantom I Rolls-Royce, with the chauffeur in the front and two hawks perched on a bar in the back. She alighted, more concerned with her birds than the boys' hunger; she thought the hawks might like to stretch their wings. So she unleashed them, flew them from her gloved hand, and cast out the remains of the partridge she had had for lunch at Claridge's as a lure; then she retrieved them, climbed into the car again and drove straight back to London, and the boys missed their tea as well as the midday meal.

Aware of her selfishness and disregard for others, Billy also resented her reminding him all the time to keep himself neat and tidy. Not that he was as grubby as most small boys; in fact a precocious elegance was evident in the studied negligence he affected. For all that, in his mother's eyes he could never shine enough – she no doubt wanted to see in him a reflection of herself – and every letter urged him to be sure to brush his hair, clean his teeth and cut his nails. These exhortations came from all over the world – for she enjoyed travelling, especially in luxury – and the envelopes with Cuban, Mexican, Romanian and Turkish stamps instilled a wanderlust which inspired Billy all his life. He certainly could not have acquired it from his father, whose only ventures abroad were on his own to Monte Carlo for two weeks a year.

Though his mother often treated Billy off-handedly, she sometimes, surprisingly, wrote as from one adult to another. A letter from the Ritz in Paris, 'my spiritual home', describes one of her regular shopping forays: 'I have not bought much – one ensemble from Lanvin, blue with a fuchsia top, and a fuchsia three-quarter coat . . . one turquoise-blue and dark-brown half-country day frock from Goupy . . . one evening blouse in gold lamé, three hats, lots of shoes . . . ' What a fifteen-year-old English schoolboy was supposed to make of this, there's no telling.

Billy's own introduction to the Continent was a summer holiday in Hungary, where his father had founded, and his paternal uncle Godfrey managed, a large trading company exporting eggs and poultry to Scotland. In those days country estates in Central Europe were still run on feudal lines, which appealed to Billy's sense of continuity. He was allowed and even encouraged to ride the local race-horses, and enjoyed going out in the high-wheeled horse-drawn wagonettes peculiar to the region, from which his mother flew her hawks at herons and wild geese, hares and pheasants.

She never went to Hungary without her birds, which she kept in her bedroom, feeding them herself and making sure they regurgitated daily. She also brought her horses and a retinue of grooms and servants, including an Indian bearer. She had reason to be grateful to the latter when one day she released her favourite hawk a little too late for it to intercept a flock of geese she had chosen for a quarry. As it climbed to gain height, the whole flock gathered speed and disappeared over an acacia wood. Her hawk also disappeared in pursuit. She was already bewailing its loss when the Indian tied a pigeon wing to a piece of string and whirled it round his head, screaming all the time at the top of his voice. This did the trick. A speck presently appeared in the sky and the hawk was soon back on its owner's wrist.

A near neighbour was the legendary Countess Francesca ('Fanny') Karolyi, who had an immense fortune, and several houses in Budapest and in the country, but preferred to live in a fishing village on the Danube, not far from Esztergom, in a strange agglomeration of peasant cottages which she had restored and linked together. Billy wrote an account of a visit there, and a description of his hostess, the opening lines of which curiously echo the tone of his mother's letter from Paris.

She was dressed in a dark-coloured bodice with a sort of cream-coloured, perhaps originally white shirt, dyed by much use, sleeves with the edges embroidered with red peasant work, a large dark-coloured skirt and hundreds of peasant petticoats underneath, bare legs and no shoes. Her hair was fluffed out like one of Gauguin's South Sea islanders. She is known in the village as Sunflower. I think a few lines are needed to explain the floral principle of the household. The old countess (everyone refers to her as old but in reality she cannot be much over 50) dislikes being called Your Excellency or Your Ladyship, but also dislikes being called by her Christian name by the village people. So she adopts the name of a flower – Sunflower. All the other ladies who live with her are Roses – Persian Rose, Chinese Rose, English Rose, York Rose, etc. All the girls are flowers and all the men are trees. To become a Rose one must work a thousand hours for the good of the village children. Everyone refers to each other by their floral names – 'Hello, Red Rose, have you seen White Rose?' 'No, I haven't, Persian Rose . . . etc., etc.'

After lunch we went into the verandah sitting-place. There, the old countess was lying down on a peasant couch, smoking a strong cigar and feeding pigeons. The table by her side was covered with an array of ashtrays, all filled with the stumps and ashes of cigars. Her bed was covered with corn. After about five minutes of conversation the old lady threw a table napkin at me – it was much soiled and scrubbed into a dirty and untidy ball – exclaiming as she did so, 'Foot!' I, with a lightning quickness which would have done anyone credit, answered, 'Ball!', which apparently was right, as the idea was to finish off the first half of a double-barrelled word. This little game went on for about ten minutes – 'Lamp' – 'Shade', 'Tennis' – 'Court', etc., each time throwing the so-called ball at the person who was to answer the second half of the word.

When this exciting little game had got a trifle boring, the old countess suddenly told me to say something. After much hesitation and raising of eyebrows in a questioning expression, I remarked that the table was very small. She replied, 'Yes, so it can never fall.' The idea apparently was to make a line rhyming with the preceding statement as quickly as possible. This little game only lasted about two minutes, happily. Then the old lady said, 'I wish all you people would leave; I want to sleep.' So we were hurriedly and unceremoniously shooed away.

One wonders how Billy's English master would have marked this composition. Alpha-plus for observation, I hope.

Billy's academic record at Eton was not spectacular. 'Idle' figures prominently in his reports. But 'lacking in purpose' would have been more accurate. As soon as he began to master a subject, he lost interest. It was the same with games. Once he had reached a certain standard he couldn't be bothered to improve, and so he didn't really mind when heart trouble – 'nothing serious, just a murmur', was the school doctor's diagnosis – debarred him from football field and cricket pitch: he had never thought very highly of 'the flannelled fools at the wicket or the muddied oafs at the goal'. But fencing was an exception; it appealed to his swashbuckler side, and eventually he captained the school team, showing great skill not only in cut, thrust and parry but also in organising matches that gave him and his fellow *sabreurs* the excuse for a night out in London.

Doodles in the margins or on the flyleaf of grammars and primers often give a clue to youthful characters and interests. Billy used to fill them with Scottish coats of arms, delineated in great detail. Though a model son of the English establishment in manner and appearance, he was deeply conscious of his Highland background and wrote from Eton to the Court of the Lord Lyon, Edinburgh, to make sure that his own arms were recorded. What could have prompted him, though, to jot down in an exercise book every verse of the popular song '*Tout va très bien, madame la marquise*'? Membership of the Eton Archaeological Society affords another clue to his extracurricular activities, and when he was asked by one of his school friends whether he had a hobby, he replied, 'Yes – collecting old silver.'

Central Asia also held a romantic fascination for him. Poring over an atlas, he would embark in imagination on the golden journey to Samarkand or retrace Marco Polo's route to the court of Kublai Khan. The works of Sven Hedin and Aurel Stein would set him dreaming of the departed glories of Bokhara or of the long-lost treasures of the sand-buried cities of Khotan; and the mere sound of certain place-names – Hindu Kush and Karakoram and Pamir – was enough to send him soaring in his mind's eye to the Roof of the World. One day, he vowed, he would visit these regions in reality.

The year 1936 was a testing one. Billy was destined for the army, his mother having decreed that a military career was more gentlemanly than mercantile activity. He sat for his school certificate, gaining credits in Scripture, History, Latin and French, and a few months later passed into Sandhurst, 106th out of 170. This was not a brilliant achievement and, suddenly aware of his deficiencies, he drew up a plan for serious reading (a habit he was to maintain throughout his life). Balzac and St Simon figure on his list of authors, and he pursued his research into Clan history with first editions from an antiquarian bookseller, William Brown of Edinburgh, with whom he opened an account. He continued with his fencing, went shooting whenever he could and perfected his horsemanship, riding in point-to-points and often winning them.

He would never have managed on the allowance his father gave him had his parents not let him use their own accounts with various shops and restaurants. He was thus able to order more or less whatever he wanted, and to take his friends out to dinner in London whenever he liked. He was a generous host, judging by what he signed for at his favourite restaurant, Boulestin's. 'Surely I couldn't have dined there so often,' said his absent-minded father on being presented with the bills. 'You must have done, Father,' said Billy firmly.

He passed out of Sandhurst with a very satisfactory mark, was commissioned into the Royal Scots Greys, and reported for duty at Redford Cavalry Barracks, Edinburgh, in the late summer of 1938.

His regiment was then on active service in Palestine and he was posted to the 'Details' Squadron, which served as a rear headquarters and training unit. For several weeks he and a batch of other newly joined recruits were put through an intensive course on the square and in the riding school, practising fast drill on foot and mounted arms drill with sword and rifle, before being accepted as fully fledged regimental officers. Only then was he assigned to normal squadron duties and given command of a troop of thirty men with their horses.

In the spring of 1939 his squadron received orders to embark for overseas to join the regiment. The draft, consisting of about a hundred men with their horses, were given ten days' leave before entraining for Southampton, where they boarded a small and rather old-fashioned troopship for the two weeks' voyage to Haifa. Mount Carmel, rising from the mists of early morning, was Billy's first sight of the Middle East.

Palestine, which had been under British mandate since the end of World War I, was in a state of upheaval. The Arabs were bitterly anti-British on account of the Balfour Declaration* and had been in open and more or less continuous revolt since 1936, when the Higher Arab Committee was formed under the leadership of the Mufti of Jerusalem, who ordered a general strike. Arab trade and work virtually ceased throughout the country, and violence and sabotage increased. Roads were barricaded and trains derailed, and armed bands appeared in the hills. To round them up, the British government mounted a massive military operation and sent in over 20,000 troops, including the 1st Cavalry Division, of which the Scots Greys formed part.

The regiment was stationed in an old-established Jewish settlement near Rehovot, some twenty miles inland from Tel Aviv, where Billy's squadron was allotted its own quarters within the general camp area. He and his brother officers shared an unfurnished requisitioned house; the men were lodged in newly constructed tin-roofed wooden barracks. It was hot and uncomfortable for everyone but especially for the horses, which lived in fly-infested picket lines outside, but the joy of being on active service compensated for these primitive conditions.

In July Billy was detached and posted with his troop to Artuf, a small station further down the line. The accommodation here was even more primitive; he and his men lived in cattle trucks on a siding. But again there were compensations: he now had an independent

---

* On 2 November 1917 the British government had declared its sympathy with Jewish Zionist aspirations in the form of a letter to Lord Rothschild from Foreign Secretary Arthur Balfour.

command, and the responsibility delighted him. His duties were to protect his section of the railway and to flush the local rebels out of their lairs. There were plenty of them in the area but they made their presence felt only at night, by sniping at the post from a safe distance and then vanishing. Day after day Billy set out in pursuit at the head of a mounted patrol, moving from village to village and questioning the inhabitants; they were friendly but too scared of reprisals to give him any help or information. He also reconnoitred the caves in the hills where the bandits were said to be hiding and he often found signs of recent habitation, but his quarry persistently eluded him.

It was a frustrating time, but not wasted. He got on well with the local population and started to learn Arabic, and, taking his cue from the rebels, he also learnt something about irregular warfare. Ordinary regimental duties appealed to him less and less, and he was sorry when his troop was posted back to headquarters. By this time war had been declared and he was all the more impatient to be in action. But it looked as though the Scots Greys were to remain indefinitely engaged on their present task in what now seemed a backwater. He was proud of his regiment and popular with the men, but did not see eye to eye with his commanding officer, a typical unimaginative peacetime soldier, so he went on leave as often as he could – to Syria, to the Lebanon and to Egypt – and kept his eye open for more active employment elsewhere.

In the summer of 1940 he learnt that his brother, who had been badly wounded on the beaches of Dunkirk, had died in hospital. He and Gillian, though much of their lives was spent apart, had been particularly close to each other. Billy went to Eton and Gillian to Bryanston, so they met only during the holidays. Then, after he was posted overseas, Gillian had joined the Cameron Highlanders. In recent years, therefore, they had not seen as much of each other as either of them would have wished and Billy felt the blow all the more keenly. It seemed ironic to him that of the two of them the younger should have died first, having been in action after serving a shorter time. His eagerness to get to grips with the enemy was now strengthened by the urge to avenge his brother's death.

His chance came when he heard that junior officers were needed for the Somaliland Camel Corps, then being hard pressed by the Italians who had invaded British Somaliland. He volunteered, and in due course embarked at Suez in a convoy bound for Berbera, together with a number of other subalterns from the 1st Cavalry Division. Among them was a lieutenant in the Blues called David Smiley, with whom he quickly made friends. They looked forward to going into action together, but by the time they reached their destination the Italians had occupied the colony, so there was nothing for it but to sail back to Egypt.

Another opportunity occurred later in the year, when his commanding officer suggested that he might like to go to Abyssinia with five Scots Greys' sergeants to train and command the bands of irregulars who had risen spontaneously in defence of their country. Billy did not have to be asked twice. His departure coincided with New Year's Eve, and at the traditional celebration in the sergeants' mess he distinguished himself by getting through two bottles of neat whisky and dancing a reel on the table before passing out and being put to bed.

2 *The Born Leader*

Abyssinia had been occupied by the Italians for over five years. Mussolini had invaded the country in October 1935 – an utterly cynical act of aggression in total defiance of the League of Nations – and managed to subdue it only by resorting to the most ruthless measures. The regular Abyssinian forces, though heavily outnumbered, badly equipped and untrained in modern warfare, fought valiantly but were finally demoralised by the widespread use of mustard gas sprayed from Italian aeroplanes. In May 1936 Addis Ababa fell; Emperor Haile Selassie, who stayed on until the last moment, was evacuated to England in a British warship; and all organised resistance collapsed. Guerrilla activity continued, however. Bands of patriots went on fighting in the mountains and were still holding out in several parts of the country when the British, who had been held in check on the frontier ever since Italy had entered the war, decided to take the offensive.

The plan was for one column, which included the 5th Indian Division, to advance from the Sudan into Eritrea, while another, composed of South Africans and East Africans, marched into Italian Somaliland from Kenya. At the same time the patriots were to be organised as a cohesive force behind the Italian lines. Haile Selassie had already returned to Africa and was now in Khartum, preparing to hoist the flag of Abyssinia on his native soil; in no time the war drums began to rally the patriots to the imperial standard. Lieutenant-Colonel Orde Wingate was put in command of this miniature army; with a Cromwellian taste for Biblical allusions sharpened by long service in Palestine, he called it 'Gideon Force', since it was to smite the enemy hip and thigh. Several operational centres were formed, each composed of a hundred local recruits, with a British officer and five British NCOs in charge. It was to command one of these units that Billy had been selected.

But first he and his sergeants had to go through a tough sabotage course at the Middle East Commando Depot in Egypt, where they learnt to blow up trains in the approved Lawrence of Arabia manner. The knowledge that the only railway in Abyssinia, from Jibuti to Addis Ababa, had long been out of service did not dampen their ardour for demolition and each morning they happily destroyed longer and longer stretches of track laid out for them to practise on. They also learnt to make booby traps and 'surprise packets' of explosives, which their instructor facetiously told them to address to a suitable recipient. Most of them chose someone obvious, like Hitler or Mussolini, but Billy was amused to see one of his sergeants laboriously labelling one with the name of the Greys' commanding officer.

When the fun and games were over, he boarded a Nile steamer for the first lap of his journey south. He slept out on deck to the sound of the water lapping against the side of the boat and in sight of the full moon shimmering under the desert sky – 'incredibly romantic,' he noted, 'almost to the point of being boring.' The rest of the journey was more prosaic. From Wadi Halfa, where he landed in the early morning, he went to Khartum by train through a landscape of monotonous sand-dunes sizzling under the blow-lamp blasts of a violent *khamsin*, and thence by truck to a nearby camp shared between the British operational personnel and several hundred Abyssinians under training.

At first glance it looked pretty bleak, and worse still on closer examination. The straw hut he was allotted stood at the end of a long room, next to the latrines. It had no door and no carpet, and sand blew in with every gust of wind. The mess, another straw hut little larger than his own, was equally dismal and it reeked of kerosene. The almost uneatable food was gritty with sand and so was the water from the river. The Sudanese attendants should have all been sacked at once – and no doubt would have been had they not also been busy procuring women for the quartermaster. Billy felt it was his duty to put up with the same conditions as his men, but the sybaritic side of his nature sometimes prevailed over the spartan and he occasionally slipped off into the town for a more or less decent meal.

There was no proper training programme. Musketry and the familiar machine-gun drill alternated with long route marches, during which his instinctive sympathy with the Abyssinians developed into genuine affection. He admired their quick gestures and quick minds, their voices pitched high and their souls too, and he soon learnt to deal with their apparently contradictory characteristics: vanity and sensitivity, ferocity and gentleness, loyalty and fickleness. He also started learning Amharic, but since his teacher, a mysterious middle-aged Czech who had lived in Addis Ababa most of his life, was unintelligible in fourteen other languages including English, he found it heavy going; though he enjoyed tussling with the strange syntax whereby, for example, a literal translation of the perfectly simple sentence *Baklo ye-makamatu-saow mata ahun yihidal* would emerge as 'The mule who-riding-man-is having-gone is now a-going.'

At the end of three weeks – high time too, he thought – he was ordered to move forward with his unit across the frontier and link up with the main body of Gideon Force which was in action on the Gojjam heights. Three other operational centres were to move forward at the same time, and their combined numbers added to the confusion of departure. At the last moment an Abyssinian interpreter was attached to each unit, but none of them was properly equipped. No eating utensils, rations, groundsheets or blankets had been issued, yet they were expected to set out on a long march through mountainous country at the height of the rainy season. Billy was not surprised to discover that the officer responsible for local supplies had been drunk for several days.

The journey began by train. The track lay alongside the Blue Nile, and Billy was enchanted by the landscape, particularly the open expanse round the Sennar dam, where the pale blue water was intersected by strips of bright green reeds, followed by a series of crystal-clear pools teeming with duck, geese and snipe. They reached the end of the line at Suki after thirty-six hours and camped out for the night by the river, surrounded by flocks of black and white ibis. Next morning they moved on in a convoy of trucks, bumping for eight hours over the pitted riverside track to Roseiris, a spot as charming and curious as its name, with avenues of magnificent old trees lining the steep banks. The souk, or native market, was thronged with strange-looking fuzzy-haired men, greased from head to toe and naked except for a loincloth, and armed with a weird panoply of swords, spears and battle-axes. This was the last outpost of relative civilisation, so Billy took the opportunity to draw £10* – there had been no arrangements for pay in Khartum – and stocked up at the local store with tinned milk, sugar, salt, coffee, and bottles of whisky and flasks of Chianti.

Next day another bumpy drive brought the convoy to the roadhead at Um-Idla, where they spent the night and then prepared for the onward trek over the border. Each of the centres was issued with a *hamlah* – a string of about a hundred camels – many in poor condition, driven

---

* Almost three weeks' pay for a subaltern, at the then going rate of 10/6d (52.5p) a day.

by hurriedly recruited camel men from the nearby towns, who clearly knew as little about handling the beasts as the British. The first day's march ended in predictable chaos, with Billy's guide losing the way and the whole unit having to pitch camp in the dark. The hobbled camels grazed where they could; their loads were scattered all over the place; piles of machine-guns and crates of Maria Theresa dollars littered the ground; and the camel men made bonfires next to boxes of detonators, high explosive and ammunition. Billy managed to restore some semblance of order and, to avoid worse confusion, decided from then on to move by night and pitch camp at dawn, avoiding the added hardship of trekking in the heat of the day.

He had never ridden a camel before and the unaccustomed gait was a strain on his back to begin with; but after a few days he became used to it and actually enjoyed the movement, even deriving a certain pleasure from the monotonous pace of the *hamlah* itself as it padded along the narrow track which stretched, seemingly without end, through mile after mile of tall bush and scrub. From time to time the tedium and the all but total silence were relieved by a voice at the head of the column breaking into song – a rather haunting melody that seemed to hesitate in mid-air before being taken up by a second voice in the rear and then, after another bewildering pause, by the whole column in unison.

After a week a range of mountains shimmered on the horizon and a week after that the units reached the foot of the steep escarpment leading up to the Gojjam. It took them twenty-four hours more to climb to the top, where they came upon the rear headquarters of the patriot army, including the imperial suite and the Emperor himself who had arrived a month before by the same route. The vast encampment swarmed with a tatterdemalion throng armed with an assortment of weapons. Some were equipped with rifles and uniforms captured or looted from the Italians; others, half-naked, wore broad-brimmed high-crowned hats and brandished spears. Others still, blank-faced and seemingly at a loss, wandered aimlessly about, swigging *talla** from enormous gourds slung round their necks, while messengers with self-important and purposeful expressions scurried hither and thither through the inferno-like atmosphere; it was compounded of the smoke from wood fires, the stench of camel dung and a hubbub of high-pitched voices. At nightfall the eerie sound of native pipes pierced the darkness. As one of Billy's fellow officers remarked, it was probably the strangest scene since Bonnie Prince Charlie crossed

* Local beer, made from fermented grain mixed with herbs.

the Tweed with his Highlanders. 'Yes,' another agreed, 'it's a cross between Peter Pan and the Forty-five.'

At this stage Wingate decided to divide Gideon Force into two. He retained command of the larger, southern part and sent the remainder north on to the high plateau of Begemder, east of Lake Tana. This Northern Force included an operational centre which was then without an officer; its commander had been badly wounded and evacuated. Billy was ordered to take his place and to move off as soon as a mule convoy could be organised. He was sad to relinquish his own centre, for he had come to know and to like his men and he considered his five Greys' sergeants by far the best of the British NCOs; but he welcomed the posting, for it meant the chance of action before it was too late. With the Italians in retreat, he had been dreading the campaign might come to an end before he had fired a shot.

It took him a week of hard trekking in pouring rain to get to the village of Isty, where the officer commanding Northern Force had set up his headquarters. The weekly market was in progress on the day he arrived and he came across several British NCOs buying eggs, honey and other local food to supplement their rations, pockets jingling with Maria Theresa dollars. They seemed utterly demoralised, complaining about their living conditions, and were contemptuous of the Abyssinians; they regarded and treated them as 'Blacks'. It was going to be uphill work, he reflected, to bring them up to his own regiment's standards.

The encampment was camouflaged in dense thickets on the bank of a stream, but Billy had no difficulty in locating it; he had only to follow his nose and ears. The approaches were ankle-deep in horse and mule dung; there were no picket lines and the animals grazed where they wished, while the flies surrounded them in an almost solid curtain. Every tree and every bush concealed a bivouac or an arbour crowded with soldiers and with their wives and womenfolk too, all of them chatting, quarrelling and singing non-stop. Pots and pans as well as rifles and submachine-guns hung from the branches, and boxes of ammunition were stacked dangerously close to the hearthstones of innumerable fires.

Billy's first impression of his commanding officer was not very favourable. He found him lying half-naked on a fur rug in a clearing littered with scraps of paper, dirty plates, flasks of *tej** and

---

* A beverage made from fermented honey but more intoxicating than ordinary mead.

a miscellaneous collection of weapons. His personal appearance –
straggling beard and unkempt hair* – matched his surroundings. But
his conversation was informative as well as entertaining and with a
few well-chosen verbal strokes he was able to put Billy abreast of the
situation.

In addition to Northern Force, which consisted of three operational
centres including Billy's and numbering about 300 in all, there were two
patriot groups in the area. The one, about 700 strong, was commanded
by Fitaurari Birrou, a great territorial magnate and a nobleman in the
old tradition, brave, dignified and kind and, by Abyssinian standards,
entirely unambitious. He was Minister of War at the time of the Italian
invasion and had recently been appointed Governor of Begemder. His
camp was situated less than a mile away. The other belonged to Dedjaz
Danyo, a feudal lord who exercised nominal control over 6000 to 7000
rifles and, though he held no official position, was in effect master
of the whole province. He had established his headquarters on a hill
above Birrou's camp. The two leaders were at loggerheads, and one
of Billy's duties was to keep the peace between them and maintain
daily contact with both.

Birrou's own quarters consisted of two large army tents, which he
had converted into a handsome reception hall and a sleeping apart-
ment; but his men lived in considerable squalor out in the open and
slept wherever a tree or a bush afforded shelter. He was surrounded
by private secretaries, military secretaries, financial secretaries, political secretaries and propaganda secretaries, who seemed to spend most
of their time hanging about their master's tent, flattering superiors,
bullying underlings and spying on one another. They constantly spread
alarmist rumours and were ready to make off at the first sign of danger.
Birrou spoke no English and discussions with him were conducted in
French, in which the commanding officer of Northern Force was not
proficient, so until Billy's arrival liaison with Birrou's retinue had been
restricted, to say the least.

Danyo's entourage, consisting of handsome, well-built Amhara
hillmen, was much more impressive. Their long black hair stood
on end, reminding Billy of the bearskins of a company of Grenadiers
after a parade in the rain, while their knee-breeches and long yellow
shirts recalled woodcut illustrations in *The Canterbury Tales*. All were

---

* Many of the British personnel in Gideon Force grew a Wingate-like beard
and let their hair grow long – Billy himself was to do so later on – not necessarily
in emulation of their eccentric commander but as a protection against flies and
mosquitoes, and also as a symbol of their disregard for army regulations.

heavily armed, though their ammunition belts were often filled with empty cartridge-cases to conceal the lack of live rounds for, unless after a battle, an empty belt revealed that the wearer was too poor to buy ammunition. Except for his hair, which sprang up from his forehead and out from his temples instead of hanging down the back of his neck in ringlets, Danyo himself looked rather like King Charles II. Beneath the smart Italian tunic, still bearing the medal ribbons and regimental insignia of the dead Carabinieri officer from whom he had stripped it, he wore a long silk shirt and, round his waist, a red velvet cartridge belt and pistol holster embroidered with gold. His headquarters consisted of a permanent *tukul*, or native hut, where he and his personal retainers lived, and half a dozen other *tukuls* where his military commanders and sub-chiefs were billeted.

Billy's introductory visit was a formal occasion. Danyo welcomed him on the threshold of his *tukul* with a ceremonial embrace, then, drawing aside the finely woven woollen arras which screened the interior from the eyes of the common soldiers and countrymen massed outside, ushered him in and seated him at a small table next to a sort of dais which served alternately as a throne and a bed. His retinue squatted in order of precedence on leopard-skin rugs spread on the mud floor. Presently some slave girls appeared carrying large wicker baskets filled with cartwheels of millet bread and bowls of red-pepper sauce, which they deposited among the guests. Then slave boys entered staggering under the weight of whole sides of raw meat, to which each guest in turn helped himself, reaching up and cutting off a slice with his own knife before smothering it in the sauce and bolting it down, while still more servants circulated with huge earthenware jars of *tej* and *talla*. The meal took place in silence, and as soon as each guest had eaten and drunk his fill he rose to his feet and according to custom left without a word of thanks to his host or even a salutation.

Danyo had a charming personality and perfect manners; he was also moody, vain, irresolute and incapable of concentration, but, for all his shortcomings, a man to be reckoned with. Northern Force were entirely dependent on him for information, transport and protection. Birrou and his staff even depended on him for their food and were terrified that he might wander off and leave them in the lurch. They therefore allowed him to lie, cheat and baulk every plan; while he on his side appeared to have no intention of doing anything more active than supplying Birrou with *tej* and raw meat. After much persuasion, however, he agreed, but with the utmost reluctance, to go into action and carry out, in conjunction with Billy's centre, a large-scale ambush on the road north of Debra Tabor, where the Italians were still holding out.

There were many delays. Northern Force had no reserve rations, so food supplies had to be bought locally. Then pack mules had to be obtained to carry them and to transport ammunition for two heavy machine-guns, and this took time. But at last, early in April, the long column consisting of Billy's two platoons and a hundred of Danyo's patriots set off on the approach march lasting three days. For the first two the troops advanced swiftly and in reasonably good order, though Billy was perturbed that no scouts or patrols were sent out. But on the third day, as they drew closer to the target, discipline broke down. Danyo himself started the rot by ordering his trumpeter to blow the 'Prince of Dessye's March', a popular patriot tune he had adopted as his personal anthem, and it must have alerted every Italian post in the area. Inflamed by the fanfare, without any attempt at a tactical formation, his men streamed across the road in a disorderly mob. Luckily it was almost dark and they were able to take cover for the night in a thickly wooded valley.

For all his musical braggadocio, Danyo had already lost heart and he kept inventing excuses, even at this late stage, for cancelling the operation: he had insufficient troops; his men refused to fight during Lent; the place chosen for the ambush was unsuitable, and so on. But Billy was adamant and next day, accompanied by one of his sergeants, he went back to the road to make a reconnaissance and choose positions for his two machine-guns. Danyo had refused to join him unless he were allowed to bring his whole force with him – a ludicrous suggestion considering the noise they would have made. That night – again without the help of Danyo or his patriots, who were either too lazy or felt it beneath their dignity to do manual work – Billy and a small detachment of his own troops prepared the demolitions; they dug up a couple of culverts, built two stone walls and filled them with hand-made booby-traps, placed anti-tank mines under the surface of the road and laid an electrically detonated explosive charge under a small bridge. Then he moved up the rest of his men and they settled down for the night.

Early in the morning they heard the noise of vehicles in the distance; then they saw a dozen troop-carrying trucks puffing out clouds of black smoke from the coarse oil of their diesel engines, moving along the road in close formation and so slowly that Billy could hardly resist the temptation to open fire. 'It was like watching a salmon move to take a fly,' he recalled, 'and I had to control the instinct to strike before he had hooked himself.' A few hundred yards further on, the trucks passed out of sight as they moved into the dead ground under the brow of a hill; but Billy knew they would re-emerge when they entered the ambush. He waited in great suspense for this to happen. But minute after minute passed, no vehicle appeared, and the noise of engines grew fainter and finally stopped altogether – the convoy had come to a halt. For a moment he thought that the enemy had smelt a rat, and indeed they may have. But before he could decide what action to take, there was a flash, followed by an ear-shattering explosion, and a column of smoke and rubble spurted high into the air – his senior British sergeant, in position round a bend in the road, had seen the convoy halt and on his own initiative had detonated the explosive charge under one of the leading trucks on the bridge, blowing to kingdom-come the thirty soldiers travelling in it.

At once battle was joined. The enemy – a 300-strong company of Italian-led native levies – poured out of the remaining vehicles and opened fire simultaneously, and the rattle of machine-guns, the crack of rifles and the thud of hand-grenades rose to a crescendo. Billy's forward sections bore the brunt of the counterattack and they would have been overrun had he not ordered them to the rear. Danyo's patriots covered their withdrawal, then in their turn pulled back to a hill overlooking the road from where they were able to keep the enemy pinned down. A stalemate ensued. Desultory fighting continued for the rest of the day, to the sound of small-arms fire broken from time to time by complete silence or punctuated by the boom of cannon from one of the outlying forts round Debra Tabor. Late in the afternoon this artillery fire intensified and the enemy was enabled to withdraw under cover of a creeping barrage, and the battle was over.

'A bit of an anticlimax', was Billy's verdict. But Danyo was already celebrating a victory with such infectious jubilation that Billy had no difficulty in joining in. In fact, their combined forces had not done too badly. Considering the initial intensity of the fighting and its subsequent duration, the number of casualties they suffered – fourteen killed and twenty-three wounded – was relatively small and could almost be discounted when balanced against the experience the survivors had gained. All in all, the operation had been more than just worthwhile.

In the early hours of Easter Sunday the Italians withdrew their troops from the outlying forts, leaving Debra Tabor isolated. To launch a frontal attack against the defences was out of the question (though Danyo, now that he had tasted blood, was all for it) for the town was strongly fortified and garrisoned by a brigade group at full strength and supported by heavy artillery. The Northern Force commander therefore decided to blockade it and to move his unit closer.

By the beginning of May he had established his headquarters in one of the forts which the Italians had just evacuated, with the three operational centres and Birrou's court and Danyo's patriots encamped on the edge of a nearby plateau. There was a most splendid view. 'From the sentry's post in our camp,' Billy recorded, 'I could see the broad plain of Fougara, with its green pastures intersected by countless streams and punctuated by clusters of tall dark trees; beyond these, the yellow sands of the desert and bush, and further off still, range upon range of blue and mauve hills. Far away to the west, I could see the whole of Lake Tana, glistening silver-grey and pale blue, with its dark islands in the centre. It was all so beautiful that I often forgot why I was up here at all.'

Northern Force's task was to block the approaches to Debra Tabor and to undermine the garrison's morale with harassing operations and perhaps bluff them into surrender. This was easier said than done. The 'little rains' had just started and the patriots, anxious to regain their villages and plough their land before the 'great rains' made work impossible, began to disperse.* Soon the only troops left were the three operational centres, and their position was increasingly precarious. Ammunition and supplies were running low, their wireless set had broken down, and the only means of communication with Wingate's headquarters was by runner. Nevertheless, by ambushing and destroying all enemy traffic and by shooting up all the foraging parties sent out by the Italians (who were equally short of provisions), they managed to invest Debra Tabor so closely that not a grain of wheat or anything else could enter the town.

Billy was fascinated by the attitude of the local population. 'During a battle,' he noted, 'the country people don't run away. Those who have arms hasten towards the sound of firing, probably in search of loot. You can easily tell where the fighting is, because the whole countryside seems to be moving towards it. There are also strange groups of unarmed peasants, shrouded in white robes, who sit perched on top of the hills watching the battle. They seem totally indifferent to the outcome of the fight and never volunteer information, but if asked they are quite ready to give full military details of the enemy positions and movements of the various leaders.' They were particularly willing to give information to Billy, when they saw that his friendliness towards them was genuine and that he had bothered to learn a few words of

---

* The 'little rains' on the Ethiopian plateau generally last from the beginning of May to the middle of June. A relatively dry period intervenes before the oncome of the 'great rains' in mid-July. These continue until the beginning of October.

their language. As a result, he could pinpoint his important mortar and machine-gun targets, economise on ammunition, and fire with greater accuracy.

By mid-June the beleaguered garrison was beginning to show signs of strain. They counterattacked less often, sent out fewer patrols, and made greater though not more effective use of their artillery. Desertions among their native levies were so frequent that Billy organised several collecting posts to lead them back to his camp. These deserters were all regular soldiers, some with very long service in the field, and far better trained than his own irregular troops; so he was delighted when they volunteered to join forces and serve under him.

As soon as the little rains ceased, Danyo's patriots began to drift back. Birrou and his retinue also reappeared. It was like vultures gathering for the kill. Soon they were strengthened by the arrival of several other British-led units: one company of Shoan irregulars, another of Punjabis, a squadron of Skinners Horse, and a Royal Engineers detachment. It could now be only a matter of weeks, even days, before Debra Tabor surrendered. In fact, negotiations for the surrender had already started. Billy had been in touch with a French-speaking Italian officer, and on 5 July he entered the town under a *laissez-passer* to discuss terms and make arrangements.

Next day the combined British force assembled on an open meadow just outside the walls, to take formal possession. Billy led the triumphal entry, with a colour party with fixed bayonets escorting the Ethiopian flag, and a trumpeter playing the 'Prince of Dessye's March'. It was a far cry from regimental soldiering with the Scots Greys, and no one would have taken him at that moment for a regular British cavalry officer. In fact an older colleague who had not seen him for several months scarcely recognised him: 'I had known Billy McLean as a gay and lively boy not long past his twenty-first birthday. He now looked twice his size and twice his age, with a great yellow beard and hair falling to his neck – the reincarnation in the wet Amhara hills of some Gaelic chieftain of the Atlantic isles.'

As soon as the ceremonial surrender parade was over, the Italian officers and NCOs were segregated from the native levies. The former were sent off to Dessye under an escort of Skinners Horse, while the latter were given the choice of making their own way back to their villages or engaging under the British until the end of the campaign. In fact they had no real alternative; they knew that if they tried to travel home across country, alone and unprotected, they would almost certainly be attacked by the local peasantry or by armed brigands who would rob and then either kill them or sell them as slaves in the nearest market. Thus an entire colonial battalion, the 79th, came under Billy's command in addition to his operational centre. This combined force, numbering some 950 men, was facetiously named McLean's 79th Foot, and he was given the temporary rank of captain.

For several weeks he found himself immersed in administrative and disciplinary problems. His men had helped themselves to the stores left behind by the Italians and were conducting a lively trade in arms and ammunition. To put a stop to this, he had to resort to the sternest measures: the culprits were given the choice of paying a fine of one Maria Theresa dollar, or receiving one stroke of the lash, for every round of ammunition that could not be accounted for. Misappropriation of a rifle incurred a proportionately harsher punishment. He also had to deal with endless complaints about food and clothing and with quarrels over wives and women. He was still acting as liaison officer between Birrou and Danyo, in addition to his other duties, and much of his time was spent in settling disputes and keeping the peace between them. Continual rain added to the tedium of these petty concerns.

'There seems to be nothing of interest to see or do,' he confided to his diary. 'I can only think about dull everyday matters: rifles and ammunition, rations and pay, the welfare and quarrels of the men in my charge. . . . Maintaining discipline becomes almost an aim in itself, not pleasure in the punishment but satisfaction in punishing the wrongdoers. Have I become callous to the suffering of those punished by my orders?

'I wish there were some more books available. Without books or intelligent conversation one's mind becomes slovenly and lacking in spirit. All my thoughts seem muddled, longwinded and uninteresting. Perhaps this is what war does to the mind.'

The scene of action had now shifted to Gondar, some hundred miles to the north, where the terrain and the weather made it impossible for regular troops to be maintained in the field. It was therefore left to the patriots, together with several other irregular units like Billy's – a force of roughly brigade strength, named Douglas Force after the major in command of it – to deal with what remained of the Italian army in Abyssinia. Transport presented a problem, as usual. But, by scouring the countryside and paying through the nose, Billy managed to secure enough mules to carry his supplies and equipment; and on 13 August, in the confusion and disorder that always prevailed at the outset of a trek, he marched out of Debra Tabor at the head of his battalion.

In their exuberance at leaving, several soldiers fired their rifles into the air. Ammunition was so precious that Billy halted the column at once and had the offenders flogged on the spot, *pour encourager les autres*. Progress was slow because of the large number of camp-followers. The wives and women accompanying the soldiers would set off every morning well in advance of the main body, but they were so heavily laden with cooking utensils and other household goods that they were soon overtaken and fell by the wayside, obstructing the road for miles. Within a week, however, the 79th and the rest of Douglas Force were in position on the high ground overlooking the Gondar plateau. Their immediate task was to isolate the town from the outlying forts surrounding it.

Billy set up his own headquarters at Aiva, 'one of the most attractive places I have ever made camp in: green rolling country with fields of maize and millet, thickly wooded streams, and large expanses of bright yellow flowers.' No sooner had he settled in than he went into action, shooting up enemy patrols and laying ambushes along the roads. What impressed him most about the troops in his new command was their propensity for looting. Even under heavy machine-gun fire they would swarm on to the enemy trucks and ransack their contents before taking cover and firing back. 'I was far too close for my liking,' he recalled after one of these engagements, 'and people seemed to be dropping all round me, and the air whistling with bullets from all sides. My own bodyguard machine-gunner was in one of the trucks, helping himself to blankets. One or two enemy dead and dying were lying about, but nobody took much notice. Nothing mattered except the loot.'

For several weeks, while the rains lasted, the only troops in action were Douglas Force and the patriot groups. Between them they successfully blockaded Gondar and captured several of the outlying defences. But the complete reduction of the area was beyond their strength and towards the end of October they were reinforced for the final assault by two regular infantry brigades and a battery of 25-pounders. These were the first orthodox units that Billy had seen since the beginning of the year, and he was not at all sure that he liked the look of them. Compared to his own motley warriors with their exiguous armoury and improvised equipment, the regulars' smart uniforms, their motor transport and all the paraphernalia of modern warfare, seemed positively alien. Realising how unregimental he himself must have appeared to them, he had his hair cut and his beard shaved off before reporting to brigade headquarters.

The brigadier himself was charming, but made it clear that there was no love lost between the regular army and 'Wingate's lot'. Guerrilla activity seemed beyond the grasp of the average military mind. Nevertheless, despite the arrival of further reinforcements including a light armoured detachment, the guerrillas were the first to enter Gondar. At dawn on 27 November the artillery started pounding the town, while the infantry and Douglas Force advanced on it steadily. The advance was checked by a demolished bridge. This had to be repaired for the armoured cars and tanks to cross a river denying them access to the last fort before their final objective. It was called Azozo. But guerrillas need not wait for bridges. Billy was over the river and away, and his men had already looted Azozo and stormed into Gondar with the rest of the patriots by the time the first regular officer arrived to accept the surrender of this last pocket of Italian resistance.

3 *The Student of Intrigue*

The Abyssinian campaign had given Billy the chance of a lifetime. He had seized it and proved his worth. Major Douglas recommended him for the Military Cross, but such was the attitude of the powers that be towards irregular officers that most of the recommendations from or for a member of Wingate's Gideon Force were simply ignored. The Abyssinian authorities were not so petty and awarded Billy the Distinguished Military Medal of Haile Selassie I, one of only four ever awarded by the Emperor to foreigners (the other three being bestowed, incidentally, upon generals). Brigadier Dan Sandford, the Emperor's principal military and political adviser, also gave Billy the following letter addressed to the Deputy Director of Military Intelligence, GHQ Middle East:

> This is to introduce Captain N. L. D. McLean, R.S.Greys, who came into Gojjam with an operational centre in February 1941, and has been engaged in operations with the Ethiopian* patriots ever since, ending up with the successful Gondar campaign.
>   This officer is a born leader of 'irregulars' and should not be left to cool his heels in Middle East, if there are similar jobs to be done.

Apart from being a born leader, he had been quick to appreciate a vitally important principle of irregular warfare which Wingate himself brought to his notice, namely that without a strike force under his direct command no leader can effectively decide on an objective or impose any plan of action. It was lack of such a force that had hamstrung T. E. Lawrence and restricted his role in the Arab revolt to that of technical adviser and paymaster. Billy took this lesson to heart and later, as we shall see, he put it to good use.
    Fond though he was of the Scots Greys, he had no wish to return

---

* 'Ethiopia' instead of 'Abyssinia' was not in current use until after the war. I have treated the two names as interchangeable.

to regimental soldiering and looked forward to whatever unorthodox assignment Middle East headquarters had to offer. Meanwhile there was the business of disbanding his unit, the sadness of bidding farewell to men he had grown to respect and admire, the sorrow of leaving a country he had grown to love. He was in no hurry to depart and it was not until the end of January 1942, after being honoured with an audience with the Emperor, that he started off for Cairo.

Communications were so disrupted that it took him two weeks by road and rail to get as far as Khartum. Like any other healthy young man with an interest in native customs and culture, he had not confined himself to observation and theory. Here is his description of an encounter on his last night in Abyssinia: 'She was not very attractive. She was also extremely shy and nervous. But she was an expert on the job. She left next morning about 6.30. She did not smell in the least, except for a tinge of garlic on the breath.' Now, on his first night back in the Sudan, he decided to sample the local talent and, with a cavalier disregard for rules and regulations, made his way to one of the many native brothels, all of which he knew to be out of bounds to British personnel.

No sooner had he selected an inmate to his liking than the place was raided by the military police. By a happy coincidence one of the posse was a trooper from the Greys and he recognised Billy at once. 'Quick,' he said, 'hide before the corporal finds you,' and Billy dived under the bed. But searching under beds was a matter of routine; Billy was discovered, and cut a rather sorry figure as he emerged. The corporal was no less embarrassed but had to do his duty, and to be seen to be doing it. He formally arrested Billy, escorted him outside to a waiting truck, sat him down in the front seat – and then disappeared. Short of shouting out loud 'Now beat it!', he could not have done more. Billy didn't hesitate. He too disappeared, and so avoided an unpleasant visit to the Deputy Assistant Provost Marshal, but at the cost of giving up what he had risked so much to get – 'a pity,' he ruefully recalled, 'as she was particularly attractive.'

A week later, after travelling by train to Wadi Halfa and thence down the Nile by boat, he arrived in Cairo where his letter of recommendation secured him a posting to Special Operations Executive,* an

---

* For security reasons, however, it was never at that time mentioned by name, or even by the initials SOE. Its members referred to it simply as 'the firm'. To others it was known, under a succession of cover-names, as MO1 (SP), MO4, and towards the end of the war, when its nature was less clandestine than paramilitary, as Force 133. But, for all these aliases, Rustem Buildings, the large block of flats which served as the firm's Middle East headquarters, was known as 'secret house' to every taxi driver and hall porter in Cairo.

organisation formed at Winston Churchill's instigation for the purpose, to use his own words, 'of setting Europe ablaze'. Its task was to organise resistance, sabotage and guerrilla activity in enemy-occupied countries, and to that end a number of allied missions had already been infiltrated into Crete, Greece and Yugoslavia. Billy volunteered for the Yugoslav section, but before taking up his duties he was given a month's well-earned leave. He decided to spend it in Cairo and moved into Shepheard's Hotel.*

Cairo at that time was the crossroads of the free world, the Clapham Junction of the war. No one could get from America or Britain to India, the Far East, or indeed to Russia, without passing through it. There was thus a constant stream of visitors – exiled kings, ministers of state, commanders-in-chief, members of parliament and journalists – on their way to Moscow, Delhi, Chungking, Singapore or Canberra. Peter of Yugoslavia held court in Jerusalem before retiring via Cairo to London. George II of Greece preferred London to Cairo, but his exiled government preferred Cairo to London and stayed in Africa. It was in Cairo that talks were held with Romanian and Bulgarian emissaries seeking to make peace, and in Cairo as well as London that the Jewish Agency in Palestine strove to forward its political and military aims. There were also many of Billy's brother officers on leave in Cairo or in transit from the Western Desert, several of his friends serving in the British embassy, and a number of Egyptian families to whom he had letters of introduction. He was therefore able to enjoy a wide variety of social life.

What he enjoyed just as much was discovering the city on his own, taking long solitary walks through the Muski, window-shopping in the bazaars, or climbing up to the citadel in the evening to see the minaret-punctuated townscape gilded by the dying rays of the sun. His was not the tourist's Cairo of the pyramids and the sphinx, the museums and the mosques. Sightseeing for its own sake did not appeal to him. But wandering the streets enabled him to take the pulse of the place and immerse himself in its indefinable atmosphere. This was to become a practice of his in every town he visited on his subsequent travels.

When he reported for duty to the Yugoslav section towards the end of March, he was disappointed to find that no specific job had been allotted to him. For several weeks he hung about the office, studying the files, reading reports from the field, and generally familiarising himself with the situation. He also started to learn Serbo-Croat. But

---

* Tara, which was later to be his home-from-home in Cairo, had not yet come into being.

the only operational task he was given was to act as conducting officer to a group of Yugoslavs who were parachuted into their homeland in mid-April. He embarked with them in a Liberator from a desert air-field at 5.30 one afternoon, saw them safely out of the aircraft above the dropping-zone, and was back at his point of departure at 5.30 next morning. Not a very illuminating experience, he thought, but it gave him some idea of what to expect should he ever himself be parachuted into enemy-held territory.

The prospect of this happening began to seem more and more remote; in fact the mission he had escorted proved to be the last one dropped into Yugoslavia, or anywhere else in the Balkans, for many months to come. On 26 May, after a lull in the fighting since the beginning of the year, Rommel launched the Afrika Corps to the attack. He kept advancing and by the end of June he had captured Tobruk. Meanwhile SOE activity ground to a halt. No aircraft or submarine could be spared for cloak-and-dagger operations across the Mediterranean; even staff cars were commandeered in support of the battle. Flushed with success, Rommel pushed forward towards the Nile delta. Cairo itself was now threatened, and panic seized GHQ. Farcical scenes ensued, as an eye-witness later described: 'It was widely known that there could be no general evacuation of the delta. There was simply not enough road or rail transport to undertake a retreat to Palestine or to the Sudan. Orders were given to burn documents. The bulk were simply burnt in the open. But then the wind got up and a mass of secret documents were blown away little more than scorched, rising like so many phoenixes from their ashes and pursued all over the city by irate and frenzied staff officers.'

In the circumstances Billy saw no immediate future for himself in SOE and so, in the hope of being more usefully employed, had himself transferred to another secret organisation. This was MI9, which had the job of helping allied prisoners of war to escape from enemy-held territory and retrieving members of the armed forces who had managed to avoid capture but were still on the run. There were British, Australian and New Zealand soldiers who had taken part in the Greek campaign and had failed to get away when the expeditionary force had withdrawn. Some of them had made their own way back to Egypt, but there were still more than 2000 at large on the mainland and in Crete. For their benefit MI9 had organised escape routes across the central Aegean, from the Sporades to the Ionian coast of Turkey, and, since it did not depend on submarines or aircraft, it could go on operating with commandeered caïques while SOE was effectively closed down.

Billy has left no record of his MI9 career and his diary gives no clue. It says that he arrived in Istanbul on the morning of 23 July and reported to the British naval attaché. Subsequent entries give the impression of a life divided between tourism, society and the pleasures of the table; there are accounts of sailing in the Sea of Marmara and of picnics on the island of Halki, of excursions to Smyrna and other seaside towns, and of lavish meals with cultivated Turks and rich Levantines. This ostensibly leisurely existence was a perfect 'cover'. The Turkish authorities knew all about MI9 activity in neutral Turkish waters and on neutral Turkish soil, but were prepared to overlook it provided it was not too conspicuous. So Billy was more discreet than ever.

But he recorded his impressions of Istanbul – 'the town was quite heavenly' – as he approached it for the first time by sea in the evening, and also a little later, on his way to Smyrna, in the light of early morning: 'We made a wide circle round the old city, which through the mist looked like some opium-eater's vision: clear, rather grey water and, emerging from the mist, here an embattled wall, there a group of cypresses, then a cluster of domes and minarets. The mist and the sea and the city seemed to melt into one another, the mist turning into sea, the sea into masonry, and the masonry back into mist.'

As in Cairo, it was the general effect more than any particular feature that appealed to him and, again, he showed little interest in sightseeing. Antiquities bored him and even in Ephesus, which he visited one afternoon from Smyrna, he found little to admire apart from the site itself. To gain an overall impression of it, he climbed to the topmost tier of seats in the theatre, from where 'the view was heaven. . . . But then wherever there is blue sky, bright sun, green trees, the sea and a few hills, the view always *is* heaven!' He sat down, relishing the solitude and silence.

Presently he began to ponder on the influence of landscape on the human heart and mind. How civilised the Ephesians must have been, he felt, to have chosen such a spot for their city. Yet all that now remained of their civilisation were these disappointing ruins at his feet. One thought led to another and he found himself being granted the sort of revelation that was vouchsafed to St Paul on the road to Damascus. As though in a dream he envisaged Western civilisation likewise reduced to ruins. 'Lo, all our pomp of yesterday / Is one with Nineveh and Tyre!' – Kipling's doom-laden couplet accompanied the mental image. Simultaneously a surge of patriotism narrowed his field of vision so as to encompass the ruins not of the West as a whole, but of one country only, his own, which, for all his Scottish blood, emblazoned its name in his mind's eye as 'England'. The ghost of an England that had ceased to exist haunted his imagination.

This apparition in due course dissolved, but not before setting him on a parallel line of thought which seemed less a nightmare than a warning. Though England had not in reality ceased to exist, there was still a risk of her immediate postwar decline and ultimate extinction. It needed no prophetic eye to foresee even now the eventual dismemberment of the British Empire. But even if this was inevitable, as he feared, there was no reason for him not to try to postpone it for as long as he could; for though he did not share Lord Curzon's belief that the Empire was 'after Providence, the greatest instrument of good the world has ever seen', he was convinced that whatever might take its place would serve the world far worse. This conviction was to dictate his personal and political conduct for the rest of his life.

We have it on Billy's own authority* that his MI9 duties left him with 'a great deal of spare time on his hands'. He put it to good use by taking Russian lessons and starting to learn Turkish as well. He also began to study the Koran and to learn more about Islam in general. Though he was never tempted to become a Muslim, the teaching of Mohammed appealed to him and he found the ritual of the mosque, the unhurried synchronised movements of the worshippers and the sonorous rhythm of their prayers, infinitely moving. His subsequent interest in other religions no doubt stems from this earlier experience.

To this period, too, may be traced the beginnings of the gastronomical appreciation that enhanced his later life. He had always enjoyed good food but the exotic Turkish fare, which he now sampled for the first time, flattered his palate to a hitherto unimaginable degree. The very name of one of his favourite dishes, *imam bayildi* ('the imam swooned'), seemed to transform the stuffed aubergines of which it is composed into objects of Epicurean worship. To know how anything he ate was prepared added to his pleasure, and so he made a habit of jotting down not only the most complicated recipes but also the 'correct' way of dealing with something as simple as a raw fig: 'Hold the stem in one hand and, with the other, decapitate the fruit as you would an egg; then cut in four and peel off the skin.'

Istanbul, as befits a city which is a terminus for the most cosmopolitan railway train in the world, has long been a traditional centre of espionage and international intrigue. In Billy's day it lived up to its reputation as possibly never before and probably never since; for, apart from MI9, it housed the secret organisations of many other countries,

---

* In a report he wrote four years later, on his return from Sinkiang in 1946 (see Chapter Five).

both allied and enemy, and pullulated with agents working on each side and sometimes on both. The atmosphere might have been created deliberately to satisfy Billy's natural urge towards clandestinity.

The heterogeneous population included refugees from the Caucasus and Central Asia, with whom he found himself in immediate sympathy. Natives of those distant and romantic lands that had fired his youthful imagination, they seemed to step straight out of the books that had been his favourite reading at school. They talked to him with sadness and nostalgia of the homes they had left behind in the great mountains and on the boundless steppes. They described the last days of the khanates and the long-drawn-out struggle of their countrymen against the Russians; they gave him eye-witness accounts of the upheaval of the Bolshevik revolution and of the turmoil of the years that followed. He never tired of listening and was able to compare their stories, which sounded rather fanciful at times, with the factual and more sober reports of some Polish intelligence officers and experts with whom he had made friends and who were even then engaged on subversive activity in the area that came to be known as the soft under-belly of the Soviet Union.

His interest in Central Asia also brought him into contact with several Turkish professors with whom he discussed the problem of pan-Turanism, a movement which had grown up among the minorities in Russia as a retort to pan-Slavism and which aspired to unite all the Turks in the world, whether within the frontiers of Turkey or beyond them, from Adrianople to the Chinese oases on the Silk Trade Route. Nothing had come of it, and Billy's political instinct told him that nothing ever would; but improbable causes appealed to the knight errant in him and he tucked the subject away in his mind for future reference.

Meanwhile the situation in the Western Desert improved beyond all expectations. Rommel's impetus had exhausted itself and his advance on the Nile had been checked at El Alamein. GHQ breathed a sigh of relief and returned to normal. By the end of October the Eighth Army was ready to pass to the offensive and by mid-November Tobruk was once again in British hands. The tide had turned; the Germans were on the run; the pressure was off Middle East Command, and aircraft were again available for SOE operations. Billy therefore asked to be posted back to Cairo. He arrived there shortly before Christmas and reported at once to Rustem Buildings. But not to the Yugoslav Section. Another country now claimed his attention.

4 *The Irregular Warrior*

Albania had come under Axis domination several months before the outbreak of the war. On Good Friday, 1939, Mussolini had suddenly invaded and quickly overrun the country, and King Zog, Queen Geraldine and their infant son Prince Leka were forced to flee across the border into Greece. When Italy declared war on France and Great Britain on 10 June of the following year, British retaliation included hatching plans for an Albanian revolt against the Italian army of occupation. They were drawn up by one of Billy's Eton friends, Julian Amery, who was then working at the British legation in Belgrade, ostensibly as deputy press attaché but in reality with the local branch of 'D' Section.*

Julian, not yet twenty-one, had crammed a great deal into his young life. A son of the distinguished statesman Leo Amery, he had imbibed politics with his mother's milk, and been dandled at the age of four on the knees of Lloyd George, and kissed on both cheeks by King Feisal of Iraq. At Oxford, where he read Modern Greats, he had hobnobbed with more than one future prime minister and, while still an undergraduate, had served in Spain during the civil war as *Daily Express* correspondent on the nationalist side. World War II broke out while he was on holiday on the Dalmatian coast; he reported at once to the legation; and within a few months had been co-opted into 'D' Section as an Albanian expert. In fact he knew nothing about Albania; but then no one else in the section did either. Starting from scratch – or, to be more precise, from an introduction to the two most important Albanian exiles in Belgrade – he built up a clandestine courier system and was soon receiving regular reports from the whole of north and central Albania down to the capital, Tirana. But when the Germans invaded Yugoslavia in the following summer, his intelligence network

* 'D' Section – distinct from 'C' Section, the Secret Intelligence Service – was the forerunner of SOE.

fell to pieces, his agents went underground and nothing more was heard from them.

Since then Albania had been an unknown quantity. To Billy this represented a challenge. He volunteered to re-establish contact with the country and submitted an operational plan. SOE accepted it and agreed to infiltrate him, with the rank of major, in command of a five-man mission.

As his second-in-command he chose David Smiley, the lieutenant in the Blues (now promoted to captain) whom he had first met on a troopship in the Red Sea after both of them had volunteered for the Somaliland Camel Corps. They had met again more recently in Cairo and David at once pounced on the opportunity of joining him on the Albanian venture. The other members of the mission were Garry Duffy, a Royal Engineers lieutenant, and an expert in mines and demolitions; Corporal Williamson, a wireless operator; and Elmaz, an Albanian with a fair command of English, who was to act as interpreter. Several weeks were devoted to parachute training and to what David called 'the dirty tricks course' – i.e. the standard training for agents in the field, which included sabotage of all types, the use of secret inks, tapping telephone lines, lock-picking and safe-blowing – and in April 1943, with mini-compasses concealed in fly-buttons and many other such devices sewn into their uniforms, they drew their weapons and gold, issued in 1000-sovereign bags, and set off by train for their jumping-off point, an airfield outside Derna on the Libyan coast, which was then being used for operations into Yugoslavia and Greece.

Rather than drop them 'blind' into a country where they had no contacts, SOE had arranged for them to be received by a British mission already established in the mountains of Epirus, from where they would make their way across the nearby border into Albania. For security reasons they were kept confined like prisoners in the Derna camp, which seemed unnecessarily bleak after the gaiety and comfort of Cairo. They were therefore all the more eager to be off without delay. But at the last minute Elmaz got cold feet, and so it was without an interpreter, and with half a dozen words of kitchen Albanian between them, that they landed in enemy territory.* Billy later described his feelings at the time:

* This was not so desperate as it sounds. Interpreters, or anyway locals with a smattering of French or English, could usually be found on the spot. Those of us who operated in civilian clothes were, of course, already fluent in the language of the country. Others, like Billy and David, picked it up as they went along and managed to understand and to make themselves understood in a surprisingly short time.

I found the operational jump one of the most pleasant I had ever made – far more pleasant than the five training jumps. It was also less difficult than I had imagined. Sometimes in Cairo, after a debauched night, I would lie on my bed in the afternoon and imagine the scene in the aircraft – the green light and everyone looking ghostly and strained, and outside very cold and black; the hollow feeling in the pit of the stomach; the slipstream rushing by and the absolute certainty that it would knock one against the side of the fuselage so that the parachute would not open properly, or perhaps not open at all; the unknown land below, so cold and dark and menacing. But in fact it was a piece of cake. Like nearly everything one is anxious or worried about, it is much less bad than one's idea of it. This, of course, is also true of the good things one hopes to happen; they also almost always fall short of one's expectations or desires. Possibly only boredom and hate, illness and bad temper, quarrels and unsuccessful human relations are worse than one imagines.

No sooner had he landed than he found himself surrounded by a band of bearded Greek guerrillas, whose vociferous welcome drowned the sound of the bells of the sheep and goats grazing on the dropping zone. Presently the British officer in charge of the reception, a young captain, came up and introduced himself: 'I'm John Cook. You're McLean, I presume?' Leaving David and the rest of the party to collect and sort out the arms and supplies that had been dropped with them, Billy set off at once with Cook on the two hours' march to mission headquarters, the monastery of Romanon, a collection of grey-stone buildings in the form of a medieval castle with its chapel, bakery, storehouses, living accommodation and stabling set round a broad fortified courtyard. David joined him there next day and together they laid their plans.

The Italians, they discovered, controlled all the main roads and the most important strategic centres of Epirus. The rest of the area was in the hands of the guerrillas, who were divided into two main factions: the followers of EAM, the communist-dominated National Liberation Front; and a right-wing group known by the initials EDES, standing for the National Republican Greek League. They were already at loggerheads and on the verge of the civil war that eventually broke out between them. But this was of no direct concern to Billy and David; their only aim for the time being was to get into Albania as quickly as possible. So after three days spent organising a convoy they pressed on, accompanied by Cook with an escort of EDES guerrillas and ten mules carrying their stores.

After a nine-hour march over winding mountain tracks, they

reached a spot beyond which their escort would go no further, for the village ahead was in the hands of ELAS (the Greek Popular Liberation Army), the military wing of EAM, which controlled the surrounding countryside. Billy and David therefore went on alone and, much to their relief, were warmly welcomed by the ELAS partisans who, by means of the local grapevine telegraph, had already learnt of their recent airborne visitation. A new convoy was organised, a fresh escort was provided; and a further four-day march, during which they were received with open arms and given a triumphant send-off in every village through which they passed and in which they spent the night, brought them to Drymades, only a hundred yards from the frontier. Here they had the luck to run into a couple of Albanian partisans, whom they sent back with a note asking to meet their leader. Three days later they received a reply permitting them to enter Albania.

The villagers over the border received them no less warmly than had the Greeks – many of them were in fact ethnic Greeks and did not even speak Albanian – but Billy was aware of a subtle difference in their welcome. Whereas in Greece he had been conscious of deep friendship and respect for the British, the generosity of the Albanians seemed to stem from a traditional sense of hospitality towards any foreigner rather than from spontaneous affection or sympathy with an ally. This was confirmed when he met the local guerrilla leader, Bedri Spahiu, who turned up with his çeta, or band, consisting mostly of young men whose political beliefs were evident, for their caps all sported a red star and they gave the communist clenched-fist salute. Spahiu appeared to regard Billy's presence in Albania with suspicion, not to say hostility, and bluntly informed him that he could advance no further but, on the contrary, would be well advised to return to Greece at once.

Billy knew enough about Balkan politics to understand Spahiu's attitude. Greece had long had designs on this part of Albania, which fervent Greek nationalists openly called Northern Epirus, and Spahiu evidently thought that the British, with their Greek connections, had come to assist Greek irredentist movements and to raise Greek bands on Albanian soil. Billy and David were unable to convince him that this was not the case, so there was nothing for it but to make their way back to Drymades. Before leaving, however, they persuaded him to forward a letter to partisan headquarters near Tirana, in the hope of its reaching a senior staff officer who might prove a little less intransigent.

Though disappointing and frustrating, this first contact with the Albanian resistance movement was not all in vain. Back in Drymades, Billy set to work on a report based on the information he had gleaned from Spahiu, which was later supplemented by material based on his own subsequent experience. This was the gist of it:*

As soon as the Italians invaded Albania, the communists began to lay their plans and by the end of 1941 they had fielded several *çetas* in the mountains. These formed the nucleus of the National Liberation Movement (LNC) which came into being a year later. Although comparatively weak among the backward tribes in the north, the LNC was by far the best-organised group in the country as a whole, and the only one which was active against the Axis. Like the EAM in Greece, it was communist-dominated, but, again like the EAM, it was careful to disassociate itself from the Communist Party proper. This was the organisation to which Spahiu belonged, after transferring his allegiance from the Fascist Party, which he had previously espoused.

It was only a few weeks before Billy parachuted in that the more conservative elements in the country formed a loose, rather inactive organisation called the Balli Kombëtar, or National Front. A little later, another right-wing party was formed by the so-called Dibra League of Bajraktars or northern chieftains. Finally, there was the Royalist or Zogist Party, closely allied to the Balli, which owed much of its strength to the personality of its leader, Agha Abas Kupi, who had been one of Julian Amery's most useful contacts in Belgrade. Napoleonic in character and appearance, Abas Kupi had originally been against King Zog and then, poacher turned gamekeeper, had become the staunchest of Zog's gendarmerie commanders. In 1939, by holding up the Italians for thirty-six days, he had covered the King's escape and was thus regarded as a national hero.

Work on his report kept Billy busy. He also had plenty to read, having brought with him a miniature library which included the complete works of Shakespeare, Keats and Shelley, Voltaire's *Dictionnaire Philosophique*, and novels ranging from contemporary whodunits to the Russian classics. But on David's hands time lay heavy. He was never happier than in action, and so he volunteered to slip back into Albania by a different route. With an EAM guide and a couple of mules he disappeared over the border and Billy did not see him again for a month,§ though they kept in regular contact by courier.

---

* At the risk of jumping the gun, but to enable the reader to grasp more easily the events that follow, I have summarised the whole of Billy's report, although it was not completed until several months later.

§ For an exciting account of David's activity during this period, and of the activities of the mission in general, see his *Albanian Assignment* (Chatto & Windus, 1984).

In due course a messenger turned up in Drymades with a favourable reply from the LNC central committee. Billy at once retraced his steps into Albania, this time with the rest of his personnel, wireless set and stores, and eventually rejoined David in the village of Leshnjë, the headquarters of another *çeta*. It was an attractive spot, perched halfway up the side of a steep mountain. Walnut and cherry trees punctuated the terraces of maize; sparkling streams tumbled down the precipitous crags above; below, a broad valley spread eastwards and forests of beech smoothed out the contours of the savage landscape beyond. Furthermore, there was a small plateau nearby which would make an ideal dropping-zone. Supplies which Billy requested by signal – for by this time Corporal Williamson had made contact with Cairo – were indeed dropped there shortly afterwards. The operation took place without incident; the containers landed accurately on the dropping-zone – but all the boots that had been ordered for the partisans turned out to be so small that only children could have worn them.

On 23 June 1943 – I record the date in full, for it was a historic occasion – Billy set off for the nearby village of Malakastreo to meet Enver Hoxha, Secretary-General to the Central Committee of the Albanian Communist Party and a leading member of the general staff of the LNC. This was SOE's first contact with the man who already controlled half the country and later ruled the whole. I have mentioned Hoxha's feelings towards Billy in my preface. Billy's reaction to him was reciprocal. Hoxha was a big man of about thirty-five, with too much flesh and a flabby handshake. A dyed-in-the-wool communist, he was naturally suspicious of the British mission; but, having heard of the recent supply drop, he no doubt saw on which side his bread was buttered and invited Billy and his group to move to a new base at Shtyllë, a day's march away, where the LNC would produce *çetas* for them to train and equip. These were to form the nucleus of the First Partisan Brigade.

Shtyllë was a village of some fifty houses situated at the head of two valleys. As headquarters, the mission was allotted a school building which had been converted from a disused mosque. It was ideally placed, standing some way outside the village, with a good view of both valleys and with a constant supply of fresh water from a nearby stream. Here they remained for two months, receiving supplies by parachute and training the partisans to use the weapons that were dropped. They also carried out a number of operations, laying mines on the main roads, ambushing enemy convoys and blowing up strategic bridges. Returning one day from one of these sorties, they heard of the arrival of a German division at the nearby town of Körçe. This was their first news of Germans in Albania.

Some days later an Italian air force deserter attached himself to their headquarters, and that night there was an alarming incident. Their dormitory was so cramped – all of them dossed down on the floor (there were no beds) in one small room, the rest being crammed with arms and equipment – that they had to step over one another if they wanted to move around. David woke in the dark to the sound of a scuffle and dimly discerned two figures in what appeared to be mortal combat. Billy had seized Williamson by the neck and was slowly throttling him. David broke up the fight and both contestants came to their senses. It turned out that Williamson, on his way outside to relieve himself, had stepped on Billy by mistake. Billy had been dreaming that the deserter was a double agent who had come to murder him – nightmares of this sort were not uncommon in enemy-occupied territory – and, mistaking Williamson for the Italian, had reacted accordingly. Strangely enough the deserter disappeared in the morning. They were worried he might have returned to his unit to give them away, but they had misjudged the poor fellow. They found him outside, murdered by a partisan who wanted his boots.

Billy gradually extended his field of operations and found himself in need of reinforcements for areas further off. Three other British missions were therefore dropped in, one after another in the course of three weeks, and placed themselves under his command. The first, he despatched to the Dibra region to contact the *bajraktars*. The second went up north to join Abas Kupi and his Zogist *çetas*. The third included Peter Kemp, an old friend of Julian Amery – they had met while taking cover in a ditch during the Spanish civil war, in which Peter served on Franco's side. He was eager to get to Kosovo, the Albanian-speaking district of Yugoslavia, but Billy and David found him such good company that they were loath to let him go.

Instead, the three of them set off together for the Barmash area, where the newly formed First Partisan Brigade was to go into action for the first time. The target was a German column moving down the main Körçe–Lestovik road. But at the last moment the brigade commander called off the attack, on the grounds that the road was overlooked by a German post.

'How many men are there in it?' Billy asked.

'I don't know,' was the answer, 'but about a platoon.'

'Do you mean to tell me,' Billy exclaimed, 'that eight hundred partisans can't wipe out eighteen Germans?'

Only later did he discover that the commander had received

orders not to engage the enemy but to keep his brigade safe and ready for future action against political opponents. Seething with anger, he turned to Peter. 'I'm damned if I'm leaving here without having a crack at something,' he said. 'David's got to get back to Shtyllë to receive the drops we're expecting, but if you agree I thought we might try to shoot up a lone staff car. Of course it's a purely Boy Scout operation, but at least it should work off some of our bad temper.' Peter agreed at once and – much to their surprise, for he was a gentle and timid young man – Stiljan Biçi, their French-speaking interpreter, volunteered to go with them.

We decided [Peter later recorded] to lay our ambush just before dusk in order to have the protection of darkness for our escape should the action go against us. In the early evening we made our way slowly towards the road, while the dying sunlight dappled the hills in a splendid contrast of ochre and indigo. We chose a spot a mile north and out of sight of the German position; here the hills reached almost to the road, and fern and bushes gave plenty of cover without obstructing our view in either direction. We hid ourselves behind a bank above the road; Stiljan crouched beside me, Billy stood ten yards to our right watching and listening.

The sun had set. In the still, clear light before dusk the land seemed deserted; the only sound I could hear was Stiljan's heavy breathing, showing that he was feeling the same nervous tension as I. We had agreed to attack only a vehicle travelling by itself; but now I remembered that it was the practice for a staff car to precede a convoy at a few hundred yards distance, and I prayed that we should not find ourselves in a trap. Besides our pistols and submachine-guns each of us carried two phosphorus smoke grenades to cover our retreat in an emergency, but I had little faith in their protection if we should run into serious trouble.

Faintly from the south came the sound of a car. We heard it a long way off, the noise of its engine rising and falling on the twisting mountain road. I saw Billy staring through his field-glasses; then he stiffened:

'It's a German staff car, all alone; don't fire till I give the word.'

The car turned the last bend and came into full view, a grey saloon approaching at about twenty-five miles an hour – a perfect target. As I heard Stiljan cock his Schmeizer I pressed forward the safety-catch of my Welgun. Then Billy stood up, his Schmeizer at his shoulder.

'All right, let 'em have it,' he ordered quietly.

We opened fire simultaneously. Within a few seconds the wind-screen and side windows were shattered, the body scoured with the marks of our bullets. The car continued on its way for about twenty yards, then slewed in a cloud of dust and came to a halt at the side of the road. The driver sat slumped over the wheel, two men lay huddled motionless in the back, but from the front seat a figure leapt out and, crouching behind the car, returned our fire with his pistol. Changing their magazines, Billy and Stiljan continued firing, but at this moment my Welgun jammed. . . . Throwing it aside I drew my .45 and began to fire carefully aimed shots at the place where I imagined the German to be. Suddenly I heard Billy shout:

'Give me covering fire, boys! I'm going down.'

'For Christ's sake stay where you are!' I shouted back; but I was too late. Throwing one of the smoke grenades, which landed well short of the car, Billy scrambled down the slope; Stiljan, urged by me, redoubled his rate of fire. Unfortunately the thick cloud of phosphorus smoke effectively hid the car from our view, although it did not seem to hide Billy from the German; we could hear the crack of his pistol and see spurts of earth fly from the bullets round Billy's feet. I knew Billy was going down not only to finish off the German, but to collect any documents in the car, and I shuddered to think how we should get him away if he were hit. I threw a smoke grenade, hoping to give him extra cover; but by now Billy himself had thought better of it and was climbing back towards us. In a moment he was safe.

'I think we'd better beat it,' he gasped, 'while the score is still in our favour.'

We raced down into a gully and started to climb the ridge beyond. . . . I too was anxious to be gone, remembering that one of the first rules of an ambush is not to linger on the scene of the crime. . . . Billy, however, was in no mood for haste. The danger, he maintained, was over and now was the time to relax and rest before the long journey home. Pulling a tortoiseshell comb from his breast pocket, he began to pass it in long, leisurely strokes through the thick blond hair that swept back from his forehead.

'Don't be so damned windy, Peter,' he protested with a careless laugh.

Towards the end of August an Italian punitive expedition, heralded by an artillery barrage which scored a near hit on the mission's headquarters with the very first shell, put an end to their sojourn at Shtyllë. They just managed to move themselves and their stores out of the village before it was reduced to smouldering ashes. But this was the Italians' last throw. By the time the mission had established a new base fifty miles further north, Italy had surrendered to the Allies and an armistice was signed. Billy at once contacted the nearest Italian garrison, but it was too late – the local commander had already gone over to the Germans, as indeed had the commander-in-chief himself and many other senior officers. Several thousand other ranks, however, joined the partisans and so did some Bulgarian deserters. Meanwhile the Germans tightened their grip on the country.

Less than a month after the mission had moved into its new headquarters, the monastery of Santa Maria, tucked away in the thickly wooded mountains near Lake Ohrid, a signal came from Cairo to say that more British personnel were to be dropped into Albania, including a senior officer who would take over Billy's command. A suitable dropping-zone near the village of Bixha was reconnoitred and prepared, and a fortnight later the new mission landed without incident in two separate groups. The first was headed by the senior officer, Brigadier Davies, affectionately known as 'Trotsky', and the second included his staff captain, Alan Hare, a contemporary of Billy at Eton and also a friend of David.

As old hands in the field, Billy and David were surprised and rather scornful of the staggering amount of kit the newcomers brought with them. All that camp furniture, all that orderly-room stationery – why, there was even a typewriter! – seemed too regimental for words. But regimentalism was clearly what Trotsky was after. Almost the first remark he addressed to Billy next day was, 'Well, McLean, I noticed there was no stand-to this morning.' Billy did not admit that there had been no stand-to on any other morning either. 'We shall start stand-to tomorrow,' Trotsky went on. 'What time does the sun rise?' Billy had no idea; he and David were seldom up at that hour. 'What time would you say, David?' he asked, smartly passing the buck. 'Six o'clock,' came the impromptu reply. 'Right,' said Trotsky, 'stand-to tomorrow morning at five o'clock.' Billy and David humoured him. They got up at the appointed time, stood to for the required hour, then stood down and went straight back to bed.

To do him justice, Trotsky was not as hidebound as he seemed. Though he insisted on his own officers being properly dressed, he turned a blind eye on the sartorial fantasies in which Billy and David indulged. Their uniform consisted, as the mood took them, of jodhpurs or corduroys, a grey shirt or a khaki one, a broad dark-red cummerbund or a regulation Sam Browne belt, commando boots or Albanian sandals, and, for headgear, an astrakhan kalpak or a white felt fez – no matter which, as far as Billy was concerned, so long as it was adorned with his regimental badge, a silver eagle, commemorating a historic charge at Waterloo in which a sergeant of the Greys captured the imperial standard of the French 45th Regiment. This manner of dress was deliberate. It reflected the irregular nature of their activities, which Billy had been careful to organise on guerrilla as opposed to military lines. Luckily they were punctilious about shaving, for Trotsky discountenanced the wearing of beards – 'None of that Wingate stuff here,' he said. But Billy found the new mission unduly ceremonious and cumbersome. He was therefore relieved to receive a signal ordering him and David to report back to Cairo.

It took more than a month to organise their departure. The only means of leaving the country was by sea and their best chance was to be picked up on the coast south of Valona, the nearest to Italy. Thither they set off, taking Corporal Williamson with them and a mule to carry the wireless and batteries. It was not much more than 100 miles as the crow flies, but they covered over twice that distance, winding through the mountains, avoiding the main roads and dodging German patrols, before they dropped down at last to the sea. A short reconnaissance revealed exactly what they wanted – a cave in the cliffs overlooking a secluded creek, which they promptly code-named 'Seaview'. Here, after signalling their map reference, they settled down to wait for the motor torpedo-boat which was to take them off.

One day passed, two days passed, a week passed – and still no boat. Signals from Cairo brought nothing but excuses, postponements and delays. Food began to run short, and also water. Luckily their mule died and provided them with meat, and an untimely storm formed puddles in the rocks which they were able to mop up with a sponge. Their cave was dark and cold and cramped, but they dared not move out of it for fear of being spotted by one of those stock figures of enemy-occupied territory – the peasant or shepherd who pops up from nowhere at the most inopportune moment.

One morning, at last, they received word that the boat was due that very night. Darkness fell and they started flashing the agreed recognition signal. After what seemed an unbearably long time they heard the sound of engines, saw an answering flash offshore and presently discerned two figures approaching in what turned out to be a collapsible rubber dinghy – a collapsing rubber dinghy, in fact, for it had been pierced by a rock on the way in and was rapidly filling with water. This did not matter much to the newcomers, two more liaison officers who were only too glad to have landed safely, but for Billy and David it was almost the last straw. They could have swum for it, but each of them had a briefcase stuffed with documents and items of intelligence which it would have been a pity to leave behind. So they pushed off, the one paddling for dear life, the other bailing furiously, until, just as the dinghy sank beneath them, they reached the side of the MTB and flung their cases up on deck. Then friendly hands reached down and dragged them out of the sea.

Three hours later, after an uneventful crossing of the Adriatic, they reached Brindisi, then cruised up the coast to Bari and from there flew on to Cairo, where they spent several weeks being debriefed, writing their report and wallowing in the delights of Tara. In their report they drew two main conclusions:

1. The LNC was the principal force with any fighting capacity in the centre and south of Albania, but it was up in arms against the nationalists in the north.
2. The nationalists (meaning all those who were not LNC) did not appear very keen to fight the Germans and, to protect themselves from the LNC, were in fact being forced to collaborate with the enemy.

These conclusions were followed by the suggestion that SOE should continue to back the partisans with military aid but should also maintain contact with the nationalists in the hope of persuading them to collaborate with the LNC and thus put an end to what now amounted to civil war.

Early in the new year they were recalled to London, where they spent a month being further debriefed and writing a more detailed report. King Zog and Queen Geraldine, exiled in England since the occupation of their country, received them several times and they were also interviewed by Anthony Eden, the Foreign Secretary. Eden suggested that they might like to return to Albania and make contact with Abas Kupi and the tribes in the north, adding that if they needed any special help from him they must not hesitate to send him a personal signal. They agreed and prepared to fly back to Cairo to make the necessary arrangements. Before leaving they heard they had been decorated; Billy was awarded a DSO, and David an MC. But there was also bad news. Trotsky Davies's headquarters had been attacked; Trotsky himself had been wounded and taken prisoner; and his mission had scattered and was now on the run.

Back in Cairo, Billy's waking hours were divided between preparations for his new mission and a very active social life. He was on the list of every Cairene hostess, both indigenous and foreign, and many a maidenly heart fluttered at his approach in palace, villa and legation. One dusky beauty in particular was so enthralled by him, and he by her, that they lost count of time when they were together and he was consequently late for the ceremony at which General Paget, GOC Middle East Forces, pinned his newly awarded decoration on his breast. But then Billy was never a stickler for punctuality.

Somehow he also found time to concentrate on the task ahead. At this stage the Allies had accepted that Romania, Hungary and Yugoslavia would be part of the Soviet sphere, while Greece would come under British influence. But over Albania there hung a question mark. There was no settled government policy towards the country and no decision had been reached about its future at the various summit meetings. Billy hoped that it might still be saved for the West. His main objective therefore was to raise the nationalists, especially the Zogists, against the Germans and persuade them to co-operate with Enver Hoxha's partisans. Since this would demand considerable diplomacy and political acumen, he asked for Julian Amery to be attached to his mission as a sort of commissar with the rank of captain, he himself having been promoted to lieutenant-colonel, and David to major. No one could have been better equipped for the job than Julian, who for his part was delighted at the prospect of active service in a country with which he had been closely connected since the beginning of the war. And so on the night of 19 April, after flying from Cairo to SOE headquarters in Bari, the three of them took off from Brindisi in a US air force Dakota and less than an hour later dropped onto the Bixha plateau, the site of Trotsky Davies's ill-fated camp.

Or rather, they should have dropped on to the plateau. But, having been launched too late and too high, they drifted and landed on a wooded crag more than a mile away. Julian narrowly missed being impaled on a jagged pine and David actually crashed into a tree-trunk a little further down. Luckily their falls were broken by deep snow. Neither of them knew how Billy had fared, for there was no sign of him. But they saw a speck of light some distance below them. They made their way toward it and presently came upon Billy's torch inserted in a snowdrift, then upon Billy himself. He had moved a few yards away so as not to present a target should anyone have shot at the light; knowing that German patrols were active, he was taking no chances. It was two hours before they were located by the reception committee – a Zogist *çeta* with a British liaison officer – who, after climbing up from the dropping-zone, escorted them to an isolated sheepfold where they all dossed down for what remained of the night.

Next morning Billy set to work. His first task was to see Abas Kupi, so he sent a messenger to announce the arrival of the mission and arranged to meet him at the village of Derije, a hard eight hours' slog to the west, which they reached at dawn on the following day. Here they were delighted and relieved to find Alan Hare. Alan had behaved with conspicuous gallantry during the attack on Trotsky's headquarters, refusing to leave the side of his wounded brigadier until given a direct order to do so.* He looked haggard from the hardships he had suffered and still limped from a frostbitten foot but was as high-spirited as ever and although he, if anyone, deserved to be evacuated, he volunteered to stay on.

Three days later Abas Kupi arrived and conferred with the mission for four hours. He was about to go on a two weeks' tour of his area and invited Billy and Julian to accompany him and his staff, while David stayed to run the base. It was already May, but in the mountains winter still prevailed. On the second day's march, however, they came down from the snows and out of the swirling mists into sunlight and saw the broad Mati valley, King Zog's own country, spread out below them like a promised land. The grass was bright green, the trees were in bud and the ground a carpet of violets, primroses, crocuses and cyclamen.

They kept on the move throughout the daylight hours, spending each night in a different village, where they were treated as honoured guests. On entering a house they would take off their boots and give up their rifles to their host, though retaining their pistols. While the evening meal was cooking they assembled with their escort round the fire, sitting on carpets or sheepskin rugs, cross-legged or reclining against their saddle-bags. Raki would be brought, accompanied by a *meze* of onions, cheese and sometimes hard-boiled eggs, and toasts were drunk to the traditional greeting of *Tungyatyeta!* – 'May your life be prolonged!' When the food was ready a low wooden table was carried in, round which they all gathered, sitting cross-legged on the floor. There were no knives or forks and they helped themselves with their fingers to dishes of roast mutton and pilaf, followed by luscious sweetmeats such as *halva* and *baklava* – a welcome change from the usual country diet of beans and coarse maize bread. It was often past midnight before they dossed down together, fully dressed, on the guest-room floor. Sanitary arrangements were primitive, the closet consisting of a can of water and a hole in the floor – often, as Julian observed, of impracticably narrow circumference – below which the household poultry were kept, and thus economically fed.

---

* His conduct was an example to the rest of the staff and earned him a well-merited MC.

There was no breakfast, but a cup of coffee or a bowl of sweetened milk fortified them for the coming day's march.

Their progress was deliberately leisurely and public, for Kupi was intent on parading them, the only British mission in the area, as an outward and visible sign of allied support. The slow pace also enabled Billy and Julian to appreciate their host's personal influence and standing and to assess the potential strength of his followers. But was he willing to work with the communists? At the end of the tour they put the question to him and to their surprise he invited them to arrange for him to meet Enver Hoxha or any other communist leader as soon as they saw fit. Then they asked him whether he was prepared to resume operations against the Germans, and he said he would gladly do so if they could obtain appropriate instructions for him from King Zog. Billy realised that the whole future of his mission depended on this royal directive. He therefore decided to avail himself of Anthony Eden's offer to communicate with him direct and on his return to base he sent a personal message to the Foreign Secretary which ended with the words: 'There is grave danger that without this measure of encouragement Abas Kupi will go the way of General Mihajlović.'*

While awaiting a reply he set out again with Julian for a tour of the Dibra region, where they conferred with various chieftains in their respective strongholds. By the time they got back, Abas Kupi was there to meet them and Eden's reply had arrived. It was not encouraging. The Foreign Secretary would not commit himself at once to obtaining the necessary directive from King Zog§ and advised Billy to 'keep the pot boiling' – an operation, Julian ruefully reflected, which in politics, as in physics, leads to the eventual evaporation of the contents. Kupi's offer, however, to negotiate with Enver Hoxha had been accepted, and the head of the Albanian section in Bari had dropped to partisan headquarters to secure the communist leader's agreement. But Hoxha was adamant. On no account would he work with Abas Kupi. His refusal seemed to indicate that he would soon attack the Zogists and therefore, as Billy pointed out, Kupi's best course was to attack

* Mihajlović was the leader of the right-wing Četnic forces, loyal to the king, who fought against the Germans when they invaded Yugoslavia. Later, when Tito's partisans turned against him, he was driven into collaboration with the enemy, and after the war he was tried by the Tito government and executed.

§ No doubt because it might have implied that His Majesty's government recognised King Zog. They were sensitive to being accused of this by the Americans, who were already critical of the support Great Britain had given to the King of Greece.

the Germans before the partisans attacked him. But Kupi could not be persuaded.

Billy and Julian went on pressing him – seemingly in vain – for two days on end, during which David, who was always bored with political discussion, must have shown his feelings; for he heard Billy remark: 'David seems to be getting restless again; we must find him something to blow up.' This did the trick. Kupi promptly spoke up: 'Let Major Smiley come to me tomorrow and I will choose him a bridge. If he will bring the dynamite, I will provide the men. Then you can tell your headquarters that Abas Kupi is fighting again.'

Kupi was as good as his word. The target he chose was the bridge of Gyoles, one of the biggest in Albania, on the main road from Scutari to Tirana and Durazzo. Two days later, with a dozen Zogists to give him covering fire, David packed charges of explosives into the demolition chambers in the concrete piers which the Germans, with typical thoroughness, had already prepared; and the bridge was utterly destroyed. Now that Kupi had proved his good faith, Bari agreed to supply him with enough arms to equip eight çetas, each of 250 men. Meanwhile, Billy heard that Gani Kryeziu, one of the tribal chiefs he had met on his recent tour, was also actively engaging the Germans, and Bari agreed to equip him as well. Other leaders were likely to follow suit, in which case they too would be supplied. With any luck the whole of north Albania would soon be up in arms. Billy accordingly called for a meeting to be held in two days' time in Lura, two days' march away, to proclaim a general uprising and to determine a plan of action.

Kupi set off at once to make the arrangements. But communist forces had already begun to concentrate along the borders of the Zogist areas and there were reports of sporadic clashes between Zogist and communist patrols. Billy kept Bari informed and pointed out that a civil war would inevitably disrupt his plans for a nationalist revolt. Bari's reply was short and robust: all supplies to the communists would be cut off if they attacked the Zogists. This was reassuring and, despite the growing tension, it was in a mood of cautious optimism that Billy, David, Julian and their wireless operator joined Abas Kupi at the appointed meeting place, a strip of grassland in the Lura forest. Several Dibran chiefs were also there by the time they arrived. Bonfires had been lit and whole sheep were roasting on spits over the glowing embers. Bottles of raki were produced and they all drank to their joint endeavour.

Summer had come and it was warm enough to sleep under the trees. Early in the morning Billy and his companions woke to the sound of voices raised in heated discussion. A courier had just arrived with news that the communists had attacked in strength and overrun Kupi's headquarters. The civil war had begun in earnest. It looked as though Billy's plans would have to be called off, for the nationalists could not be expected to fight on two fronts. But events now took an even more dramatic turn. A signal from Bari announced that a Major Victor Smith was to be dropped that very night with proposals for restraining Enver Hoxha and bringing about a truce. 'The plot is just about right for a *deus ex machina*,' Billy remarked drily.

Recognition fires were lit and shortly after midnight an aircraft circled overhead, a parachute opened, and Smith came safely down to earth. His instructions were to invite delegates from the two warring factions to a conference in Italy. 'There,' he blithely asserted, 'we can knock their heads together and make them see sense.' Billy doubted whether Hoxha would ever be brought to see sense, and pointed out to Smith that the communists were already acting only too sensibly from their own point of view. But Abas Kupi welcomed the idea of an armistice and volunteered to go to Italy himself.

The next step was to bring Smith in contact with the communists and to this end Billy decided to take him back with David and Julian to their base for a talk with Alan Hare, who had been watching the fighting and would know best where to cross the lines. But on their way they saw for themselves that Hoxha had forestalled them. His partisans had entered the Mati valley and set fire to Kupi's strongholds. As he watched the flames Billy wondered what kind of reception his own mission might expect from the communists, and was not reassured when Smith casually remarked that Bari had accepted a proposal from Enver Hoxha that his partisans should take under their 'protection' any British officers they 'chanced to meet' in Zogist territory. This was a fine time, Billy thought, for such information. But worse news was to come. A scout he had sent ahead to reconnoitre the situation came back and reported that the communists had overrun the mission's base, looted their stores, seized their wireless, and captured Alan and his operator.*

Billy, David and Julian had no wish to suffer the same fate; so they parted company with Smith, leaving him to make his own way to the communists, and went into hiding in the depths of a thick beech forest to await the outcome of his efforts to secure a truce. It poured with rain and they were drenched day and night. They were also hungry, for what food they had brought with them had to be

---

* Alan was marched south and eventually evacuated from partisan territory.

strictly rationed. But they were able to keep in daily wireless contact with Bari and thus, at the end of a comfortless week, they learnt that Enver Hoxha had rejected Smith's proposals out of hand.

Their situation was now desperate. If they left their hideout they risked being seized by their communist 'allies' who surrounded them on all sides. On the other hand, they could not hold out any longer. So they decided to make a break for it. That night, then, so as not to present too large a target – with muleteers and bodyguards, their party was twelve strong – they split up into three groups and under cover of darkness crept separately through the cordon. By daylight they were safely back in Zogist territory, and a few hours later they joined forces again in a farmhouse some ten miles from Tirana belonging to a wealthy landowner called Ihsan Toptani, who spoke excellent English and had played an important part in trying to reconcile the LNC and the nationalists. He had always kept aloof from politics but his private sympathies were unreservedly pro-British and he gave them a warm welcome, providing them with real beds, clean sheets, hot baths and civilised food – unwonted luxury after their recent ordeal. They were tempted to stay there indefinitely, but their continued presence might have jeopardised their host. Next day, therefore, they moved into the foothills and established a new base in an olive grove within easy reach of Abas Kupi, who had likewise set up new headquarters on the slopes of Mount Kruya, a short distance further north.

Here, to their chagrin and amazement, they learnt that, despite categorical assurances to the contrary, the communists were again receiving regular supplies of arms from Italy. Billy protested vigorously to Bari and asked for an explanation, and could hardly believe the reply he received. The supplies, he was told, had been dropped in answer to an appeal from one of the British officers attached to Enver Hoxha, who had persuaded him that Abas Kupi was a traitor. This officer had even had the temerity to send the following signal: 'Met Hoxha tonight [23 August]. Stated McLean, Smiley and Amery working against partisans with collaborators. Gave ultimatum they must leave Albania or hand themselves over to partisans for evacuation to Italy within five days. Otherwise partisan patrols will be sent out to capture them and bring them back for trial by partisan military court.' Bari at least had the decency to forward this message to Billy, so as to let him know what was going on and to assure him that they had told Hoxha to withdraw his threat or else all supplies to him would cease. This counter-ultimatum had the desired effect: the threat was withdrawn. But Billy still felt badly let down.

Meanwhile he heard that Abas Kupi was concentrating his forces
in the coastal range with a view to attacking and taking Durazzo, the
second city of Albania. He at once sent David off to reconnoitre the
prospect and assess the chances of success. These proved to be fairly
slim, for even if the attack succeeded, the Germans were bound to
retaliate and the Zogists would be driven out with heavy losses within
two days. Billy therefore persuaded Kupi to abandon the plan and
apply himself instead to keeping the Tirana–Scutari highway blocked.
He notified Bari to this effect and on 1 September a plane-load of
supplies was at last dropped to the Zogist headquarters.

A few days later Billy heard that a unit of Soviet troops from
Central Asia – mostly Tajiks, Kazaks and Uzbeks, who had deserted
from the Russian army and enlisted in the Wehrmacht for duties in
occupied territories – had mutinied, murdered their German officers
and taken to the hills. Remembering the principle of irregular warfare
that he had learnt in Abyssinia, he took the risk of rounding them up
and organising them into a strike force under his personal command.
Then, to test their loyalty and fighting qualities, he decided to attack
the nearest worthwhile target, a German artillery headquarters. A *çeta*
of a hundred Zogists promptly volunteered to join him. He himself led
the charge at the head of the Zogists, with Julian and the Turkomans
attacking from the other flank, while David and three machine-gunners
gave covering fire.

The operation was a complete success. The Germans fled, leaving
ten dead on the ground. Here was ample evidence to refute Hoxha's
charges of Kupi's collaboration with the enemy. Billy signalled the good
news to Bari, and once again could hardly believe their reply. Instead of
the congratulations and encouragement he expected, instructions came
for him and David to 'report' as soon as possible to Italy, while Julian
was to stay behind as 'a neutral observer', with orders to dissuade Kupi
from engaging the Germans and to hold out no hope of British support
for him if he did.

As though to add insult to injury, he was told that he and
David would be 'escorted' to the coast by the partisans. This is
what had happened to Alan, and another British officer and his
wireless operator had likewise been marched south under conditions
of calculated indignity. Billy resolved that he and David would not
be similarly humiliated. He therefore decided to ignore these instructions for the time being, in the hope of their being rescinded if the
nationalists increased their activity. Ironically, the chances of their
doing so were now higher than ever: the Germans had started to
withdraw from Albania, and Abas Ermenye, the military leader of

the Balli Kombëtar, had recently appeared at the head of a thousand followers and offered his services in the common cause.

For the next two weeks this combined force incessantly harassed the retreating enemy convoys, laying ambushes on the main road, blowing up bridges and seizing quantities of arms and equipment. Yet no more supplies were dropped to them. SOE headquarters had negotiated a formal military agreement with Enver Hoxha and were reluctant to do anything that might offend or upset him. To make matters worse, the partisans now stepped up their activity, not against the Germans but against the Zogists. Unable to fight on two fronts, Abas Kupi was forced to disband his troops. The fate of Billy's mission was therefore sealed.

After an acrimonious exchange of signals, however, he did obtain certain concessions. His instructions to hand himself over to Hoxha were countermanded; instead, a motor torpedo-boat was to be sent in to take off the whole mission, Julian included. But Abas Kupi was to be left behind. Billy was categorically forbidden to bring him out, or any of his companions, lest their presence in Italy should damage SOE's relations with Enver Hoxha. This was the last straw. Billy refused to abandon his friend and loyal ally and, at the risk of being court-martialled for taking the law into his own hands, he advised Kupi to charter a local vessel, on which the mission would also embark. At the same time he sent a personal message to Anthony Eden explaining the situation. To this he received no reply. Instead, another signal arrived ordering him to make his way down to an appointed spot on the coast from which the mission would be evacuated on the night of 24 October. There was nothing for it but to obey.

Back in Bari, Billy discovered that his signal to Eden had been deliberately suppressed in the SOE office, whose policy appeared to be dictated entirely by partisan interests. He therefore sent another, to which Eden replied at once, recommending that Kupi be evacuated. But the office still stalled, so he flew up to Caserta to plead his case before General Wilson, the Supreme Commander, and Harold Macmillan, the resident minister of state. Both agreed that Kupi must be rescued, and orders were given to this effect. A few hours later, however, David rang up to say that Kupi was safe: he and five companions, including Ihsan Toptani, had landed at Brindisi that very morning in the boat that Billy had advised him to charter. But for this advice, they might never have got away. As it was, they had been saved in the nick of time. With the German withdrawal from Albania, the whole country fell into Enver Hoxha's hands and, in consequence, under a reign of terror.

Billy was anxious to leave Bari as quickly as possible. He found the company of the officers in the Albanian section unbearable; one of them at least was a member of the British Communist Party and the rest held left-wing views. This was not in itself objectionable – after all, Russia was an ally – but he did mind their calling him a 'fascist spy', just because he did not share their reverence for good old Uncle Joe. It was therefore with relief that he finished his report and flew straight back to London.

5 *The Oriental Traveller*

In London Billy met with a warmer reception than he had been given in Bari. Lord Selbourne, the cabinet minister responsible for SOE, received him with great kindness and, having read his report, expressed complete sympathy with his views. Billy had not minced his words. His two missions to Albania had convinced him that although Russia was Britain's ally today, it would be the West's adversary tomorrow. He therefore felt it was his duty not only to fight Hitler's Germany and Hirohito's Japan, but also to oppose the spread of the communist doctrine with which the free world was bound to find itself in conflict as soon as the war was over.

In Europe hostilities were already drawing to a close; it was only a matter of months before the Germans were defeated. The centre of gravity in the struggle against the common foe would then shift to the Far East, where a clash between Soviet, American and British interests was very likely to occur. The uneasy truce between Chiang Kai-shek, the nationalist generalissimo, and the communist leader, Mao Tse-tung, might well develop into a gigantic Asiatic version of the recent conflict between Abas Kupi and Enver Hoxha. Billy felt that his experience might be put to good use, if only in trying to avoid in another territory the mistakes that had been made in the Balkans. He therefore volunteered for duty in China, and in the spring of 1945 flew out to SOE headquarters in Ceylon.

Together with two or three score other operational officers, including some of his Tara colleagues, Billy found himself installed in a camp near Colombo. It was a far cry from Cairo. Accommodation consisted of a number of *bashas*, or huts, built of lashed coconut-palm fronds. These had been put up only a few months before but were already being eaten away by white ants and other destructive insects. The space under the flooring was occupied by cobras and pythons. Scorpions were a daily hazard; one had to be careful to shake out one's jungle boots every morning before putting them on. The damp was appalling; freshly

laundered shirts and shorts came back from the *dhobi* looking and
feeling like limp rags, and leather equipment was covered overnight
with a dusting of penicillin-like mould.

Billy spent several weeks here, increasingly impatient for a posting.
But none materialised. The Americans, already deployed in strength
on the far side of the Himalayas, were hostile to any British mission
being sent to China; SOE would be allowed to operate only in Burma,
Malaya, Siam, French Indo-China and the Dutch East Indies. Many of
his brother officers found a niche for themselves in one or another of
these countries, but China still beckoned and Billy was all the more
determined to get there. He therefore decided to act on his own and
flew up to Delhi, where he felt he would have more opportunity of
realising his dream.

His instinct was correct. Julian Amery, whom he found staying at
Viceroy's House, had just been offered the post of military adviser
to the British consul-general designate to Kashgar, the largest city in
China's westernmost province, Sinkiang; but he had had to refuse it
as he was about to fly back to England to stand as a candidate at the
forthcoming general election. The job was now Billy's for the asking.
He asked, and was duly accepted.

Sinkiang, or Chinese Turkestan, was right up his street: a remote,
mysterious land and a potential bone of contention. In the early thirties
it had come under Soviet rule, but the Chinese had recovered control
of it in 1942, when Russia had had to concentrate all its forces against
Hitler. Two years later, however, when the tide of war on the Western
Front was running in their favour, the Soviets turned their eyes once
more to the East and their attitude toward China stiffened. In Sinkiang
this resulted in a revolt which broke out in February 1944 among the
nomads in the north-west of the country. Later that year there were
large-scale raids into the south from the Soviet Union, and these were
still going on. Raiders kept crossing the frontier in bands from 200 to
300 strong, armed with mortars, machine-guns and rifles, and after
two to three days' pillaging would make their way back with the loot.
It was the sort of situation that appealed to Billy's sense of adventure
and also to his appetite for political intrigue.

Sinkiang had an additional attraction for him: it was a melt-
ing pot for different races, 80 per cent of whom were Muslims
of Turkish stock. Turkis, Uzbeks and Tartars inhabited the oases
around the Takla Makan desert; Kazaks wandered over the bare
windswept steppes of the north and along the wooded slopes of the
Altai, while Kirghiz tribes roamed the Pamirs and the Tien Shan, or
'Heavenly Mountains'. Billy was also aware of the country's strategic

importance. Should the Soviets assert themselves again in Sinkiang, they would gain control of the 5 million Muslims living there and thus be able to influence the 12 million Tungans, or Chinese Muslims of north-west China. This would increase Soviet prestige in the Muslim world as a whole, and would also afford Russia a territorial base for the political penetration of Tibet and Kashmir. The governments of India, Afghanistan and Great Britain therefore had a considerable interest in the preservation of a friendly Chinese presence in Sinkiang, and this was Billy's brief. He would be playing an active part in the Great Game, as described in one of his favourite books, Rudyard Kipling's *Kim*.

Preparations for the expedition were already under way. The consul-general designate, Gordon Etherington-Smith, had scoured the bazaars and shopping centres of Delhi for the stores and equipment that would be needed for a 700-mile trek, and these were now being packed in cases of the right size and weight for pony transport. Billy also stocked up with such creature comforts as whisky and cigars, and on 4 June he and his companion set out on the first leg of their journey, by train to Rawalpindi, the last railway station on their route. From there they continued by car, through the hills of Jammu and along the Kashmir valley as far as Srinagar – an enchanting drive, which Billy described in a letter to one of his numerous girl friends: 'The valley is a mass of lovely lakes, rivers and streams, with villages of wooden houses clustering on the banks, balconied temples rising straight out of the water, and superb seventeenth-century Moghul gardens adorned with summer-houses, fountains and waterfalls.'

At Srinagar he and Etherington-Smith – they were not yet on Christian-name terms – were invited to stay with the political resident while they waited for a favourable weather report. It had been a hard winter and the passes ahead were still blocked. The residency, which reminded Billy of a Victorian vicarage, was extremely comfortable but rather too dull and respectable for his taste; so after a couple of days he moved into one of the gaily decorated houseboats on the lake. The neighbouring vessel was occupied by a Chinese gentleman on holiday with his Indian wife who, having no other language in common, conversed in pidgin English; and Billy was amused by their daily quarrels, which invariably ended in the self-same way, with the husband turning on his wife and screaming: 'Well, anyway, you slut, you are nothing but a fucking Black!'

At the end of a week news came through that road conditions had improved sufficiently for the travellers to resume their journey; but in fact it was not by road but by water that they started out, gliding smoothly away from Srinagar in two *doongas*, the small flat-bottomed

river boats of Kashmir, on which they were conveyed along the winding
Jhelum river and then across to Bandipur, on the far side of Wular
lake, where their caravan of eighty-two ponies awaited them. Loading
up took several hours, but at last they were on their way. They rode
along the valley for three or four miles and then began to climb steeply,
zigzagging up the side of the mountain through thick pine-woods, until
they reached the *dak* bungalow just below the Tragbal pass, where they
halted for the night. These bungalows, or rest-houses, maintained by
the local authorities and providing basic accommodation for a nominal
fee, were spaced along the route at one-day's-march intervals, so that
wayfarers might always find shelter. Billy and Gordon (as we must now
call him, since Billy by this time did) were thus spared the trouble and
discomfort of camping out in the open.

They almost lost count of the stages as they penetrated day after
day deeper and deeper into the heart of the Himalayas, now toiling
through thick mist and snow five feet deep as they crossed the highest
passes, now dazzled by the sun and nearly fainting from the heat as they
plunged into chasm and valley. On one stage they would find themselves plodding along dark and narrow gorges; on the next, ambling
through meadows studded with irises, primulas, forget-me-nots and
daisies; and on the stage after that, scaling saw-tooth ridges from which
they gazed in awe at a succession of snow-covered peaks receding into
the distance as far as the eye could see. The sight of Nanga Parbat in
particular left an indelible impression on Billy, 'its jagged, unclimbed
crown soaring in one sweep up to the very heavens.'

For days on end they followed the course of the Indus, through a
landscape of scorched sand, shingle and rock, without a tree, bush or
verdure of any kind, and eventually emerged on to a broad plain which
provided a delightful contrast: green fields, tall trees, watercourses,
plantations and – wonder of wonders – a small town of mud houses,
the first human dwellings they had seen since setting out from Srinagar
six weeks before. This was Gilgit, capital of the district of that name,
which though nominally part of Kashmir was administered by a British
political agent responsible to the viceroy. Here they stayed for over a
week, while their equipment was transferred to another caravan which
had been sent to them from Kashgar; then, escorted by a detachment
of the Gilgit Scouts, a locally recruited militia commanded by British
officers, they took to the road again.

A further four days' march brought them to Baltit, capital of
the mountain state of Hunza, where the ruling mir, or prince, a
most engaging character who spoke good English, invited them to
stay in a pleasant modern bungalow attached to his own medieval

castle. Here, for two days, they were cordially entertained, lavish feasts alternating with performances of local dancing – a refreshing interlude before re-embarking on the rigours of the trek. Ahead lay what they knew to be the hardest stages, through the narrow defiles and deep gorges of the Karakoram, named after the black gravel of which the range is composed. The surface consisted of loose detritus – at times it seemed as though the entire massif was crumbling to pieces in some vast process of disintegration – and patches of scree, which clung to the slopes in seeming defiance of the laws of gravity, presented a further succession of hazards. Trusting their own two feet more than their ponies' four hooves, they both dismounted, and were thankful they had done so when they saw one of their pack animals slither on a stone-shoot and plunge to its death into the river hundreds of feet below.

Three stages further on they encountered an even greater obstacle – the Batura glacier, one of the largest in the world, thirty miles long and between two and three miles wide. Though they crossed it at its narrowest point, it took them the best part of a day to negotiate the desolate stretch of boulders and rubble contorted into innumerable waves and troughs; it was like treading on an ocean turned to stone yet for ever in motion, for rock and ice alike kept shifting and heaving and cracking under the warm rays of the sun. But on the far side of the glacier the going was good, and for the next week they climbed uneventfully and steadily up to the Mintaka Karaul pass which, at a height of 15,000 feet, divides India from China. They had reached the Roof of the World, and Billy for the first time set eyes on the regions he had romantically envisaged all those years ago at school. Straight ahead stretched the green upland pastures of the Pamirs. The wind blew cold off the snow-capped heights, but after the heat and airlessness of the Indus valley it was like a breath of paradise and the two travellers inhaled it as deeply as the rarefied atmosphere would allow. Then, spurred on by the excitement of having at last reached Sinkiang, they set off at a brisk pace on the long descent into the grasslands.

Presently they caught sight of a group of mounted figures moving towards them. It turned out to be a patrol of frontier guards, awkwardly perched on great shaggy yaks. The men, who were all Turkis, escorted them to the nearest post, a fort of mud walls pierced with loopholes – so reminiscent of a *Beau Geste* film set as to appear almost unreal – where the Chinese commander received them as hospitably as lack of a common language permitted. Gordon had spent several years on the staff of the British embassy in Chungking, but his Chinese was not equal to the task of carrying on a long conversation. Luckily he and Billy had by now picked up a few words of Turki, and so managed, through a Turkic–Chinese interpreter attached to the garrison, to converse with their host, after a fashion.

On this side of the frontier there were no more *dak* bungalows or rest-houses in which to halt for the night; from now on they had to rely on the local authorities for their accommodation. They were thus escorted during the remainder of their trek from one fort to the next, or else, where no fort or any other permanent building existed, arrangements were made for them to be put up by Kirghiz families in the *aquois*, or felt tents, that were maintained at regular intervals along the route at the expense of the Indian government, for the benefit of the *dakchis*, or runners, who carried the consular mail between Kashgar and India. The Kirghiz were very poor but, to Billy's surprise and pleasure, their staple dish, *katelama*, was as rich as any sweetmeat he remembered from Istanbul. It consisted of flaky pastry made from flour, yak butter and fat, saturated with black honey and topped with clotted cream which, being made from yak's milk, was even thicker and tastier than normal Turkish *kaimak*.

In due course they started descending into the foothills, and one morning they came upon something they had not seen for more than two months: a motor road. At this point they were still three stages short of their destination – that's to say it would have taken them three more days to reach it at caravan pace – but a truck had been sent from Kashgar to pick them up, so, leaving the pony train to follow, they climbed in and drove off. In no time at all, it seemed (though in fact it was about four hours), they reached the outskirts of the town – an oasis in the midst of a barren desert – and then the massive mud walls of the old city. A few minutes more, and they had drawn up at the front door of the British consulate and were being ushered inside by the Consul-General, whom Gordon had come to relieve. He had good news for them: Japan had just surrendered, the war was over.

For some reason, which Billy never discovered, the British consulate in Kashgar was known as Chini Bogh, or the Chinese Garden. In fact it was an entire village, with its own bakery, foundry, and other work-shops, as well as stabling for a score of horses and accommodation for a hundred people. Billy was allotted the south wing of the main building, with a bedroom, bathroom and private sitting-room, and quarters for his personal servants. He was thus totally independent. In every other way he was also his own master. Though still a member of SOE, he was not engaged on SOE activities – indeed, now that the war had ended, there were no longer any enemy-occupied territories in which to operate. What, then, was the purpose of his present assignment? By and large, whatever he himself cared to make of it; his brief could be interpreted as he saw fit. For the time being, of course, there was no question of his taking any sort of action; all he could do was observe and report. But first of all he had to take his bearings and see how the land lay.

He started off by rubber-necking like any foreign tourist, ambling through the dusty streets of the old city, listening to the story-tellers on the steps of the Id Mashit mosque, bargaining with the merchants in the bazaars. One of the first things he noticed was the way the inhabitants appeared to shy away from him. He soon discovered why. When Sinkiang had been under Soviet influence, anyone known to have anything to do with the British had been put in prison or forced to leave the country. People remembered those days and were still scared of being seen conversing in public with a British subject, for fear of being persecuted should the Soviets reassert their sway. But they did not seem at all unfriendly and he felt it would be only a question of time before they ceased to be embarrassed by his presence in their midst.

As for the Chinese he encountered, they too, though perfectly cordial, seemed to hold aloof. Not without reason, as he well knew. In the past the British had often fomented Muslim rebellions in Sinkiang in order to extend their influence there in the interests of India. The Chinese were therefore understandably suspicious of a continued British presence in the country, and the fact that the recent Muslim raids were instigated by the Kremlin did nothing to diminish this suspicion; it merely put the Chinese on their guard against the Russians as well, and above all against the local population whom they had even more reason to fear and distrust. The Kazaks in particular were a constant threat. They had rebelled twice during the previous year and the three northern districts of Sinkiang were still in their hands. Where would they strike again? And when?

That very autumn, as it turned out. And on several fronts at once. In the south five rebel columns, armed with rifles, machine-guns and mortars, pushed through the passes leading from Russia on to the Pamirs, drove out the Chinese garrison (carrying out in the process horrible atrocities in true Central Asian style) and advanced almost to Kashgar. In the north another group thrust eastwards and were not halted until they were within a hundred miles of the capital, Urumchi. Smaller groups raiding even further east then cut the road between Urumchi and central China. If the native population had joined in the uprising the Chinese would have been unable to hold the country; but the Turkis, although averse to Chinese rule, were not prepared to risk their necks or property in order to restore Soviet rule, under which they had been equally oppressed for eight years. The rebel advance therefore lost its momentum and both sides settled down to prepare for the next round. Conditions were so disturbed, however, that all the routes out of Sinkiang remained closed. So Billy found himself marooned. Not that he minded. The duration of his assignment had never been determined and in any case, with winter setting in, he would not have been able to leave the country until the following spring. He looked forward to at least six months more in Sinkiang, and prepared to make the best of his sojourn.

The first task he set himself was to improve his Turkic, so as to be able to converse with at least one section of the local population. Gradually he managed to overcome their distrust and, when away from the watchful eyes of the police, they would talk freely on almost every subject and even criticise the Chinese officialdom. They introduced him to their own form of falconry and often asked him out on expeditions in the desert, where they would hunt hares, pheasants and duck with goshawks (which were slower than peregrines, but easier to train) or, mounted on shaggy Kalmuck ponies, chase gazelle with the *qara qush*, the black eagle of Central Asia. At night they would crowd into the mud hut of a peasant or into a Kirghiz *acquoi* and sit on the floor drinking tea flavoured with red pepper, roasting gazelle meat *kebabs* over an open fire, smoking *charas* (home-grown hashish) and discussing the day's sport.

The only other foreign mission in Kashgar was the Soviet consulate-general, and the Russians often invited their British counterparts to dinner. The parties were usually a success, because they were very good hosts and provided great quantities of 54-per-cent-proof vodka which they knocked back as heartily as their guests. When it was their turn to come to the British consulate, however, they were always on their best behaviour and hardly drank at all, thereby inhibiting their hosts and casting a gloom over the proceedings. Having discovered that Billy was a Scotsman, they never tired of questioning him about Scottish nationalism and explaining to him, much to his amusement, how he and his compatriots were being oppressed by the brutal British capitalists. Little wonder, then, that he preferred the company of his Turki friends to theirs.

The winter of 1945–6 was said to be the mildest that Kashgar had known for over fifty years. Since the temperature nevertheless fell far below zero Fahrenheit, Billy dreaded to think what a harsh winter here might be like. Although he wore several layers of woollen clothes, a fur cap with ear muffs, and a padded sheepskin overcoat, he still felt naked in the blasts of the *buran*, the prevailing icy wind. But in due course the weather improved, and the advent of spring, which seemed to occur all of a sudden, made him realise how quickly the months had passed, and how pleasantly.

Unable to recover the territory they had lost to the rebels, the Chinese came to an agreement with them, and as a result the road to Urumchi and beyond was reopened. It was now possible to get back to India by way of central China, and Billy decided to return by this route to Delhi.

Even travelling by car and aeroplane, it took him just as long as his pony trek over the Himalayas. The distance was infinitely greater, of course, but what really consumed the time were the constant delays *en route*. He would find himself again and again in the middle of nowhere, without knowing how long he would have to wait or by what means he would be able to continue his journey; but a judicious mixture of bribery, persuasiveness and audacity in due course invariably secured him a seat in a vehicle or on an aircraft. Landscape always had a dual appeal for him: he appreciated it for strategic as well as aesthetic reasons. So as he drove down the imperial highway from Hani to Lanchow – through the so-called Kansu Corridor, almost 2000 miles long – he kept picturing the hordes of barbarians who for centuries had invaded China from this back door; then he pigeonholed the vision in a recess of his mind for future reference. As for Lanchow itself – his first experience of civilisation within the Great Wall of China – he was as much impressed by it as any savage Pict might have been on stumbling upon the first civilised outpost on the Cumbrian side of Hadrian's Wall.

He arrived back at Delhi at the end of June, thirteen months after he had left it, and, since SOE had ceased to exist, came under the orders of the Director of Military Intelligence, who instructed him to write a detailed report on the situation in Sinkiang. Meanwhile he stayed at Viceroy's House as the guest of Field-Marshal Lord Wavell.

The cold war that he had foreseen as a result of his experiences in the Balkans now seemed more inevitable than ever. The Iron Curtain – a phrase that had been coined only a few weeks before – was already a recognised feature of Soviet policy. These factors were uppermost in his mind when he drafted his report, and to a large extent they coloured its contents. In his opinion there was a serious danger that the Russians might occupy Sinkiang. After all, they had done so before – until the

Chinese had re-established their own supremacy – and three northern districts of the country were still in the hands of rebels who were citizens of Soviet Turkestan. Sinkiang, however, seemed to him to be one of the few areas of Central Asia where retaliation in the cold war might still be possible. The native population, he claimed, would be the deciding factor. Many of them, discontented with Chinese rule, looked across the frontier for help from their fellow countrymen in the Soviet Union – a tendency that had been skilfully exploited by the Russians. On the other hand, being Turkish, they were anti-Russian by tradition and, as Muslims, anti-communist on principle; and these ethnic and religious differences could equally well be exploited by the British.

Yes, but how? Well, first of all, by setting up an intelligence network and propaganda machine aimed at encouraging native aspirations for a united and independent Turkestan. If these aspirations were realised under British auspices, Soviet influence in Central Asia might be effectively obstructed. The organisation could be based on Kashgar, where the British consulate-general already had useful contacts with the Turki population and certain Indian traders, and where Billy himself had earmarked a number of potential agents among the students and technicians being trained in Alma Ata and Tashkent; or on Urumchi, where there were three possible lines of penetration into Soviet Asia: through the Uzbek immigrants, the Kazaks of the Altai mountains and a handful of White Russian refugees. There could be another base at Tashkurghan, where it would be possible to canvass the Tajiks, Whakhis and Kirghiz living in the Chinese Pamirs. Finally, there were refugees from Sinkiang now living in India, some of whom could possibly be usefully recruited, as Billy saw for himself when he left Delhi for several days at a time to visit their camps in Kashmir, Peshawar and Bophal.

He also visited Afghanistan and, thanks to a cousin who had served as minister in Kabul, came to know most of the leading Afghan politicians and all of the royal family. From them he obtained permission to make a tour of Afghan Turkestan and the other provinces north of the Hindu Kush, where no private individual had been allowed to travel since the beginning of the war. Here was a heaven-sent opportunity to extend his field of activities, not to mention the chance of further adventure, and he hastened back to Delhi to make the necessary arrangements. His headquarters were only too willing for him to take up the Afghan invitation and readily agreed to a further plan which he now proposed – namely, to travel to Afghanistan by road, then drive on through Iran and the Middle East, skirting the soft under-belly of the Soviet Union for most of the way.

He was allotted as expenses no more than the cost of a single air fare to London, so the only vehicle he could afford was a second-hand Chevrolet station-wagon, in which, on a sunny autumn morning – 19 October 1946, to be precise – he drove off in triumph, accompanied by his friend Charles Rankin, the viceroy's assistant private secretary.

At the outset of their journey they continued to enjoy the sort of viceregal conditions to which they had grown accustomed, spending the first night in Lahore, at Government House, as guests of the Governor of Punjab; the second in Peshawar, at Government House, as guests of the Governor of the North West Frontier Province; the third (after crossing the border into Afghanistan by way of the Khyber Pass) in Jalalabad, at the British consulate, as guests of the Consul; and the fourth in Kabul, at the British embassy, as guests of the Ambassador. But from there on the going grew rougher, both for the vehicle and for themselves.

North of the Hindu Kush board and lodging left much to be desired. But Billy didn't mind; he always enjoyed contrast. Besides, he was delighted to find himself again in an atmosphere and landscape that reminded him of Sinkiang. After threading through the claustrophobic gorges in the mountains it was a relief to come out into the open, almost steppe-like country traversed by herds of horses and sheep and dotted with the round felt tents of the nomads. Above all he was delighted to be back among Turkomans: 'To me they are like a breath of fresh air from Central Asia, with their round red faces and slit eyes and their gaily coloured quilted coats, huge turbans and high-heeled riding-boots.'

After three days' driving along a surprisingly good road – it had just been repaired for the King's forthcoming tour of the northern provinces – and three nights spent in one-horse towns providing primitive food and accommodation at exorbitant prices, they reached the valley of the Oxus and, in the words of an earlier English traveller in these parts, 'felt the presence of the river thirty miles away as one feels the presence of the sea before seeing it.' They also felt the proximity of the Soviet Union, for the Oxus marks the frontier between Russia and Afghanistan; but, as far as Billy could make out, there was absolutely no communication between the two countries, not even contraband traffic.

Heading westwards and parallel to the frontier, along part of the route that Marco Polo had travelled nearly seven centuries before (but in the opposite direction) they eventually reached a point where the metalled road petered out into a desert track which

slowed down their advance and imposed a severe strain on the old
station-wagon. First the fanbelt broke, then the clutch burned out;
finally something happened to the gearbox – neither of them knew
exactly what, for neither was mechanically minded – and they were
brought to a halt in the middle of nowhere. But they were in luck.
Before they could even decide what they were going to do, a truck
miraculously materialised and towed them all the way to Herat, the
nearest big town and the last before the Iranian border. Here they
stayed in a reasonably comfortable hotel while their car was being
repaired. The chief of police undertook to find them the spare parts
they needed, and the governor of the province put his own car and
chauffeur at their disposal. But the charms of Herat soon palled –
the bazaar was a disappointment, the mosques nothing to write home
about – and the week they spent there seemed more like a month by
the time they were able to drive on.

They had not gone very far – just over the frontier in fact – before
they were in trouble again. Ominous clanks and vibrations heralded a
loss of engine power and it was long after dark when they finally crept
into Meshed, the capital of the Iranian province of Khorasan. Here they
were delayed for yet another week, while their car was repaired – but
extremely badly repaired, for two days after resuming their journey
they broke down yet again in a god-forsaken place called Shahroud.
This time there was nothing for it but to carry on by train to Tehran
and make arrangements there for the vehicle to be retrieved and put
in order in a proper workshop.

Nearly two months had elapsed since their departure from Delhi;
they were still only a little over halfway to Cairo; and now they were
faced with further delay. But if they had to cool their heels somewhere
en route, they could not have chosen a better spot than the Iranian
capital. They moved into a large hotel in the centre of the town and
for several days gorged themselves on caviare. 'For the first time in my
life I had a surfeit of the stuff,' Billy admitted, and they soon stopped
ordering it for breakfast as well as for every other meal and even
between meals. Much of their time was spent at the British embassy,
where they both had friends and where they celebrated Christmas
and the New Year; and, thanks to a little diplomatic pressure, the
station-wagon was ready for the road again by the middle of January.
But Charles Rankin was too ill to drive on. A duodenal ulcer sent him
hurrying back to England by air and Billy found a new companion for
the rest of the journey in Norman Derbyshire, the Assistant Oriental
Secretary, who had served in the embassy for some time and spoke
fluent Persian.

They headed first towards the Caspian Sea, in the direction of the Russian border, through the province of Azerbaijan which had been under Soviet influence until a few weeks before. In 1941, in order to oust the pro-German Iranian monarch and safeguard allied interests, Russian forces had occupied the north of the country and British troops had landed in the south. When the objective had been achieved, the British withdrew; but the Russians remained and did not evacuate their zone until May 1946. In the meanwhile the so-called Democrat Party, an instrument of Soviet policy, had set up an autonomous government in Azerbaijan, while a Kurdish movement for autonomy took place in Mahabad, near the Iraq frontier, also with Russian encouragement. Iranian forces finally marched on Azerbaijan and the democrats withdrew into Soviet territory, blowing up bridges and roads behind them. But these demolitions had clearly not been carried out by expert engineers, for Billy and his companion had no difficulty in driving right up to Astara, the frontier post on the Caspian coast.

They arrived there after dark and were halted by sentries thrusting their cocked rifles into the car. They asked if the travellers were Russian and, on being told they were British, flashed cigarette lighters and matches in their faces as though to verify the statement. Although Billy and Norman, muffled up in fur hats and fur coats, must have looked almost like caricature Muscovites, the soldiers cheerfully accepted their identity and without even a glance at their passports escorted them to their colonel, who invited them to dine in the officers' mess and to share his own quarters. Their host proved to be a man of great charm and hospitality, a typical Persian of the old school, intelligent, easygoing, pleasure-loving, somewhat idle, fairly incompetent and thoroughly corrupt – that at least was Billy's immediate impression – but very favourably disposed towards the British and eager to help his guests in any way he could.

Next morning he took them to a spot from where they had a good view of the Soviet positions on the far side of the border. A line of stone barracks and wooden observation-towers stretched all the way from the coast to the foothills, protected by a single-strand barbed-wire fence patrolled at intervals by pairs of sentries. Billy thought it would be quite easy to slip through these defences, and was not surprised to learn that there were several crossing-points in constant use by smugglers. Otherwise, as on the Russo-Afghan border, there was no communication at all between the two countries.

From Astara a secondary road led inland through the mountains, the shortest way to Tabriz and points west. Billy and Norman took it but found themselves blocked by snow at the very first pass. They had to return to the coast, then drive nearly all the way back to Tehran before rejoining the main highway. So it was not until several days later that they reached Tabriz, the capital of the province, where they stayed at the British consulate-general – but only for one night, for the Consul-General manifested an immediate antipathy which they heartily reciprocated (though his wife made amends by slipping them a bottle of whisky when they said goodbye to her). Then they set off again.

A morning's drive northwards brought them to Julfa, on the Armenian border, the only official entry point into the Soviet Union that Billy had so far seen, but which he had no wish to use. So they headed west again, hoping to leave Iran by way of Turkey, and in the stretch of no-man's-land between the two frontier posts they became stuck fast in a snowdrift. There was nothing for it but to struggle ahead on foot. The Turkish officials, amazed by the visitation of two foreign pedestrians, gave them a warm welcome and plied them with coffee and cigarettes. They could do nothing to help, however – the snow lay even deeper further up the road – and advised them to retrace their steps, find some oxen to pull their car free, then drive back the way they had come. This they managed to do, with surprisingly little trouble and after only twenty-four hours' delay in the little frontier town of Maku.

As there was no other road into Turkey, they decided to drive south towards Iraq, stopping on the way at Mahabad, which the Kurds chose as the capital of the autonomous republic they had declared thirteen months before. This venture, like that of the Azerbaijan democrats, had recently been quashed and the ringleaders were still in prison under sentence of death.* But a group of rebels, some 2000 strong, was still at large fifty miles or so to the north, and Iranian troops were assembled in force at Mahabad, prepared to attack them should peaceful negotiations with them fail. Billy spoke to one of the officers, a tubby little captain in command of a motorised artillery battery, who referred to the Kurds as 'wild, dirty people. . . . Just look at them,' he went on, indicating the crowd in the streets. But Billy found them more attractive than most Iranian crowds. His instinctive sympathy with any ethnic minority or tribal people – and the Kurds are both, having no homeland and being scattered over the frontier regions of five adjacent countries§ – no doubt prejudiced him in their favour. Besides, they

---

* They were hanged a month later, on 31 March 1947.

§ The Kurdish population has been variously estimated at between 6 and 12 million, divided among Turkey, Iraq, Iran, Syria and the USSR.

had appealed to him ever since he had learnt at an early age that his hero Saladin was not an Arab, which is what most English schoolboys assume a Saracen to be, but a Kurd from northern Iraq.

The leader of the nearby rebel group was also from Iraq. His name was Mullah Mustafa Barzani, who was born into a tribe long famous for its fighting qualities.* The Barzanis had been in the forefront of every rebellion: against the Turkish authorities when Iraq was part of the Ottoman Empire; against the British during the British mandate that followed the end of Turkish rule; and against the Baghdad government after Iraq had become a sovereign state in 1932. Mullah Mustafa was himself interned in 1935 for his revolutionary activities but escaped eight years later, and within a few months had assembled a tribal force so large and well armed that the government agreed to treat with him and to discuss Kurdish grievances. He continued nevertheless to raid police posts and seize government property with apparent impunity, which encouraged other tribes to join him. Alarmed by the consequent spread of Kurdish nationalism, the authorities finally decided to take action. An army column sent up to restore law and order met with ignominious defeat and failure; but when air force planes began to take their toll of Barzani property and morale, Mullah Mustafa had no alternative but to withdraw over the border into Iran. He arrived just in time to lend his support to the newly proclaimed Mahabad republic. Now, thirteen months later, he was on the run again, yet also again in the process of negotiating with the authorities.

Intrigued by what he had heard of the man's character and career, Billy tried to get in touch with him. He particularly wanted to see how such an essentially feudal figure could have become the apparent champion of a Soviet-sponsored movement. So he drove out to the Barzani camp with the Iranian colonel in charge of the negotiations. But nothing came of the visit. Mullah Mustafa had already made up his mind to pull out, and two days later redeployed his forces toward the Iraq frontier.

Billy himself subsequently headed in the same direction, aiming to enter Iraq by way of the Ruwandiz pass, but found that this road also was blocked by snow. He had no alternative but to drive back to Tabriz, then south again to pick up the Tehran–Baghdad highway. The remainder of the journey was something of an anticlimax. Baghdad, Amman and Jerusalem were the only memorable stopping-places on

---

* I give these particulars here to avoid repeating them later. In time to come, though he could not have foreseen it at Mahabad, Billy was to have more to do with Mullah Mustafa.

a route that seemed increasingly more tame the closer he drew to his destination. But Cairo itself had lost none of its charm during the two years he had been away, and he lingered there for nearly a month before flying on to London.

6 *The Neophyte Civilian*

The end of hostilities brought many young servicemen down to earth with a bump. War being the state of exception that it is, they had lived, some of them for the whole duration, in a sort of cloud-cuckoo land, absolved from everyday responsibilities, commitments and problems. They had had their conduct dictated to them, their thinking done for them. So it was hard to adjust to normal existence, particularly for those who had been too young to have had a job before joining up. Whatever career they now chose, they would be starting at a disadvantage, handicapped by the lack of the experience and training they would have acquired during the years they had spent fighting, and perhaps also hamstrung by resentment at having to accept a humbler position and a smaller salary than employees of their age had reason to expect. Though pay in the armed forces was nothing to write home about, many new recruits to civilian life found themselves worse off than they had been in the services.

In this respect Billy was more privileged than most. He had been commissioned, and so already had a job, before the outbreak of hostilities. Moreover, his job being what it was, the war, far from interrupting it, had enlarged its scope and increased its significance. Not that all his colleagues subscribed to this opinion. There were some old diehards who could hardly wait for the war to end 'so that we can get down to proper soldiering again'. But 'proper soldiering' had never appealed to Billy and the prospect of returning to his regiment, from which he had been absent for so long, was disconcerting. He was the first to admit that his paramilitary activity had accorded him a higher rank than his military seniority warranted, and had also bestowed on him, as an allied representative in enemy-occupied territory (necessarily a *rara avis*) an inflated position of importance which owed as much to circumstance as to his own qualifications and ability. Even so, that rank and that position had been his; he had proved worthy of them; and he felt that a lower rank and a lowlier position, both of which he

would have to accept if he stayed in the army, would restrict whatever
talents he had developed. He had mastered the tactics of guerrilla warfare in Ethiopia. He had sampled the politics of guerrilla warfare in
Albania. He had had no other political experience, but was eager for
more. Besides, a political career would enable him to continue to serve
his country. He therefore applied to resign his commission, on the
ground that he wished to stand for Parliament. The War Office duly
accepted his resignation and he moved into bachelor chambers in
Down Street, London, entered his name on the Conservative Panel,
and started a course of public speaking at the Conservative Central
Office, pending his adoption as a prospective candidate.

He had served nine years and nine months in the army. Had
he completed ten years he would have received a gratuity of £1000.
As it was, he got nothing. 'How typical of Billy!' was the verdict
of his friends, some of whom perceived in his premature gesture a
patrician disregard for money, whereas others saw mere inattention.
Both interpretations were correct, for both traits were intrinsic to his
character.

Many other, sometimes contradictory, attributes contributed to
his nature. Superficially he was the model of a man-about-town and
a pillar of the Establishment. He lived in Mayfair. He belonged to
several West End clubs. He lunched and dined out every day of the
week, and attended every fashionable dance and wedding. He spent
weekends in ducal houses and, though he no longer hunted and had
never been keen on fishing, went shooting at the appropriate country
seats. An allowance from his father of £1000 a year – almost double
an MP's salary at the time – was not enough to keep him in the
style which he took for granted, and he soon had an overdraft so
large that his bank would never have allowed it had it not been
guaranteed by one of his richer friends, Colin Mackenzie, whom he
had known since early boyhood. This worried him as little as had
the forfeiture of his gratuity. For all his expensive tastes, however,
he was not as frivolous as he seemed and his occupations were not
exclusively Woosterish. In addition to the course of public speaking,
he persevered with his Russian and Turkish lessons, and began to
read widely and attentively in order to fill what he considered to
be gaps in his education. Biography and politics competed for his
favour with comparative religion. English and French classics also
vied to be included in his curriculum. But, like a secret drinker who
hides the bottles under his mattress, he kept his learning to himself,
concealing it as though it was a vice to be ashamed of or as though
he feared being thought 'intellectual' – to his mind, or at least on his

lips, a mildly disparaging word. He preferred to parade his worldly persona.

His natural dichotomy revealed itself in various other ways. Havana cigars (he never smoked cigarettes), fine wine and vintage port and, oddly for such a sophisticated palate, sweet liqueurs like Kümmel and Cointreau were his usual complements to a meal; but if they or even the meal itself were unavailable, he made a virtue of it, playfully telling himself and anyone else who cared to listen that abstinence was good for body and soul alike. From within the votary of Epicurus, the ascetic was always willing to emerge.

Likewise, the man of action contained a lazybones. A friend called on him one morning, just before noon, and found him still in bed. 'I'm working,' he explained, partly by way of excuse and partly in jest, as he indicated half a dozen newspapers cascading from his breakfast tray, across the counterpane and on to the floor. Similarly, the member of the pack would become the lone wolf, as he slipped away from the crony-crowded bar at White's to a table for one in a restaurant where he was sure of seeing no one he knew. Contrast was all.

As a final example of this symbiosis – for the catalogue of odd bed-fellows must end somewhere – the lounge-suited or dinner-jacketed or tail-coated denizen of London ballrooms and dining-rooms, the kilted son of the Highlands and the tweed-clad guest of the Shires (to list but a trio of his different overt selves) cohabited with the robed and turbaned nomad of the desert, the felt-shod and fur-muffled nomad of the steppes, and many another outlandish *alter ille* which, like the several working parts of a machine, constituted his physical and mental organism.

Demonstrably, therefore, Billy was already a man of many parts, with a wide variety of experience and a mind broad enough to encompass a host of seemingly conflicting aspirations and accomplishments. He was blessed to a marked degree with *areté*, that ancient Greek virtue which English schoolboys are prone to mistranslate, or rather half-translate, as 'goodness' or 'valour' or 'virtue', but which more properly connotes 'all-round excellence'. This augured well for his chosen career.

Several of his closest friends were involved in politics or were otherwise politically connected. Julian Amery, though defeated at the first postwar general election, which returned Labour to power, was destined for higher office in time to come. His father too lost his seat in 1945 – till then he had been Secretary of State for India – but his house, 112 Eaton Square, which to Billy was a second home, continued

to be such a hive of Conservative activity as to constitute an alternative
shadow cabinet. Leo Amery's socialist successor at the India Office was
Lord Listowel, Alan Hare's eldest brother, and Alan himself for some
time toyed with the idea of a political career. (His choice of party led
to his being deprived of the salmon which Billy's mother gave to each
of his friends every year: hearing he might be standing as a socialist, she
crossed him off her list.*) Harold Macmillan's son Maurice was another
strand in what was to become, through intermarriage, a close-knit
political network: his sister Catherine married Julian Amery; and
he himself married the Honourable Katharine Ormsby-Gore, whose
brother David became Minister of State for Foreign Affairs and whose
own services to the Conservative cause were to earn her the title of
dame. Hugh Fraser, the younger brother of Lord Lovat and a future
under-secretary for the colonies, and Rowly Winn, who became joint
parliamentary secretary at the Ministry of Agriculture after succeeding
to the title of Baron St Oswald, completed the intimate circle of friends
whose political views, while not always identical, reflected the image of
Tory government.

There was also Anthony Eden. As we have seen, he had singled
Billy out for special treatment during the war. Since then he had
continued to befriend him; and even though Eden was now out of
office, it could obviously do Billy no harm to be in the good books
of a former foreign secretary who was likely to rise even higher with
the return of a Conservative government.

If punctuality is the politeness of kings – and it was a king himself who
is supposed to have said it was§ – then Billy was anything but regal.
Three years before, in Cairo, he had turned up almost too late to be
decorated. Since then his unpunctuality had become a byword. Close
friends with whom he had made an appointment took it for granted
that he would be late, and timed their own arrival accordingly. Those
who knew him less well, or were meeting him for the first time, would
regret having turned up on the dot, only to be kept waiting half an hour
or more. One could almost judge the degree of anyone's intimacy with
Billy by how late he himself made a point of being – or, for that matter,
she herself; for when it came to keeping people waiting, Billy made no
distinction between the sexes. His girl friends soon grew used to this,
and paid him back in his own coin.

* Had she but known how far in the opposite direction his political allegiance
was finally to shift, she would have reinstated him straight away.

§ Louis XVIII: *L'exactitude est la politesse des rois.*

The girl he eventually married evolved a theory which pretty well exonerated him, namely that his mental alarm-clock was wrongly set. If he happened, for instance, to be at a cocktail party in one part of London, prior to dining in another part at a given hour, the alarm in his head would ring precisely at that hour, *on* time, but not *in* time to prevent his arriving late for dinner. Wearing a wristwatch did not help at all; he was always too engrossed in conversation to consult it. 'Unavoidably delayed' was his usual excuse, and these indeed were the first words his wife-to-be heard him utter. It was at a dinner party where he and she knew all the guests except each other. Their hostess introduced him to her – 'Daška Kennedy' – and placed them together at table. The unusual Christian name intrigued him and so did its bearer, who struck him (as he told her after they became engaged) as the second most beautiful woman he had ever seen, *the* most beautiful being a Turkish princess he had met only two weeks before. Daška had hurt her hand and had her arm in a sling, so Billy had to cut her meat for her – which brought them closer together literally as well as figuratively, the very process entailing a certain intimacy or collusion.

She was nevertheless surprised to hear from their hostess two days later that he had asked after her and said he would like to see her again. She welcomed the idea, and another, smaller party was arranged. After dinner they went on to a nightclub and then Daška, who had driven up for the evening from the country, gave the others a lift home before dropping Billy off last of all. They stopped outside his rooms and sat chatting in the car for half an hour, during which she sensed he was falling in love with her, and found herself reciprocating his feelings. 'How old are you?' she suddenly asked. 'Twenty-eight,' he replied, and added in the same breath – for he realised what lay behind the question, but it was too late now to make himself out any older – 'and three-quarters!' 'Well, I'm thirty-two,' she said, 'and I'm married and have four children.' Then she told him more about herself.

Her maiden name was Ivanović, she came from Yugoslavia, and her parents were divorced when she was six. Her mother then married the shipping tycoon Božo Banac, and although custody of Daška and her two brothers had been given to their father, it was their stepfather and their mother who brought them up. For five years the family lived in London, where Banac had his business headquarters, but the great depression following the Wall Street crash of 1929 caused him to lay up his fleet of eighteen vessels in Dalmatia, and the household moved back to his home ten miles south of Dubrovnik.

Dubrovnik was a favourite port of call for British yachtsmen with a discerning eye – not for nothing had the lovely old city republic been known as the 'Pearl of the Adriatic' – and many of them, with letters of introduction from London, dropped in on the Banacs. Soon there was a regular flow of British visitors, including the Duke and Duchess of Kent, who came to stay for several summers in succession; and Daška, who was already bilingual, found herself speaking English more than her native tongue. She seemed fated to marry an Englishman, and she did. Her wedding to Geoffrey Kennedy, a distinguished and successful consultant engineer took place in 1938, and she had lived in England ever since.

If either Billy or Daška thought it was wiser in the circumstances not to see each other again, neither was able to take the decision. The very next morning he rang her up and asked her out to dinner at the Ritz and she accepted without demur, especially when he told her, as though there was safety in numbers, that he was inviting another couple as well. So she drove up again for the evening from her home near Guildford.

Since her fellow guests were unknown to her, she could not tell if they were already there when she entered the hotel lobby on the dot of eight, the time they had been asked to foregather. But she saw straight away that Billy was not. She waited for half an hour; still no sign of him. Vexed and disappointed, and at the same time rather relieved – for she now had a very good reason, almost a desire, not to see him again – she decided to wait no longer; but as she passed the reception desk on her way out, she heard her name pronounced by the hall porter, who was at the telephone. When she told him who she was, he said there was a gentleman on the line who wished to speak to her. It was Billy, of course. And of course he had been 'unavoidably delayed'. But he begged her not to leave, and she relented.

By the end of the evening, after the other couple had left and they had gone on to a nightclub on their own, it seemed useless to pretend that their mutual attraction could be lightly dismissed or easily resisted.

More than a year went by before Billy was given a constituency to nurse. Part of this time he spent, a dutiful son, staying with his parents at Glencalvie. But never for longer than two weeks at a stretch; he could not bear being away from Daška a moment longer. She, on her side, came up from the country as often as she could and they lunched together most days of the week. This arrangement, though better than nothing, was far from perfect for either of them. But they saw no way out of the dilemma; for she recoiled from the idea of divorce and he too quailed at the thought of breaking up a marriage.

He was adopted as the Conservative candidate for Preston South in September 1948. Less than a month later his father and uncle, both of whom happened to be too ill to travel, asked him to go out to Hungary to see what could be salvaged from their trading company, which had recently been nationalised, and another month passed before he got back to England. By this time his mind was made up. The long separation from Daška, and the prospect of even longer separations dictated by a political career, persuaded him to take the plunge and he greeted her on his return with the words: 'Well, if you get a divorce, I'll marry you.'

This was not the most elegantly phrased proposal, but she accepted. For she too had come to a decision. The atmosphere at home was now so intolerable that even the children had begun to notice. 'Why is it, Mummy,' they asked, 'that you never smile when Daddy is here and you're perfectly happy when he's away?' Rather than risk their witnessing an open quarrel between mother and father, she thought it better for them to see their parents separately. So she asked for a divorce, left the house,* and moved in with her brother Vane and his wife, who lived nearby, so that she was able to be with the children every day while her husband was at work in London.

Early in the new year she and Billy went through the farcical rigmarole which divorce in England in those days entailed. They booked into a hotel in Stratford-upon-Avon under a false name, and made sure that the chambermaid saw them sharing a bed. In due course the case was heard and the decree came through – on 4 July. Billy was in Rome when Daška telegraphed the good news: 'Independence Day!'

Billy had gone to Rome on a secret mission in connection with his old stamping-ground, Albania.

Since 1945 Enver Hoxha's régime had been in full swing. People's courts were dealing out death sentences by the hundreds to 'war criminals', a term that included anyone whose sympathies were non-communist. Private estates had been abolished; all religious activity was suppressed; and bogus elections, at which there were no opposition candidates, had resulted in the formation of a national assembly composed entirely of Hoxha's supporters.

---

* Even though the house belonged to her, the court in due course decreed that she had left 'home' and therefore awarded custody of the children to Kennedy.

In May 1946 Albanian artillery opened fire on two British cruisers sailing through the Corfu Channel, which Britain regarded as an international waterway, and a few weeks later Albania declared a three-mile exclusion zone to foreign shipping. On 22 October explosions severely damaged a couple of British destroyers sailing from Corfu port in defiance of the three-mile limit and killed forty-three members of the crews. The waterway had been mined.

In October 1947 the UN General Assembly set up a special committee to investigate allegations that the Greek communist forces, disbanded the year before but now again in action against the Greek national army, were being equipped and provided with safe havens by Albania, Bulgaria and Yugoslavia. The committee found that Albania was the worst offender and recommended a stern condemnation of that country which might prepare the ground for any future action.

In June 1948 Stalin expelled Tito from the Cominform, and Albania found itself out on a limb. Julian Amery, since 1945 the Conservative candidate for Preston North, had visited Greece that summer and was quick to appreciate the situation. 'The position of the Albanian state,' he observed, 'is particularly precarious. Albania is separated from the rest of the Cominform by a deviationist Yugoslavia. . . . A number of political outlaws are still in the mountains, and news of recent purges suggests that the Albanian Communist Party is deeply divided between Stalinists and Titoists. In the face of a popular revolt the régime would be hard put to defend itself.'

Billy echoed this opinion. He and Julian might have been accused of wishful thinking – and after their wartime experiences in Albania they understandably had an axe to grind – had their view not been confirmed by an independent witness. Guy Menant, the French Minister in Tirana, who was now the main source of the few dismal scraps of information about Albania that reached the Western world, reported: 'The arrival on the frontier of sizeable numbers of allied troops would be the signal for a spontaneous uprising through Albania.' The moment for action seemed ripe.

But what form was this action to take? The open use in peacetime of allied troops against a small country with a gallant anti-Nazi record was clearly out of the question. Too many people in Britain, including most of the Labour government, were still singing the praises of dear old Uncle Joe, and public opinion would never have countenanced any overt move against a Soviet satellite. Secrecy was therefore of paramount importance. A special committee was formed to study the possibilities, and towards the end of the year the Prime Minister,

Clement Attlee, gave the official go-ahead for a small-scale clandestine subversive operation.

The plan was to infiltrate groups of agents and saboteurs recruited from anti-communist Albanians in exile, who would organise a general uprising and topple the Hoxha régime. From the political point of view there could be no objection to it. If successful, it would boost the morale of anti-communists throughout the Soviet empire and might well initiate a chain reaction that would roll back the tide of Soviet imperialism. On moral grounds too, since Stalin was trying to over-throw the pro-Western government in Athens, it seemed reasonable for Britain to try to overthrow the pro-Soviet government in Tirana. As Julian pointed out, 'You can't apply the Marquess of Queensberry rules to one side and not to the other.' But there was a serious snag – money, or rather the lack of it. Britain was in the throes of postwar austerity and, as a Foreign Office man remarked to Billy, 'Church mice do not make wars.' The special committee therefore decided to ask for American co-operation. Washington agreed, and by the spring of 1949 the plan had begun to take shape.

One of the first to be involved was Alan Hare. He had transferred at the end of the war from SOE to SIS, the Secret Intelligence Service, but such was his security that even Billy and Julian had been unaware of it until they too were roped in. They had kept in touch with Abas Kupi and with several other Albanian leaders who had fled their homeland after the communist take-over and whose followers were now living in refugee camps in Italy. The team would have been incomplete without David Smiley, who had risen to be second-in-command of the Blues after going to staff college and serving as Assistant Military Attaché in Warsaw. So he too was in at the start.

At the beginning of May, Alan, Billy and Julian flew out to Athens. Greece, being the only pro-Western country adjacent to Albania, was the obvious springboard for the operation; but first the Greek govern-ment had to give its assent. There was only one person who could authorise such a sensitive and potentially embarrassing use of Greek resources: Field-Marshal Papagos, the Greek army commander. But he was too busy to see a trio of young Englishmen with ostensibly no official position. They solved the problem by obtaining, through an old SOE comrade-in-arms, an introduction to one of the Field-Marshal's closest friends. They took him out to lunch at a taverna outside Athens where there was no chance of their being overheard, and put their cards on the table. Forty-eight hours later they had the Greek government's authority to go ahead with the scheme.

Meanwhile David Smiley, seconded from his regiment in Germany, had recruited a team of instructors in sabotage and guerrilla warfare, and flown out to Malta to set up a clandestine training school for the potential agents. These now had to be selected, and on 18 May the trio flew to Rome for discussions with the leaders of the Albanian exiles. With their help it did not take long to pick the men they needed from the various refugee camps. Hundreds volunteered, but the scale of the operation restricted the number required to thirty; and they in due course, with no documents, precious few possessions and not a word of English, were smuggled into Malta.

On 25 May the trio flew back to London to report on their progress and to meet their American counterpart, Robert Low, who had just arrived from Washington; and a month later they all flew out to Rome to conclude arrangements with the exiles. Their first task was to get the various factions to co-operate with a view to forming a representative Albanian government after liberation. The royalists under Abas Kupi were at loggerheads with the republican Balli Kombëtar, and both were sworn adversaries of the National Independents. There were also several other groups, none of whom was united except in their fervent opposition to communism. It took many days of intensive discussion to work out a compromise acceptable to all; but agreement on the formation of a national committee was finally reached on 7 July. Now all that remained was for King Zog to accept it.

The Albanian royal family had moved to Egypt in 1946 and were living in a large villa in Alexandria. It was here, on 14 July, that Billy, Julian and Robert Low met the King after flying from Rome to Cairo. The meeting started badly. 'We rather blundered in,' Billy later admitted, 'proud of having pulled off the Rome agreement, and we imagined that the King would accept what we put to him.' But far from accepting it, the King reacted angrily. Under whose authority, he asked, had this agreement been reached, and this 'government in exile' created? By what right had the British and Americans made such decisions and appointments? He, Zog, alone could represent Albania; no one else.

Without the King's assent there was no hope of the operation getting under way. It was therefore absolutely essential to win him over. With a few well-chosen words Julian managed to do so. 'Amery's performance was masterly,' Low recalled. 'I've never seen such diplomacy in my life. He was like Talleyrand.' The King relented. He would not support the committee publicly, he said; on the other hand, he would not oppose it. This was enough for the Anglo-American delegates. They flew back to Rome with the goods news that the thirty volunteers could now proceed with their training in Malta. This was to last several weeks. So Billy, having for the time being nothing further to do in Italy or Egypt, decided to fly home.

Now that Daška's divorce had come through, she and Billy were free to marry, and so, though they were not officially engaged, he notified his parents. As was only to be expected, his mother was disappointed by his choice – a divorcée with four children, and a foreigner to boot. She would have preferred any of his English girl friends, especially one belonging to the aristocracy; on the other hand, it was a relief to know that her future daughter-in-law was not a pauper. The Banac fortune, which had survived first the depression and then the war, had multiplied under the management of Daška's mother, who had succeeded her husband on his death in 1945. Lack of money therefore presented no impediment to the marriage.

To be on the safe side, however, Mrs McLean sent her husband to London to meet Daška and report back what he thought of her. Billy had arranged for the meeting to take place in his rooms, but went out on some errand or other and failed to return in time; so that Daška and his father, both of them punctual, had to introduce themselves and sum each other up on their own. By the time Billy returned, 'unavoidably delayed' as usual, the ice was broken: his father had been completely won over by Daška, whom he welcomed as his future daughter-in-law – 'subject', he added, as though suddenly remembering the purpose of his mission, 'to my wife's approval.'

Billy's next move was to take Daška to stay at Glencalvie and introduce her to his mother. Since the war his parents had had to do without servants, unable to find anyone willing to work in such a remote and isolated spot. They no longer had a chauffeur and neither of them could drive, so they had to hire a taxi every day to do the shopping in the little township of Ardgay, sixteen miles away, while their two Rolls-Royces stood idle, one in a local garage, the other in store at Harrods. Mrs McLean did all the cooking and sat down to dinner in her apron; but she insisted on the others being formally attired, the two men in dinner jackets and Daška in an evening dress. Afterwards Billy and his father cleared the table and did the washing-up, their black ties hovering incongruously above the kitchen sink, before rejoining the ladies in the drawing-room, where Daška was then subjected to three separate jets of Havana-scented smoke, for Mrs McLean enjoyed a good cigar as much as did her husband and her son. It was a trial by fumigation, which she passed with flying colours, earning her future mother-in-law's full approval and consent.

In due course she and Billy were married at Caxton Hall Register Office, but he wanted a religious ceremony as well, and, moreover, a Catholic one. He thought Catholicism was the only 'grown-up' Christian religion, and the Roman the only rite appropriate to the dignity of the Church. Besides, it was the faith in which Daška had been brought up – her father's faith, not her mother's which was Serbian Orthodox – and he felt that she should marry in no other. She had lapsed, as he knew, but he was sure that a course of religious instruction would redeem her. He suggested it; she complied; and it did.

They decided to hold the church service in Rome, where Daška had a cousin, a monsignor and former secretary to the Pope, who would make the arrangements. In Rome Billy would also be able to keep an eye on the Albanian committee. But he had to nurse his constituency as well, and therefore could not be out of England for more than a fortnight at a time. He and Daška left for Rome at the end of August, but the monsignor was not yet ready for them; so they went on to Sicily, honeymooning in advance lest there be no time later. The arrangements for their marriage had still not been made when they returned to Rome, so they came home to England.

Billy spent the next six weeks between London and Preston, occupied with constituency affairs but also following the progress of the Albanian operation. The first batch of volunteers had finished their training in Malta, and on 28 September nine of them embarked on a small fishing boat and headed towards the heel of Italy. Three days later, at sea off Otranto, they transferred to another vessel, ostensibly a private yacht but fitted with a powerful engine and with secret compartments and dummy fuel tanks, installed, just as the captain and crew had been chosen, especially for the operation. The yacht then set off for the Albanian coast, which it reached at dead of night, making a landfall at 'Seaview', the creek from which Billy and David had been evacuated during the war. From here the nine agents, after being ferried ashore with their arms and equipment, made their way inland.

Though they had two wireless sets, they gave no sign of life for several days. To keep in contact with them, Alan Hare had established a radio base in the north-east of Corfu, overlooking the channel and the Albanian coast. Here he listened in every day at a pre-arranged hour, but it was not until 12 October that they came on the air. Their brief and hurried signal announced that three of the nine had been killed in an encounter with a police patrol, a fourth was missing, and the remaining five were on the run. This augured ill for a second group of eleven who had been put ashore two days earlier by the same means as before but further north. They too kept silent, except for a couple of indistinct and incoherent messages. Clearly something had gone wrong, and so, when they next came on the air, Alan ordered them to make their way over the border into Greece.

The sixteen survivors, after being arrested by the Greek frontier guards and imprisoned in Yannina, were released through SIS intervention and taken to a 'safe house' in Athens. The information they brought was alarming. The first group had fallen into an ambush almost immediately after striking inland. Police and military forces had previously surrounded the coastal area, and patrols were active everywhere. The Albanian authorities seemed to have been forewarned about the landings and had not been taken by surprise. The second group reported similar conditions and activity in the area where they had been put ashore. This confirmatory evidence pointed to one of two things: a gross breach of security or treachery at a high level.

The operation had in fact been betrayed. But this did not come to light until January 1963, when Kim Philby defected to Moscow. In his memoirs, published five years later, he describes how he rose to a senior position in the British Secret Service while serving all the time as a Russian agent. Posted to Washington in the summer of 1949, he was given the important task of co-ordinating CIA and SIS participation in various Anglo-American ventures. He thus knew every detail of the Albanian operation and was able to report the forthcoming landings to his Soviet contact in London in time for Hoxha's security service to take action.

Despite this initial reverse, Washington and Whitehall decided to continue with the operation and sent further groups of agents into the field. Most of them were killed or captured and nothing was achieved. In the light of what we now know, this does not seem surprising. But at the time no one could have suspected such a disaster, and Billy and his colleagues were still optimistic about the final result. At the end of October he and Daška again flew out to Rome, and this time their mission was successful. At 11.30 in the morning of 14 November they were married at the Church of SS Luca e Martina al Foro Romano. Two days later they were back in London, and next morning they set off for Preston.

7 *The Parliamentary Candidate*

Billy had already laid the groundwork for his parliamentary campaign. Since his adoption he had spent as much time as he could with his prospective constituents, and had won them over. Now, with Daška by his side, his popularity soared. Her presence enhanced his reputation, surrounding him with an aura of romance. Her religion endeared her to the large Roman Catholic community, and her beauty endeared her to all. The local press, reviving the name by which she was known in pre-war Yugoslavia, never failed to refer to her as 'The Pearl of Dubrovnik'.

In his campaign speeches Billy voiced his hopes, his plans and his misgivings. He denounced materialism as 'a worldly, evil doctrine' and 'the real enemy of our generation'. To combat it, Britain needed to regain her faith in Christianity, and in this process all denominational schools had a vital part to play. 'I am a strong believer,' he said, 'in religious instruction in the schools. Every parent ought to have the right to choose what instruction his children should receive, and I shall do everything possible to further these views.'

He inveighed against the Labour government that had been in power since 1945, and blamed the postwar food shortage on its wasteful bulk buying. Rationing, he pointed out, was still in force in Britain although it had been lifted in most other European countries. During the height of the submarine blockade, he added, Britain was better fed than she was now. If the Conservatives were elected, they would rely on private traders who really knew about buying food from overseas at the lowest prices; and first priority would be given to buying animal foodstuffs to enable the farmers to raise more meat and poultry at home. He also blamed the high cost of living on reckless government expenditure and the expense of the nationalised industries, especially railways and coal. The Conservatives, he said, were pledged to stop further nationalisation; to hand back nationalised industries to private enterprise where this was practical; and, in those industries where nationalisation had already gone too far, to decentralise and cut out waste.

On foreign affairs, the issue that concerned him most, he spoke with the deepest conviction. The only way to deal with Russia, he asserted, was for Britain to be strong; and the best hope of preserving peace and freedom lay in the combined strength of the British Commonwealth and Empire and a united and free Europe. Only through developing the resources of the Empire, he believed, could Britain recover her economic independence; socialist talk of exporting enough goods to America to bridge the dollar gap was a pipe dream.

'I also believe,' he concluded, 'in the freedom of every person to lead his own life in his own way, provided he does his duty towards his God and towards his neighbour. I believe today that the only way through the difficulties which lie ahead of us is to combine freedom with social justice. This is the Conservative way. Our aim is to create a property-owning democracy.'

But the electorate was not yet ready for this, either at Preston South or in the country as a whole. At the general election of 23 February 1950 Billy lost to the socialist candidate (but by only 149 votes); and Labour returned to power, but with such a reduced majority (of eight, as against 186 in 1945) that no one expected the government to last more than a few weeks. In the event it lasted almost two years, and during that time the economic situation deteriorated even further. The dollar gap grew wider than ever before. The loss of Iranian oil (for Iran had meanwhile nationalised the Anglo-Iranian Oil Company) meant that Britain had to find a further £125 million worth a year. By the time the next general election was held, the country was on the verge of bankruptcy.

Billy embarked on married life in a style which even his mother could not fault. Number 5 Gloucester Square, the house that Daška had bought after moving from the country, was a far cry from bachelor rooms in Down Street. It was big enough for all her children – she had made a point of this – for they, though in paternal custody, were allowed to stay with her for three weeks in the year. Besides, she was sure they would come home for good as soon as it was legally permissible for them to choose which parent they wished to live with. To the ten-year-old twins, Tessa and Marina, the choice would be open in six years' time; seven-year-old Alexander would have to wait a little longer; and five-year-old Caroline would join them last of all. But in the end the whole family would be gathered together under one roof, hers, of that she was certain.

The large house with its appropriate complement of servants enabled Billy to entertain on a scale to which he had always aspired but had never yet attained. He could now return all the hospitality he had enjoyed as a bachelor, and Daška willingly rose to the occasion. She thought nothing of giving a dinner party for twelve twice and even three times a week; nor did she mind, as did some foreign wives, the British ritual of post-prandial sex-segregation – luckily, because Billy really enjoyed hobnobbing over the port with the men while the ladies kept to themselves in the drawing-room. Carried away by the conversation, he would often forget the time and linger in the dining-room unduly; so one evening she decided to teach him a lesson. She hustled all the ladies upstairs, then waited in the drawing-room alone. Presently the men moved back, still so immersed in their discussion that they sat down and went on talking without noticing anything amiss; she had to draw their attention to their wives' disappearance. 'Where on earth have they gone?' Billy asked. 'They got tired of waiting,' she replied. 'Some of them went home, and the others went on to a nightclub.' But she couldn't keep a straight face for more than a minute or two before summoning the absentees downstairs. Billy was only slightly abashed.

Like every newly married couple, they kept discovering fresh aspects of each other's personality and behaviour. She found herself wondering, for instance, why he never wore an overcoat. 'I suppose I must have,' he said, when she asked him if he had ever owned one, 'but I can't remember when.' He certainly did not miss it, and she thought no more about it until someone rang up one day and left a message asking him to come and collect an overcoat he had left behind a couple of years before. But Billy couldn't be bothered. 'It was an old one,' he said, 'and I never liked it.' So she bought him a new one. It lasted exactly a day. He put it on in the morning and in the evening he came back without it, having left it on the seat of a taxi. Once again he did nothing to recover it, 'as I'm obviously not meant for overcoats'.

His attitude to clothes in general was off-hand. He dressed conventionally and always looked well turned out; but this was due more to his natural elegance than to any sartorial skill. At the end of the war he had had several suits made on the cheap in India – 'run up by a little Hindu round the corner,' as a clothes-conscious friend remarked – and though they fell short of Savile Row standards he was perfectly satisfied with them. Not so his mother: she begged him to get rid of 'those dreadful garments', and to order some decent suits at his father's tailors. To humour her he complied, without settling who was to foot the bill. In the end it turned out to be Daška. Many years afterwards, during one of his absences abroad, she was sorting out his mail to see what he might want forwarded, when she came across the tailors' invoice accompanied by a 'final demand' for immediate settlement, failing which the matter would be referred to their solicitors. She sent them a cheque at once.

Billy realised more clearly every day that no one with his temperament could have had a better wife; no other character could have been more closely attuned to his than hers; no other personality could have so fully complemented his own. She understood the moodiness that assailed him from time to time, which even his best friends never suspected and he himself found difficult to explain. The idea of himself as a bird in a gilded cage was absurd; yet the sensation he sometimes had of being trapped was undeniable, and so overwhelming that he could not trust himself to speak. There were days when neither of them uttered a word to the other; and she was invariably the first to break the silence, with an apology which he felt ashamed of not having proffered himself but which restored him to normality.

There were days, too, when separation from her children seemed to create the sort of void that even a husband cannot fill; but if she ever felt anxiety about Billy's reaction to them, it was dispelled the very first time they came to stay. Long before the three weeks were over, he had become as deeply attached to them as if they had been his own. He may have appreciated them all the more for not having had to endure them as infants. There was something to be said for having a family all ready made. He treated them like adults, and they returned the compliment by roping him into their circle and making him feel he had belonged to it for ever.

Meanwhile, in addition to his constituency duties, Billy found himself involved in affairs of a less parochial nature. His interest in the ethnic minorities and Iron Curtain refugees led to his introduction to an organisation whose semi-clandestinity had an immediate and irresistible appeal. Its very name, the Antibolshevik Bloc of Nations, was music to his ears and its avowed intentions coincided with his own ideals. Its members, representatives of the various peoples under Soviet domination, aimed at nothing less than the annihilation of communism and Russian imperialism and the restoration of independence to every subjugated nation. The methods it proposed – internal subversion and covert encouragement of national aspirations in every ethnic group within the Soviet Union and in every satellite state – were also similar to those Billy himself had advocated at the end of his report on Sinkiang. The organisation was based in Munich, and early in the new year he flew out there for talks with some of its senior members.

He spent ten days in an atmosphere of political intrigue, in which he felt entirely at home. The ABN office in Dachauerstrasse was a hive of activity and conspiracy, and a veritable Babel. On his first visit he was buttonholed by a young White Russian bishop who harangued him for over an hour in an incomprehensible mixture of languages. Then he was cornered by a Croat general who addressed him in equally incomprehensible French. On subsequent visits he conversed through an interpreter with the president of the North Caucasian Committee whose members, composed of Iranian-speaking Ossetians, Caucasian-speaking Avars, Dargins and Lezgians, and Turkic-speaking Balkars, Karachays, Chechens and Ingushes, used Russian as a common tongue. With the Turkestan National Unity Committee there was no problem: all its members, whether Uzbek, Kazak, Kirghiz or Tajik, spoke Turkic, which Billy himself also understood. Talks with the Azerbaijan and Georgian leaders occupied the remainder of his stay. He had no time to confer with the representatives of the nineteen other nations belonging to the Bloc. But he made a point of driving out to Ingolstadt to visit a group of Kalmucks, the only survivors in Europe of a Mongol-speaking Buddhist tribe that he had first come across in Sinkiang.

In Tsarist times there were 200,000 of them, refugees from Central Asia, living on the steppe between the Volga and the Don. Most of them in due course returned to their homeland and those who stayed came to be known as Kalmucks, from the Turkish for 'remain'. Before the revolution there were two regiments of Kalmucks serving in the Russian army and during the civil war 5000 of them resisted the Bolsheviks until they were forced to withdraw to Turkey, where they were disbanded, small groups of them finding asylum in Yugoslavia, Bulgaria, Czechoslovakia and France. In the early twenties, when Lenin proclaimed an amnesty for refugees, they returned to Russia and settled once again on their steppe, where they were overrun during the last war by the advancing Germans and conscripted into the Wehrmacht. Later they formed part of one of the Cossack regiments which the Allies handed back to Russia at the end of hostilities. Almost all of them were then shot. But a few managed to escape and eventually found their way to Ingolstadt, thankful to be alive and wanting nothing more than to be left in peace.

In many ways the Kalmucks were more to Billy's liking than the rest of the Antibolshevik Bloc. Most of the other national committees seemed to be at loggerheads and unable to agree on a concerted policy or a co-ordinated line of action. But he felt his time in Munich had not been entirely wasted. He was now more aware of the refugees' potentials and also of their requirements, while his mere presence amongst them had encouraged them to believe that they were not forgotten by the free world.

A few months later a commission from the *Manchester Guardian* to report on the newly created Republic of Indonesia gave him an opportunity to revisit the Far East for the first time since the war. He found the situation there confusing. An independent republic of Indonesia had come into being a few days after the Japanese surrender. Then four years of conflict between Dutch troops and Indonesian nationalists had resulted in the Netherlands transferring sovereignty at the end of 1949 to a federal state called the United States of Indonesia and consisting of the Republic of Java and Sumatra and sixteen other non-republican states and autonomous territories. But within a few months the republican troops were in action against the troops of the federal states, and a unitary republic was restored. Immediate resistance to this new constitution took the form of widespread guerrilla activity.

The guerrilla activity [Billy wrote] is generally attributed to thugs and common thieves. This may be true in Jakarta and other large towns, where almost every night cars are stolen and houses burgled. But it is not so in the forests and mountains, where many young men who formerly fought hard for the independence of their country are still serving with the bands. They continue to live as guerrillas mainly because they cannot find an alternative means of livelihood. They may also prefer the excitement of the life of an outlaw – which in parts of Indonesia local tradition has long accepted as a profession – to the humdrum work of the fields or on the estates.

The guerrilla bands exist in many parts of the country but are strongest in West Java, especially in the triangle Bandung–Tasikmalaya–Chiribon, where many of the largest produce estates are situated. This area is also the haunt of Dar-ul-Islam, the fanatical Islamic guerrilla organisation whose ranks are said to include ex-members of Westerling's forces* as well as some communists. The activities of the bands – murder, arson, extortion, and kidnapping for ransom – are directed as much against Indonesians as against Europeans, or even more so. By means of threats and terrorism the bands extort money from the Chinese merchants and food from the

---

* 'Turk' Westerling, so named because he was born in Istanbul, had served as a captain in the Dutch colonial forces and after the declaration of independence he formed a private army to clear Sumatra of the 'bandits and terrorists', as he called the republicans. He was eventually discredited and deported to Europe, where he adopted the career of an opera singer.

villagers and up-country estates. These bands are a heavy burden on
the peasants and a hindrance to the economic recovery of the country.
They are also a source of trouble to the administration and a constant
threat to security, though they are not yet able to challenge effectively
the authority of the central government, chiefly because there has
been little or no co-ordination of their activities.

On his way back to Europe Billy found himself in Pakistan with a few
weeks to spare, so he was able to renew his acquaintanceship with the
leaders of the Turkestani refugees in Rawalpindi and Peshawar whom
he had met five years before on his return from Sinkiang. They told
him they were as keen as ever on working under British auspices for
a free and independent Turkestan, which he himself still advocated as
the best means of counteracting Soviet influence in Central Asia, and he
undertook to plead their cause should he ever be elected to Parliament.

Another ethnic minority in whom he was interested, the Pathans,
lived astride the north-west frontier. The status of these warlike Muslim tribesmen had for centuries been a bone of contention between
the Afghans and the British in India, until an agreement was reached,
and a treaty signed, in 1921. But, with the transfer of power in India
in 1947, a tense situation had arisen between Afghanistan and the
newly created state of Pakistan. The Afghan government declared
all former treaties with Great Britain null and void and staked out a
claim for a separate Pathan state, to be named Pakhtunistan, which
would include much Pakistan territory. Not unnaturally the Pakistan
government strenuously resisted the idea and, though Billy had talks
with a number of Pakistani politicians, he was unable to meet any of
the advocates of Pakhtunistan as they were all in custody or under
house arrest. So he decided to visit Afghanistan to hear the Afghan
point of view.

There was no air service between the two countries and he
had to motor over the Khyber pass via Jalalabad, as he had done
five years before. Since then the road had fallen into disrepair and
it was only after making several detours along unsurfaced tracks that
he reached Kabul late at night, grimy and exhausted. In the course of
the next few days he conferred with the Afghan Foreign Minister, the
Minister of War and other government officials, all of whom told him
that Pakhtunistan was eventually inevitable, for the idea of a separate
Pathan state appealed not only to the tribesmen themselves but to the
Afghan people in general.

So there seemed to be no way out of the impasse; on the
face of it, the issue was cut and dried. Or was it? Billy felt there

was something fishy about such intransigence, something about the official attitude that didn't quite ring true. His experience of the East had taught him to suspect the obvious – in this part of the world nothing was ever as simple as it was made out to be – and his instinct told him to delve below the surface for further information. Sure enough, the investigations he undertook, among the many unofficial contacts he had made during his previous visits, cast a very different light on the situation. They revealed that the idea of Pakhtunistan had been promoted by greed and lust for power. At the time of partition the rulers of Afghanistan thought Pakistan would be too weak to last as an independent state and had decided in due course to grab what they could from it, pleading the Pathan cause to justify their claim. But the tables had been turned. Pakistan not only still existed but had become progressively stronger; meanwhile the Afghans had grown poorer and were in no position to lay down the law. So Pakhtunistan was far from being an inevitability; in fact the Afghan government went on backing it only to divert the people's attention from the lamentable internal conditions of the country.

This was another simplification, of course, but it seemed more plausible to Billy; and he felt he was nearer the truth about Pakhtunistan by the time he flew back to England to prepare for the general election.

It took place on 25 October 1951. This time the Conservatives won, but it was no landslide victory; their majority was only sixteen. By exactly the same number of votes Billy failed to be elected at Preston. There had been one recount when he had lost at the previous general election. This time there were no less than three. The first count gave the Labour candidate a majority of six votes; but the returning officer announced there was a discrepancy of forty-seven in the total number of voting papers, and a recount was ordered. The second count resulted in the Labour candidate's majority increasing to twenty, and the tension mounted as Billy asked for a second recount. This resulted in his opponent's majority increasing again, to twenty-three, but a further discrepancy was disclosed in the total number of papers, and the returning officer ordered a third recount. Finally, at three in the morning, after five and a half hours' counting, the mayor declared the Labour candidate elected by a majority of sixteen votes.

Being defeated by this narrow margin was galling enough. Worse still was the thought that his mother might have contributed to his defeat. She had graced his campaign with her presence; but could well have lost him those crucial votes, Preston being unused to flamboyance such as hers, by appearing on his platform puffing away at a positively Churchillian cigar.

                                   *   *   *

Billy's articles on Indonesia had been published in August and were so well received that the *Manchester Guardian* commissioned him to write another series, on South-East Asia in general. This time he planned a more protracted tour, of six months at least, for he no longer had a constituency to nurse. His second defeat at the polls had decided him to abandon Preston, although he wrote to Anthony Eden, 'I still intend to stand elsewhere at the next general election or, if I am lucky enough, at a by-election before then.'

He started his tour at Jakarta, which he reached in June 1952, towards the end of Ramadan, when 'all Indonesian thought was on coming feasts and brightly coloured clothes and presents to be given or exchanged. It was almost impossible to talk seriously to any prominent Indonesian figures or, for that matter, to any Indonesian at all; they were all too busy with their families and their holidays to bother about strangers.' Even when the holidays were over, government officials and political leaders proved to be 'just as elusive as they were last year. They always seem to disappear whenever there is a specific question to be answered, or an unpleasant fact to be faced. It is as if they vanish into the jungle in the middle of a conversation, leaving no trace except a slight rustling of the branches to mark the place where they have last been.' Even so he managed to interview a number of them, and to paint a delightful word-picture of each. Here, for instance, is his impression of the socialist leader Sjutan Sjahrir:

> The Ministry of Information arranged for me to have an interview with Sjahrir in his house. I was kept waiting on the verandah until a servant came out and asked my name. He then went back inside. A little later he came out again and asked why I wanted to see Sjahrir. He then disappeared for good. At last the door opened slightly and a small, shy creature sidled out, like a field-mouse emerging from a hole. He smiled nervously, sat down coyly, and stared at me with huge, soft, vacant eyes. So this was Sjahrir, the dynamic leader of the Indonesian national revolution! For the first ten minutes I could get no sense out of him. He just stared absent-mindedly, sometimes at me, sometimes at the ceiling, or giggled and coughed foolishly, or made disjointed remarks, tugging at his hair with his hand. Then suddenly he livened up and by the end of fifteen minutes was talking intelligently, wittily and to the point.

Security in Jakarta had improved enormously in the last year. Europeans were now able to live there without having their cars stolen and their houses burgled. Apart from this, the situation remained much the same. There was little new to report, so Billy moved on to Indochina.

The war between the French and the Vietminh was entering its seventh year, but, on the surface, life in Saigon was pleasant, easy and safe. The hotels were full, the restaurants thronged. There was no shortage of food – fresh meat and vegetables often arrived by air from France – but Billy found the cost of living prohibitive at the official rate of exchange. Luckily there was a thriving black market in currency.

As usual, he spent several days 'taking the pulse' of the place and drinking in the local atmosphere. Then, through the British minister, to whom he had a letter of introduction, he met the military commander of South Vietnam and also the head of the information service, who gave him a general review of the situation. But much of their information was irrelevant and conflicting, so he decided to find things out for himself.

His first visit outside the town was to the area of swamp and jungle some hundred kilometres to the south, where the Vietminh were particularly active. Only the night before, in fact, two of their frogmen had swum downstream under water and blown up a bridge, which was still being repaired when he drove up in the army jeep he had been allotted. The men at work on the repairs were from the Foreign Legion and it was strange to hear the NCOs barking out their orders in German, though he knew this was the language most commonly used in the Legion, in which thousands of ex-Wehrmacht veterans had found refuge. He was to hear many other languages in the course of the next few weeks – Arabic, Berber, Meung, Mung and Senegalese as well as Vietnamese and French – for the army in Indochina was as foreign as the Legion itself. It was the sort of army that appealed to him, and reminded him of his own soldiering in Abyssinia.

He spent nearly a month in Cochin-China, accompanying ambushes and patrols, before flying north to Tonkin where the fighting was heaviest of all. Many of the villages of this region changed hands every few weeks, as one side or the other advanced or retreated, and the wretched inhabitants were subjected alternatively to 'pacification' by the Franco-Vietnamese troops and 'liberation' by the Vietminh. During an operation in the Red River delta he went forward to within half a kilometre of a Vietminh-held village and, from the top of a church tower, watched the population scatter as French artillery opened fire with devastating accuracy. Then he joined a platoon of

Algerian *tirailleurs* splashing through the paddyfields in their heavy
boots with mud up to their knees as they prepared to search the houses,
uttering gleeful cries in guttural Arabic as they battered down the doors
and smashed the furniture, loosing off every so often with their rifles
and tommy-guns. Once again he was reminded of campaigning with
his Abyssinian patriots.

None of the other troops in Indochina came up to the standard of
the Legion. The Senegalese were considered too stupid for anything
more demanding than guard duty; the Vietnamese never stopped
chattering and smoking even when laying an ambush. There were
also four private armies, whose fighting qualities left much to be
desired but who fascinated Billy because each of them belonged
to a separate politico-religious group. The most important were the
Cao-Daists, whose cult combined Christianity, Islam, Buddhism and
Confucianism and whose saints included Christ, Mohammed, Buddha,
Confucius . . . and Victor Hugo. Then there was the UMDC, or Union
for the Defence of Christianity, a medieval Catholic movement headed
by a rich Eurasian landowner. The third, the Ben Sugen, were a gang of
thugs who terrorised the Chinese in Cholon; and the fourth, the Hua
Hua, an armed group of militant Buddhists whose record of extortion
and murder and torture hardly conformed to the faith they claimed to
defend. The French put up with these contingents, and even supplied
them with arms and equipment, because they knew that if they were
disbanded the territories under their control would be overrun by the
Vietminh.

If Billy found some of the ethnic formations somewhat less than
perfect, he had nothing but admiration for the French officers who
commanded them. This handful of Westerners guarding Indochina
for the free world against communism were comparable, he thought,
to the Crusaders defending Jerusalem for Christendom against the
infidel. Back in Saigon they enjoyed a free-and-easy life, high pay,
good food, plenty of wine, local women, opium if they wished, and
constant opportunities for loot and pillage. But on active service they
had to contend with physical discomfort in the dark mud towers where
they lodged and with the daily risk of being killed in an ambush on the
roads or in a night attack on their posts. If captured by regular Vietminh
troops, they faced the prospect of years in a communist prison camp or
trial by a 'people's court'; and the possibility of torture and mutilation
if they fell into the hands of irregular Vietminh supporters. Most of the
junior officers had come straight from France and lived in conditions
which most British subalterns would have considered intolerable, being
stationed all alone for months on end, even for a year without a break,

in the midst of a hostile population and miles from the nearest town or European. It was their belief in *la mission civilisatrice de la France* which kept them up to the mark.

At the end of August Billy went back to Saigon to welcome Daška who was flying out to join him for a few weeks' holiday. She was rather apprehensive about the situation, but he assured her there was nothing to worry about; though the Vietminh were active on the outskirts, the town itself was as safe as houses. But apparently not as safe as hotels, or at least not the hotel where she and Billy were staying, for no sooner had he spoken than a deafening explosion shattered every pane of glass in the room and brought the plaster down from the ceiling. They learnt next day that a nearby ammunition dump had been sabotaged.

Combining business with pleasure, Billy suggested moving on to Cambodia which he had not yet visited. He and Daška had an audience with King Norodom in his gaily painted palace in Phnom-Penh, which yielded another characteristic vignette. 'Small and nervous', was how Billy described the young monarch. 'He has a strangely squeaky voice which, combined with his quick, jerky movements and a shy giggle, gives him a childlike appearance. But he never made a stupid remark during the whole conversation.'

Cambodia–Ceylon–Singapore–Malaya–Java–Bali and finally Hong Kong – the McLean itinerary was all the more enjoyable (and sometimes also all the more arduous) for being impromptu. But their holiday was over all too soon. Indeed it seemed to have scarcely begun before it was time for Daška to fly back to London, leaving Billy to continue his tour on his own. Only a couple of months elapsed, however, before he received a telegram from her which sent him hurrying home.

The telegram announced that the Unionist (Conservative) MP for Inverness, Lord Malcolm Douglas-Hamilton, had quarrelled with the local Unionist association and would not be seeking readoption as their candidate at the next general election. Here was a heaven-sent opportunity for Billy to re-enter the political arena. He had always wanted a Highland constituency, and so no sooner was he back in England than he contacted the Inverness Unionist Association. They, for their part, welcomed his approach and lost no time in choosing him as their prospective candidate to succeed the sitting member.

The adoption took place on 29 April 1953, at a crowded meeting held in the hall of the Queensgate Hotel, where Billy endeared himself to his prospective constituents with the first words he addressed to them. 'I am a Highlander,' he said, 'and my family for generations lived in the Highlands.' Though he himself, he added, had spent much of his life in

England and even further afield, he was delighted to be coming home to Inverness, where he and his wife now intended to live and which he planned to get to know like the back of his hand.

He was as good as his word. He and Daška moved into Eskedale, a house on the Beauly river belonging to their friend 'Shimi' Lovat, and during the summer and autumn they visited every part of the constituency, an area with a distinctive geography and social com-position, covering 4000 square miles of mountain and glen, town and clochan, loch and burn, as well as the islands of Eigg, Rhum, Muck, Canna, Raasay, Soay and Skye. Here they were in the heartland of the Free Kirk, where hotel visitors found Bibles in the bedrooms and where the sin of Sabbath lawn-mowing was believed to stop the grass growing. They motored more than 5000 miles over rough local roads – always with Daška at the wheel as Billy did not like driving (except, as she observed, from the back seat) – holding meetings in village halls, attending tea-parties and other social functions, and presenting the prizes at the inevitable and ubiquitous whist-drives. He was overjoyed to meet several men with whom he had soldiered in the Scots Greys in the early days of the war, but was appalled to find large numbers of deserted crofts in glens which once housed thriving communities. As he said in one of his speeches, 'the drift of the young men and women to the south is not only a human tragedy but is a real danger to the future of the Highlands and Islands and weakens the whole of Britain; for if Britain is to survive as a free independent country, she must have a sound and flourishing agriculture, in which the Highlands with their fine cattle and sheep, poultry and eggs, cereal and other crops, forestry and fishing, as well as tweed production and other industries, play a vital part.' He pledged himself to work tirelessly for the economic development of the Highlands, which, he felt, was closely linked to the prosperity of Britain as a whole.

A second tour of the area, during which he addressed a meeting, and sometimes more than one, every weekday for several weeks, kept him busy till the end of the year. And similar duties occupied most of the following year as well. A short visit to Ethiopia in March was all he allowed himself as a break from constituency affairs.

He had not been back there since the war and could not decide whether to play the part of the old Abyssinian hand returning to his haunts or to behave like an ordinary tourist. His mind was made up for him as soon as he landed at Addis Ababa and discovered to his dismay that he had forgotten almost all the Amharic he had ever learnt. It was as though he had never been there before. But he began to feel more at home when his taxi approached the centre of the town and he recognised the broad main street lined with eucalyptus trees. Sadly he noticed that European-style bungalows with cement walls and tin roofs now outnumbered the native thatch and wattle *tukuls*.

He put up at one of the three big hotels where he had stayed thirteen years before. It was still as dirty, noisy and overcrowded as he remembered it; the only change he saw was in the guests. American pilots and aircrews of the Ethiopian state airline jostled with European businessmen, foreign diplomats, and adventurers of every nationality; and there were many Ethiopians as well, dressed in Savile Row suits and speaking perfect English. It was all very progressive and up to date, no doubt, but a far cry from the feudal, medieval country that Billy had known and was hoping to rediscover. Vestiges of the old days did still exist, however, as he saw for himself two days after his arrival.

He was sitting on the front veranda, when a shiny black Cadillac drew up and out of it stepped an Ethiopian general resplendent in full dress uniform. Leaving his car to obstruct the entrance, he swaggered into the lobby and had taken no more than half a dozen strides before a couple of soldiers darted forward. Billy expected them to snap to attention and salute; instead they knelt and kissed the ground at the general's feet. And there they remained, until given permission to rise, in the traditional attitude of obeisance due to a feudal lord. The old customs had not died out after all.

Billy had some difficulty, after such a long absence, in tracking down his old patriot comrades-in-arms. Some had changed their whereabouts and even their names, as was the custom after marrying or siring a child; others had moved from the capital altogether. Many, whom he had known as junior officers or interpreters, were now provincial governors, generals, or cabinet ministers – a delightful surprise when he thought of Albania, where his wartime friends and colleagues, far from becoming the ruling class, had been driven into exile or condemned to death. He flew home, confident that as long as the present situation lasted, Ethiopia could continue to be one of Britain's staunchest allies.

The sitting member of Inverness having at last resigned, the by-election was fixed for 21 December 1954. An encouraging message arrived from the Prime Minister, Winston Churchill:

My dear McLean,

I send you my cordial wishes for success in your election campaign. You have the best possible claim to the confidence of the electors.

You are a supporter of the Government. You have your roots in the Highlands and are familiar with the special problems of that scattered region. Your distinguished war record and the political experience you have since acquired have been an excellent preparation for the day to day work of the House of Commons.

Polling day was ushered in by gale-force winds and showers of sleet and snow. But the weather did not cause any serious delay in the collection of ballot boxes from the seventy-six polling stations in the county. All of them were delivered by nightfall, and the result was declared early next afternoon:

Mr Neil L. D. McLean (Unionist)	10,329
Mr John M. Bannerman (Liberal)	8,998
Mr William Paterson (Socialist)	5,642
Unionist majority	1,331

8 *The Honourable Member*

After celebrating his victory, and also Christmas and the New Year, Billy worked right up to the last minute before leaving for London to take his seat in Parliament when the House of Commons resumed at the end of January.

Highland affairs were naturally close to his heart and uppermost in his mind. But there were broader issues that also claimed his attention, especially the situation in the Middle East. Since the war the British government had pursued, however reluctantly, a policy of gradual retreat from Egypt as from other imperial outposts. But Billy believed that Britain still had the power, and the duty, to act decisively in Middle Eastern affairs, and so had no hesitation in joining a minority of Conservative MPs – the so-called Suez Group – who were uninhibitedly committed to the forceful assertion of British authority in the Middle East or, for that matter, anywhere else. Their chairman was Captain Charles Waterhouse, a former minister and privy councillor; Julian Amery was their co-secretary with Enoch Powell; their membership included John Morrison (later Lord Margadale) and Sir Fitzroy Maclean; and they were represented in the House of Lords by Baron Hankey and Baron Killearn.

British troops had been in Egypt since 1882, partly to guarantee the safe working of the Suez Canal, partly to maintain Britain's other Middle Eastern interests. Even after withdrawing her forces from Cairo in 1947, she had continued to keep a garrison in the canal zone. But in 1954, two years after the *coup d'état* which toppled King Farouk and eventually brought Colonel Nasser to power, she agreed to evacuate the canal zone as well. The Suez Group thought the agreement was a serious threat to Britain's entire Middle East position, and said so in no uncertain terms, but, faced with a *fait accompli*, they could do little more than denounce it and warn against further appeasement. The evacuation of Britain's last military base in Egypt began shortly after Billy took his seat; it was to have dire consequences.

In April 1955 Churchill resigned the premiership because of ill health – he had had the first of several strokes two years before – and was succeeded by his Foreign Secretary, Anthony Eden, who resolved to go to the country as soon as possible. The general election of 26 May increased the Conservative majority from seventeen seats to sixty, and returned Billy to Inverness with a slightly reduced majority of 996. His pleasure in being a personal friend of the new Prime Minister was somewhat dimmed by the fact that Eden had been outspokenly in favour of the scuttle from Egypt. Their friendship, as we shall see, did not survive the crisis.

But there was good news from elsewhere in the Middle East. In the very month that British troops began to withdraw from Suez, representatives of the Turkish and Iraqi governments met in Baghdad and signed a defensive and economic pact, to which Britain also adhered two months later. This was a slap in the face for Nasser, who professed to regard the pact as an anti-Egyptian conspiracy and started a violent propaganda campaign against it. Billy, for his part, spoke up for it in a broadcast which the BBC invited him to give.

> I welcome the pact [he said] as a first step in the development of a Middle East security system in which other countries will subsequently join. The traditional Soviet policy in the Middle East has been to stir up trouble along the borders of Russia. In doing this the Soviet Union has often supported armed movements and armed revolts which come very near to being minor wars. The arming of the Azerbaijan separatist movement in 1946 and the support given to the Kurds were much more than straightforward frontier incidents; they took place well inside these countries, far behind their frontiers. I think the new pact will prove a barrier against such aggression and will give a sense of real security against armed revolts supported from outside, which have long been one of the traditional aspects of politics in the Middle East.

'I personally feel,' he concluded, 'that our accession to the Turkey–Iraq pact will immensely strengthen the defence of the Middle East, and this strength will be further increased when other countries, including perhaps Iran, also join it.'*

Being an MP for a remote constituency had its disadvantages. Billy found that commuting between Westminster and Inverness added

---

* Iran did indeed join the pact, in November, following Pakistan's adherence in September.

greatly to his parliamentary workload. Travelling to and fro by air took even longer than by train, for there was no direct flight and changing planes at Glasgow entailed an overnight stop. He also found that domestic matters occupied as much of his time as international affairs. Concerned though he might be about the situation in the Middle East, he still had to attend to problems nearer home and, for example, plead with the Chancellor of the Exchequer for the abolition or reduction of the purchase tax on shinty sticks, giving his reasons in writing and in detail:

Shinty is a national game in the Highlands of Scotland, although today in many parts it has already died out or is in danger of doing so. But the game is still worthily played, especially in Inverness and Argyll. Although shinty is a popular game in some of the most remote glens, it is not a cheap game, for a player can break several sticks in the course of a match and on every stick there is a stiff purchase tax.

I am informed that in the season 1953–54 the thirty-two clubs playing in the various competitions spent on shinty sticks and balls a total of £2832, which works out at an average of £88 10s for each club. The total amount coming into the Treasury for this purchase tax must be negligible, but it is nevertheless a considerable burden on these clubs, especially some of the smaller ones in the more remote glens.

I feel that these clubs are not only part of the Highland national tradition, but also perform a useful social function. They increase the community spirit. They provide healthy sport and entertainment, especially for the young men in areas where there are few other recreations. It is in these isolated areas, where the problem of encouraging young people to live on their crofts and farms is especially acute, that the shinty clubs play a not inconsiderable part in keeping the interest of the young people in their own districts.

I have taken the liberty of writing to you about this matter because I believe that the Government, in helping these shinty clubs by abolishing or reducing the purchase tax on shinty sticks and balls, could, without undue financial loss, show its desire to improve conditions in the remote farming communities of the Highlands. At the same time it would be proof that the Government is sympathetic to the national traditions and way of life of the Highlands.

Assiduous attendance in the House, an active social life in London, incessant travel to and from his constituency, and never-ending duties and engagements within it, began to take their toll. Billy, without realising it, was burning the candle at both ends. For some time his physical and mental stamina helped him to take the strain, but in the end even his powerful constitution succumbed. In mid-September he had a nervous breakdown.

It was at one of his many public meetings in the Highlands that the chairman, a personal friend of his, spotted that something was wrong with him, cancelled the meeting, and advised him to go home. Daška put him to bed, hoping he would get some sleep, and watched over him. But he stayed awake, reading the Bible. He looked rather odd and told her he had had a revelation: there was dirty work afoot, a conspiracy against him; certain factions in the constituency were plotting to kill him; the Freemasons and Scottish Nationalists were actually going to crucify him – he had been shown the very hill they had chosen for the ceremony. Thoroughly alarmed, Daška sent for the doctor, who gave him a sedative which ensured him a good night's rest.

But in the morning he seemed as confused as before. He told Daška that everybody had taken against him and only God was on his side. Seeing no improvement in his condition, she arranged for him to be transferred to a nursing home in London for specialist treatment. When the ambulance came to fetch him he grew more agitated than ever and cried out: 'They're going to take me away! Daška, don't leave me!' She sat up with him in the train all night, holding his hand and keeping him calm.

On arriving at the nursing home he at once asked for a Bible. The specialist advised Daška not to let him have it; instead she gave him Gibbon's *Decline and Fall of the Roman Empire*. This did the trick, or at least must have helped, for by the time he had read all eight volumes he was cured. But cured of what? The psychiatrist who examined him diagnosed a paranoid state induced by alcohol. Yet Billy had not recently increased his usual alcohol intake, which had never before had any ill effect. A second medical opinion was probably nearer the mark when it suggested that his mercurial temperament was in part responsible. Like many Celts he was subject to violent shifts of mood, ranging from euphoria to mild melancholy, and this, combined with nervous exhaustion, could have brought on an attack of hypomania (a medical term for over-excitability) which alcohol certainly aggravated.

But his rapid recovery showed that he was no alcoholic. At the end of a fortnight he was able to leave hospital and, after a short holiday in Portugal, was back to light parliamentary duties by the first week of November.

*   *   *

On 29 February 1956 King Hussein of Jordan dismissed General (later Sir) John Bagot Glubb, better known as Glubb Pasha, from the command of the Arab Legion which he had held since 1939. This event was the main topic of Billy's maiden speech, which he delivered on the floor of the House of Commons a few minutes after 5 p.m. on Wednesday, 7 March. Tradition demands that a maiden speech be non-controversial. Billy explained straight away why his might not be so:

> Mr Speaker, it is extremely difficult to make a non-controversial speech about such a controversial part of the world as the Middle East. If I should stray and make some remarks that might be thought controversial, I hope the House will extend to me the indulgence which is usual when honourable members speak in the House for the first time.
>
> I was shocked by the abrupt and discourteous way in which General Glubb was dismissed by the King of Jordan after so many years of loyal service to the Hashemite kingdom, but I was not in the least surprised. I think that many of us saw some such event coming.
>
> We ought to ask ourselves whether the hand that removed General Glubb was the same hand that killed or organised the killing of King Abdullah in one of the most holy places in the Arab world. [Abdullah, assassinated in Jerusalem on 20 July 1951, was succeeded by his eldest son, Talal, who was deposed a year later, by reason of mental illness, in favour of his son Hussein.] Was it perhaps the same hand that pushed out King Farouk and brought Nasser to power or, at least, was behind the *coup d'état*? Even if it were not perhaps the same hand, it might well have been the same forces that brought Colonel Shishakli to power in Damascus at about that time [following a military revolution in 1949; he was forced out by another *coup d'état* in 1954]. I wonder whether that hand belonged to the Mufti of Jerusalem [Billy's old opponent in pre-war Palestine] or at least one of his henchmen.
>
> Whether the young King of Jordan took the steps he did under compulsion from a group of officers who delivered the ultimatum to him that he must act in this manner, or whether it was upon his own initiative that the King took this action to forestall such an ultimatum, perhaps we shall know in a few weeks' time.* We ought to ask ourselves what have been the roles of Egypt and

---

* It transpired that Nasser had brought pressure to bear, to discourage Jordan from joining the Baghdad pact.

Colonel Nasser during these last few days in Amman [rioting had broken out in Amman, incited by Egyptian and Saudi propaganda]. Colonel Nasser has openly said that he wishes to have a unified Arab command of which the Arab Legion will form part. . . .

In any event, these happenings in Jordan are a grave blow to British prestige. This blow to our prestige has been underlined by events that followed in the Bahrain area which we thought we had under complete control.*

King Hussein and the Jordan government have said that they desire to continue their friendship with us and to continue the Treaty [the Anglo-Jordan treaty of alliance, signed in Amman on 15 March 1948; it was to be terminated, at Hussein's instigation, early in 1957, in the wake of the Suez crisis], and we welcome these statements. The reasons, however, that the King and the Jordan government have given for the dismissal of Glubb Pasha give cause for grave disquiet. . . . They said that the reason for dismissing General Glubb was that he did not follow a policy sufficiently active or hostile to Israel. That was also one of the reasons why King Abdullah was killed. Now there is news that they want recruits for the Arab Legion from the West Bank of the Jordan.§ One can imagine what would be the feelings of these new recruits from the West Bank who, if they were in the Arab Legion, looked from their outposts across the frontier at their own villages and farms on the other side. One can imagine the temptation it would be for them to commit raids across the frontier. So I believe there is grave danger of increased hostilities along that frontier.#

Before concluding I should like to say a few words about the Arab peoples. The Arabs are awakening. There is a tremendously strong force in Arab nationalism. In the development of this movement Egypt must undoubtedly play a great, perhaps, the leading, role. But I feel that our Egyptian friends and the Egyptian government

---

* On a visit to Bahrain two days after Glubb's dismissal, the British Foreign Secretary, Selwyn Lloyd, had been stoned by demonstrators during a pro-Nasser anti-British riot. It had its origins in local political agitation stirred up by Egyptian intrigue.

§ After the partition of Palestine and the war between Arabs and Jews over the establishment of the state of Israel (1947–8) the West Bank voted to join what was then Transjordan and the two were united into one state called the Hashemite Kingdom of Jordan. (But the Six-Day War of 1967 resulted in Jordan's loss of the West Bank to Israel, which has occupied it ever since.)

An accurate forecast. Border incidents were to occur regularly for several years, Jordanian infiltrations into Israel being countered by occasional savage reprisal raids into Jordan.

must realise that admiration for Egypt is not the same thing as love for Egyptian imperialism.

We should also point out to Colonel Nasser and other Arab nationalists, who feel so strongly on certain matters that they take arms from the Russians or make an alliance with the communists, the dangers in this course, because the Soviets are only using them as an instrument of Soviet policy. It is very important that the Egyptian government should not be confused about these two matters and we should tell them by all the means in our power, including the press and radio, of the dangers for them of following these policies. I should also like them to look at the fate of the Crimean Tartars and the other Muslim minorities in the Soviet Union and to ask them if they would like to share the same fate.

The crux of the problem in the Middle East lies here, in this country, where the final decision still rests about what can be done. . . . One of the decisions we have to take is whether we wish to stay in the Middle East or not. To stay is unpopular, difficult and even dangerous. To go would, I believe, be disastrous both for this country and for the people of the Middle East.

Perhaps I may quote an Arab story about the last Arab sultan of Granada. After he had lost the town to the Christians, he went with his mother up to a hill overlooking this capital and cried, and she said to him: 'Well may you weep like a woman for what you could not defend as a man.' Let that never be said of us in this country.

The sting in the tail was not lost on the Prime Minister. Speaking later in the debate, he congratulated Billy on his eloquence – he could hardly have done otherwise in public – but outside the House he never spoke to his former protégé again.

His maiden speech having firmly established Billy's reputation as an authority on the Middle East, the council of Chatham House invited him to become a member of a study group to examine British interests and policy in the Mediterranean. But no sooner had the group prepared its preliminary report than its work was overtaken by events. On 26 July Nasser nationalised the Suez Canal.

At a meeting in Inverness shortly afterwards Billy strongly denounced this 'grave insult to international conduct and law' and went on to say: 'If Colonel Nasser gets away with it, there is little doubt that he will be master of the lands and Arab peoples stretching from the Atlantic to the Persian Gulf. He, with Russian help – and they are, I believe, working much more closely together than is generally supposed

– will without doubt overthrow every Arab government friendly to us, and instal their own puppet régimes to follow the Cairo and Moscow line. They will vie with each other in their hatred of Britain and the West.'

What had been nationalised, of course, was not the great international waterway itself but the Universal Suez Maritime Canal Company, of which Britain had bought almost half the shares in 1875. The company had been operating under Egyptian law according to a 100-year concession due to expire in 1968. Nasser had jumped the gun and unilaterally ended the concession twelve years early. But it was not this narrow issue that dismayed Britain; it was the anti-British hostility implied in the act of nationalisation, and the underlying threat to the free use of the canal by all nations as guaranteed by the 1888 Convention. Nasser had not denied this Convention, but his good faith in observing it was doubted, especially by Billy and the rest of the Suez Group.* They believed that whatever law or international practice might say, it was intolerable to have the canal in potentially enemy hands.

For the next three months the two countries wrangled over the question of management. Britain took the view that Egypt should allow an international authority to control the operation of the canal, no matter its new ownership. This was the very principle that Nasser would not accept; it would destroy the entire effect of nationalisation if he were to be left with ownership but no control. He insisted on Egyptian management and refused to countenance any international supervision. Britain tried various means to make him yield. In August she convened a conference in London, inviting all the parties to the 1888 Convention; but Nasser regarded the proposal that emerged for an international Suez Canal board as an infringement of Egyptian sovereignty. A second London conference, held in September to form a Suez Canal users' association, proved equally fruitless; and an attempt at the beginning of October to secure international control through the United Nations was thwarted by a Russian veto.

In the meantime the Suez Group had been busy behind the scenes. They were in touch with a clandestine Egyptian opposition composed of monarchists and other anti-Nasserites, and Billy and Julian found themselves involved in the sort of conspiratorial activity which they both enjoyed and at which they excelled. At their own expense, and on their own responsibility, they held several meetings in the South

* Egypt had in fact been in breach of the Convention since 1951, when she refused to allow Israeli ships through the canal.

Billy in his mother's arms.   Billy's father.

Billy, on the right, with his brother Gillian.

Lance-Corporal McLean, adjutant's orderly, Sandhurst.

Lieutenant McLean with his two operational centre sergeants and two Abyssinian patriots.

Major McLean with Albanian partisans.

Lieutenant-Colonel McLean with pony and falcon in Sinkiang.

Billy and Daška marry in Rome.

(*Inset*) On their honeymoon in Sicily.

The newly-weds with
Daška's mother.

The parliamentary candidate.

Taking cover with fellow journalists in a ditch near Algiers during an exchange of fire between rival political factions (Hugo Charteris, *Sunday Telegraph*, 1962).

Entertaining Soviet VIPs in Scotland: Julian Amery (*second from left*), the Russian delegation's interpreter, the Soviet Aviation Minister, and Billy (*second from right*) between his stepson and Sergei Krushchev.

Billy, while in Yemen with the royalist forces.

From left to right: Prince Abdurrahman
bin Yahya, his nephew Iman al-Badr,
Billy, and Said Ahmed al-Shamy, the
Yemeni foreign minister.

With Daška at La Guardia.

Billy towards the end of his life.

Snorkling with his brother-in-law, Vane.

of France with some of the highly placed Egyptians they had known during and just after the war; representatives of the Wafd, colleagues of the former premier Nahas Pasha, and others who even today must remain nameless. They also went so far as to make contact, in Geneva, with members of the Muslim Brotherhood, informing only MI6 of this *démarche* which they kept secret even from the rest of the Suez Group. Their efforts resulted in the formation in Cairo of a shadow government ready to take power should an appropriate occasion arise.

Though Billy took his work very seriously, he was not above making fun of it and, in a spirit of parody but not entirely in jest, he concentrated his conspiratorial skills on the home front as well. The Amery house in Eaton Square was a Suez Group bastion. The Macmillan house in Smith Square was another. It also happened to be adjacent to the house of R. A. Butler, the Lord Privy Seal, who looked upon the Suez Group with an eye no less jaundiced than Eden's. Billy blithely declared that Butler was spying on the group and deserved to have the tables turned on him. Typically – for he made a point of courting the young – it was the Macmillans' schoolboy son Alexander (the present Earl of Stockton) whom he entrusted with the task of listing Butler's visitors and identifying them, if possible, by means of a rogues' gallery of MPs which Billy had thoughtfully provided. Flattered, Alexander rose to the occasion.

Billy spent part of the summer recess on a fact-finding tour of Syria and Iraq. The situation in both those countries confirmed his belief that Nasser was planning, with Russian help, to bring the whole of the Middle East under Egyptian domination. He witnessed pro-Egyptian student demonstrations in Baghdad, notwithstanding Iraq's official pro-British attitude, and noticed increasing Egyptian influence in Syria, where closer relations had lately been established between Damascus and the Kremlin. Sabotage, connived at if not inspired by the government, had destroyed the pipeline by which Iraq oil was carried to the coast. At a public meeting in Inverness town hall which he addressed on his return, he issued this warning: 'If Nasser gets his hands on the areas which supply Britain with oil, it will result in millions of people in Britain being unemployed.'

Meanwhile deadlock over Suez left no recourse except the use of force.

France as well as Britain had already undertaken conspicuous military preparations in the eastern Mediterranean – a bit of 'sabre-rattling' designed to convince the Egyptians of the value of making a concession. French public opinion had been quickly stirred by the crisis because of France's role in building the canal and the number of

French shareholders in the company; but many Frenchmen regarded its nationalisation less as a disaster than an unexpected chance of justifying the use of force against Nasser, whom, in the absence of an Algerian rebel leader worthy of their hate, they regarded as Enemy Number One. Plans were therefore made for an Anglo-French landing in Egypt, to take place on 6 November. But they were forestalled. On 29 October Israel launched against Egypt a preventive attack on which she had long been determined.

On 30 October France and Britain issued an ultimatum, giving the combatants twelve hours to cease fire and to withdraw ten miles on either side of the canal. Egypt naturally refused these terms and on 31 October the Anglo-French air and naval bombardment started, followed a few days later by troop landings by air and sea.

The Suez Group hailed the operation as 'a new age in this country'. But many of their fellow Conservatives were less enthusiastic and the Opposition, almost to a man, voiced out-and-out disapproval. The Labour leader, Hugh Gaitskell, was furious that Eden should have used force without consulting him. So was the President of the United States, Dwight Eisenhower, and for the same reason. Thus the country was not only divided from within but also at loggerheads with its most powerful ally.

After two days of UN manoeuvring, the American Secretary of State, John Foster Dulles, introduced a resolution calling for a Middle East ceasefire; it was approved by sixty-four votes to five, Britain and France abstaining. Then an even more serious threat loomed up for the Anglo-French expedition. Israel, having captured all her objectives by 5 November, was now willing, even anxious, to accept the ceasefire, provided that Egypt did so too. All these pressures caused Eden to waver and on 7 November Britain accepted it, but only on condition that Anglo-French troops remained in the canal zone until they could hand over to a UN emergency force.

The first UN troops landed in Egypt on 15 November. Billy himself flew out there a few days later. What he saw convinced him that an Anglo-French withdrawal would be premature. The Egyptians had blocked the canal by sinking in it forty-seven ships filled with concrete and he felt that until the waterway was cleared, and a free passage through it guaranteed, Britain and France should stand firm where they were. He stated this opinion in no uncertain terms at various meetings in his constituency and when, at the beginning of December, the government nevertheless announced the forthcoming withdrawal of the British troops, he was among the fifteen Tories who abstained from voting in favour. The Inverness Unionist Association applauded his action. 'Colonel McLean's stock will go up as a result,' said a spokesman.

The Anglo-French withdrawal was completed by the end of the month; UN salvage operations began; and the canal was reopened in April 1957, with Nasser in complete and sole control. In a last desperate bid to retrieve the situation, Billy and his Suez Group colleagues tabled the following motion: 'That this House pledges support to Her Majesty's Government in any action calculated to uphold the 1888 Convention and to redeem the undertaking given [by Sir Anthony Eden] on 30 July 1956, that the Suez Canal will not be left in the unfettered control of one power. . . . '

Nothing came of it.

Billy was convinced that Britain's retreat from Egypt would have an adverse effect on the rest of the eastern Mediterranean, where the situation was already bad enough. In Cyprus a revolutionary organisation called EOKA had started a campaign of sabotage and murder in support of the demand of *enosis*, or union with Greece. In Jordan there had been an Egyptian-inspired attempt at a *coup d'état*, which had been suppressed only by the firm stand the young monarch had taken against the pro-Nasser conspirators. Although Iraq was still on friendly terms with Britain, the alliance brought about by the Baghdad pact had been severely shaken. In Syria Egyptian influence continued to be prominent and closer ties had also been established with the Soviet Union. A general anti-Western landslide seemed to be sweeping the whole of the Middle East. Billy decided to fly out there again and see for himself what was happening.

In Amman he had an audience with King Hussein, laying the foundations of a lifelong personal friendship which also forged an enduring international bond. In Cyprus he conferred with the Governor, Field-Marshal Sir John Harding, and also, since Greeks and Turks populated the island, discussed the situation with leading politicians in Athens and in Ankara. In Baghdad he had talks with the Prime Minister of Iraq and with the Minister of the Interior, and visited the frontier areas of Syria. He would not have been welcome inside the country, where several thousand Egyptian troops had just been flown in to oppose the alleged threat of a Turkish invasion. His tour convinced him all the more that Nasser was intent on establishing, with Russian help, a Soviet vassal state in the Middle East where he hoped to assume the role of a puppet caliph of Islam ruling all the Arab nations.

At a press conference he held on his return, he stressed the importance of Anglo-American co-operation in the Middle East. 'Since the war,' he said, 'American influence has, in the main, been used against British interests in this area, starting from the time of our surrender of the mandate in Palestine and culminating in the open hostility to us at the time of the Suez intervention. . . . Had American influence been thrown behind Britain and France at that phase, the situation in the Middle East today would be infinitely better than it is.'

He went on to discuss events in Cyprus:

During the last two years Britain has made considerable efforts to deal with the lawlessness and terrorism promoted by EOKA. In spite of gloomy and defeatist talk at home that it could not be done, and the active opposition of our enemies in the United Nations and elsewhere, Field-Marshal Harding has broken the back of the terrorist movement. . . . All of us, of course, hope that it will now be possible to reach a just and lasting solution through negotiation and discussion. But if EOKA starts up again we shall be able to break them again, through the organisation and machine that has been forged during the last two years, provided the government makes the effort.

This effort would mean the stationing of soldiers and the spending of money in Cyprus. It might be necessary to keep about 10,000 men on the island and to spend two million pounds a year, but maintaining a base there would enable us to fulfil our military obligations to the Baghdad pact and to keep our friendship with Turkey, which is also vitally interested in what happens in Cyprus. . . .

Surely we remember how Nasser grabbed the canal within five weeks of the day when the last British soldier left the Suez base. The lesson to be learnt from this is that it is often cheaper to maintain a comparatively small force in a key position than to evacuate it and then be compelled into re-intervention later.

He concluded by reiterating the need for American support of Britain's policy in the Middle East:

I feel that the American government should join or give far more aid to the Baghdad pact and at the same time help Jordan in her present financial difficulties. America should also throw her full weight behind Britain in our attempts to maintain stability in the Persian Gulf, and do what she can to help us fulfil our obligations to the sheiks and sultans in that area. . . .

His statement drew warm applause. But some of his constituents criticised him for spending too much time gallivanting abroad; he would be better employed, they said, going round the West and the islands. This narrow-minded view was derided by the vice-president of the Inverness Tories, who pointed out that it was essential for Billy, as an expert on the Middle East, to keep in close touch with affairs there: 'From what I hear from my friends in that part of the world, Colonel McLean has done an extraordinarily good job of work. He is acting as a sort of unpaid under-secretary for the Foreign Office, with the tremendous difference that if he does not agree with what the government is doing out there he is perfectly free to say so.'

The criticism was in any case unjust. His constituency was not only remote; it was vast, extending from the shores of the Moray Firth and the North Sea, with its cold winds and bracing climate, to the Atlantic where the soft green hills, wooded glens and sea lochs of the west coast, and the isles of the Inner Hebrides, are warmed by the Gulf Stream. Arriving by train he entered it at the Drumochter Pass, but the town of Inverness still lay 70 miles away to the north. From there it was 60 miles to Fort William, the second largest town in the county, and 40 miles more to the thriving little fishing port of Mallaig, famous for its lobsters. Despite the sharp bends and blind corners, he loved this stretch of road for its romantic associations and would tingle with emotion each time he passed through Glenfinnan, the spot where Bonnie Prince Charlie raised the Stuart standard in 1745. It was also 100 miles of rough driving from Inverness to Moydart on the west coast, while the islands, and even some of the isolated townships on the mainland, could be approached only by sea. So merely getting from one point to another took a great deal of time.

There was now a direct daily flight to Inverness from London; it took five hours, but it was often cancelled due to bad weather. Billy much preferred the overnight train journey, waking in the morning to find the smog, smoke and soot of London and industrial England replaced by the clean pure air of the Highlands, and gazing out of his window on the fertile fields and meadows of Badenoch where once the Macpherson, Mackintosh and Grant clans quarrelled and fought. But merely travelling to and fro from Westminster took up time which he would rather have spent in the constituency itself.

Even the most critical of his constituents could not find fault with the efforts he made on their behalf in the House. Nothing was too trivial for him to attend to, provided it was in the interest of the Highlands, and he kept questioning the Secretary of State for Scotland and other ministers about such matters as the number of candidates presented for higher English at the Scottish Leaving Certificate examination; the delay in starting work on the Loch Storr water scheme for Portree and

the surrounding region; the extent of the damage done to hill and mar-
ginal farms by red deer; the number of cases of poaching deer that had
been brought to the notice of the police in the seven Highland counties
since 1 October 1956; the provision of suitable houses for tinkers in the
Highlands; the lack of BBC television services in the west Highlands
and islands and the poor quality of the existing sound-radio reception;
the unsatisfactory conditions of the access roads to crofting townships;
the number of crans of herring and their value, and the weight and
value of lobsters and other shellfish landed at Mallaig harbour that
year to date and in the preceding four years, respectively.

In one of his speeches Billy entered a special plea for the development of tourism in the Highlands:

> Tourism is perhaps one of our most sensitive industries. A bad
> rumour – a rumour of war, for example – can temporarily ruin
> the American tourist trade. This year, because of petrol rationing
> [caused by the Suez crisis], even though it was eventually removed,
> many people did not make their usual bookings in the Highlands but
> went to the Continent instead. This has already reflected a great fall
> in trade compared to last year. This year's figures of visitors to the
> Highlands have not come up to expectation.
>
> There will, of course, be great competition from abroad. It is
> extremely important that we should have the latest and most accurate
> information about amenities, prices and services offered to tourists in
> other countries in Europe, so that we can compete with them. If we
> wish to increase our tourist industries we must, in the Highlands at
> least, greatly develop the natural attractions and facilities for sport,
> skiing, fishing and so on. Unless we do this, and also provide the
> improved communications which will become necessary, there will
> be a great temptation for people from Great Britain to go over to
> the Continent. . . .
>
> The government should not be afraid to use such powers as
> they possess, and if necessary to put their hands in their pockets,
> to help the tourist industry. . . . One day, in fact, I hope we may
> have a minister who is directly in charge of tourism, it being one of
> his portfolios.

Billy's passion for the Highlands was infectious. Daška loved them
because she felt closer to him there and indeed saw more of him than
she did in London, where he often came home late for dinner, or
not at all, 'unavoidably delayed' by parliamentary duties which were
either absolutely genuine – late-night sessions in the House were not
unknown, after all – or else only an excuse for prolonged political
discussions with cronies at White's or any of the other clubs to which

he belonged.* In Inverness there was no such lure or distraction. From Eskedale they moved after a while to another house on another river, the Nairn, and this became their home for several years. At the same time, since they no longer needed a family house in London – for the children, too, much preferred Nairnside – they exchanged 5 Gloucester Square for a flat in 17 Eaton Square, right opposite the Amerys, where they stayed when Parliament was sitting.

The twins, Tessa and Marina, had reached the age at which they were allowed to choose which parent they wished to live with and, as Daška had predicted all along, they chose their mother. Though still at boarding school in England they spent every holiday with her, and at Christmas so did the two younger children. Only this once a year was the family all together, and the rarity of the occasion made it all the more memorable. The journey itself was what Alexander to this day recollects with undimmed delight: the sleeping-car he shared with Billy, and the intoxicating scent of Billy's after-dinner cigar ascending from the lower bunk to the upper. 'Oh, do have another,' he begged, and Billy didn't have to be asked twice; he lit up again, only too pleased to encourage a sophisticated taste in one so young. (Likewise, when Alexander's cousin Andrija developed a precocious appetite for caviare and Stilton cheese, Billy indulged him, and himself, by assiduously gratifying it.)

As for the girls, the Highlands spelled romance; and no one seemed more romantic to them than their own kilted stepfather. They needed little persuasion to follow suit and adopt the kilt themselves as their everyday dress. They also shared his enthusiasm for Highland reels (at which he was adept, though he never mastered or enjoyed ordinary ballroom dancing). But what pleased him most of all was the interest shown by the twins in Highland politics, or at least in his own constituency. They were barely in their teens when they took part in his first electoral campaign, serving as messengers and delivering leaflets from door to door, and they helped him at every election at which he subsequently stood. Later, when they were married, they roped their husbands in as well, to the dismay of Billy's stuffier constituents who did not consider either of the young men worthy of the job. Tessa's husband in particular was too clever by half for their liking; they thought him 'a bad lot' and, to do them justice, it must be said that Daška herself thought much the same; in fact she did her best to stop the marriage.

It was love at first sight, for Tessa at least, when she and Dominick met at the opening ball of the 1957 season. He was the son of the

* Namely, the Guards and Cavalry, Buck's, Pratt's, Beefsteak, and Shikar.

distinguished portrait painter Simon Elwes but, apart from a certain facility for caricature, he had inherited none of his father's talent and showed less interest in the arts than in the turf and the gaming table. Unpaid bills, bad cheques and brushes with bailiffs and policemen did nothing to enhance his reputation and, by the end of the summer, when Tessa's infatuation showed no signs of abating, Daška decided to take her abroad till she got over it. To her surprise, Tessa raised no objection.

Under Billy's auspices the journey was a delight; it also appeared to serve its purpose. The itinerary he chose – Athens–Cyprus–Beirut–Amman–Istanbul – provided enough novelty and variety to take Tessa's mind off her boy-friend, and at each stage she seemed less lovelorn and bereft. Little did Billy and Daška suspect that she was keeping in constant touch with him by means of sly telephone calls.

Their last port of call was Cannes, where they stayed with Daška's mother. Mme Banac had a soft spot for Billy, and he in turn was extremely fond of her. He enjoyed her conversation, her company and the pleasure of her table. Her cellar and her chef were renowned, and Billy did justice to both, managing also to slip out between meals for a ritual *pain bagnat* – that typically Niçois concoction of onions, tomatoes, black olives, anchovies, oil and vinegar spread on a half-loaf of bread – without which no visit to the Riviera would have seemed to him complete. This time, however, he had to hurry home for the reopening of Parliament, and Daška followed a few days later, leaving Tessa to accompany Mme Banac to Zurich for a change of air. The next thing she heard was that Dominick had joined them there.

As Tessa was under age, her father promptly made her a ward of court. But there was no holding her now. She and Dominick eloped, first to Edinburgh in the hope of evading the court's jurisdiction, then to Havana where they were married by a notary public, and finally to New York where they were married again in case the Cuban ceremony was voidable under British law. By this time she was pregnant and they decided to come home and face the music.

Presented with a *fait accompli*, Daška welcomed them back and accepted Dominick as her son-in-law, though she still felt he left much to be desired. But Billy had no such reservations; he had never minded scallywags, provided they were attractive and amusing. Besides, he was extremely fond of Tessa and went out of his way to make her feel that her husband was a useful member of the family. When he wanted to find out what his constituents really thought about him, it was Dominick he commissioned to find out. The result of the investigation was reassuring, though not quite what Billy had expected.

'They all love you,' Dominick reported, 'but some of them still think you spend too much time in foreign parts. Of course, they don't understand a word you say, not with that English accent of yours; and they can't make head or tail of Daška either. They've never known anyone so exotic, but they have no idea where she comes from. Yugoslavia? Russia? It's all one to them.' Then he broke into a mock-Highland tone: 'Strange things are going on up at the manse. There's the colonel married to that wee Russki, with those wee Russki bairns, and all of them up there drinking champagne and playing canoustie. . . . '

Billy found this irresistible. But, for all his wit and charm, Dominick proved to be an unsatisfactory husband. Manic depression brought about unpredictable shifts of temper, which in turn led to alarming and irresponsible behaviour. Within eight years he and Tessa were divorced, and nine years later he committed suicide.

Billy's investigations into the Cyprus troubles gave him room for thought. He had studied the island's history and he remembered what Churchill, as Colonial Secretary, had said in 1907: 'It is right and natural for Cyprus to belong to Greece; the Cypriots' patriotic devotion to what they call their mother country is an ideal to be earnestly and fervently cherished.' But even if the British had really wanted to give Cyprus to Greece, it was not theirs to give, being held in trusteeship for Turkey in accordance with the Convention of Defensive Alliance of 1878. In 1915, however, after Turkey entered the war on Germany's side, Britain annexed the island and offered to transfer it to Greece if she joined the Allies. Greece did join, but rejected the offer – unwisely, for it was never repeated. Instead, in 1925, Cyprus was made a Crown colony.

Understandably, the Cypriots were piqued. They intensified their demands for *enosis*, only to be told that the subject was closed. In 1931 their frustration flared up into an open revolt in which a mob set fire to Government House. The price they paid for this was a long suppression of their constitutional liberties. Even so they enlisted in World War II, as they had in World War I, and fought bravely in the allied ranks. Yet after the war there was no return to constitutional government or any yielding by the British over *enosis*. Some colonial officials added insult to injury by claiming that the Cypriots were not Greek at all, and never had been – a strange thing to say about a people whose ancestors had sent ships to the siege of Troy and helped Alexander in the conquest of Persia. As well might they have claimed that the inhabitants of the Greek mainland itself had never been Greek because Greece had not become a nation until the early nineteenth century. In any case, 'A

man is of the race which he passionately feels himself to be.' This
was the view held by Sir Ronald Storrs, one of the few enlightened
governors of Cyprus, who also said: 'The Greekness of the Cypriots
is, in my opinion, indisputable.'

In 1954 the Minister of State for the Colonies, Henry Hopkinson,
announced the offer of a new constitution for Cyprus, but added,
'There are certain territories in the Commonwealth which, owing
to their particular circumstances, can never expect to be fully independent.' The word 'never' was the last straw, and led inevitably to
EOKA's three-year-long campaign of violence.

If imperialism consists of one people ruling another against the
latter's will for the sake of the former's strategic or economic interests,
then there never was a more clear-cut case of it than Cyprus. But Billy
believed that it was justified on the ground that it prevented worse
evils than it entailed. The Baghdad pact was a bulwark against Russian
expansionism. To fulfil her obligations to that pact, Britain had to rely
on Cyprus as her one remaining base in the Middle East. So it was
essential for her to hang on to the island, come what may.

But the Baghdad pact was soon to be dealt a blow from which it
never recovered. On 14 July 1958 Feisal, the young King of Iraq, his
uncle, Crown Prince Abdullah, and Nuri Said, the Prime Minister, were
killed in a *coup d'état* carried out by a group of officers headed by Abdul
Karim Kassem and Abdul Salam Arif. Billy referred to 'this terrible and
barbarous act' in a speech he made to the House four days later:

I, and I am sure many others, regard those who were killed
not only as people who proved themselves great Arab patriots in
a difficult period and believers in their own country, but as great
friends of this country too. They created Iraq with our help.

Of what crime were they accused? They were old-fashioned but
they were friendly to us. That is all: they were hated for this by
the officers who killed them. I cannot help recalling the wartime
coup d'état which was made under Rashid Ali, in favour of the Nazi
Germans when this country was at its lowest ebb. I am sure that those
who struck at us then are among those who are striking at us now, not
in the interests of Nazism as before, but of communism.

The Hashemites in Iraq who were wiped out have always shown
great personal courage in time of danger and distress. King Hussein
in Jordan has shown it in the last crisis in his country, and I am sure
he will show it again. There is an Arab expression that applies to these
Hashemites: 'The coward dies a thousand deaths; the brave man only
dies once.'

What will the new government of Iraq do? None of us knows.

We can be sure that Iraq is a difficult country to rule. . . . It has a mixed Turkish, Kurdish and Arab population, and it has a division in religion between Sunni and Shia. The Iraqi government may be able to rule the country efficiently, but only by sheer violence and force. After all, many of these problems can be solved by force. Stalin solved many a difficult national question by the simple method of killing off the leading exponents of the nations concerned. The internal political difficulties which the new Iraqi government will face will be very real, and they may be forced to shed more blood in order to survive. The people of Iraq may have a very rough time and a great deal of killing may go on. This reminds me of something that a much earlier governor of Iraq – the Ommayad governor of the time – once said. He said, looking at the Baghdad crowd: 'I see heads ripe for cutting. I see blood between the turbans and the beards.' Iraqis do not now wear turbans and not many of them now have beards, but they are still a warlike and rough people, and the new government will have a very difficult time with them. . . .

The government of Iraq has so far used soft words. They have said, 'We will give you our oil and we will take your pounds.' They have even told the Turks that they want to remain in the Baghdad pact,* while telling the rest of the world at the same time that they wanted to join the United Arab Republic.§ They will use many soft speeches, such as Colonel Nasser used to us in the early days when he came to power. Our government took Colonel Nasser at his word when he said he was not against us. But within five weeks of the last British soldier leaving Egypt he grabbed the canal, and he has not looked back since. . . .

Turning for a moment to some of the immediate dangers as I see them, I think there was an immediate danger in the Lebanon of Colonel Nasser getting control. There was also a danger in Jordan. Both these dangers have been temporarily stopped,# although Iraq has fallen under the control of a pro-Nasser extremist Arab force. What of the future? I think Nasser and the Soviet Union will continue

* Kassem withdrew from the pact as soon as he felt his grip on the country was assured.

§ This was the union between Egypt and Syria, established on 1 February 1958. Less than two weeks later, as a counterweight to the United Arab Republic, Iraq and Jordan formed a federation which they called the Arab Union. Nuri Said was its first prime minister.

While Iraq was in revolution, Lebanon was in turmoil and Jordan became dangerously unstable. At the request of the two governments, American forces landed in the Lebanon, and British paratroops and infantry in Jordan, and the situation in both countries was quickly restored.

their present policy, by diplomacy, propaganda and infiltration, of expanding their power. I think there is grave danger that from Syria there will be increasing pressure on the Lebanon and Jordan. . . .

Billy felt so concerned about Jordan that he spent the first week of August on a flying visit to Amman, to see for himself what effect the Iraqi *coup d'état* had had. The situation was less alarming than he had feared, as he reported on his return:

During my stay I was particularly struck by two facts. The first was that although there has recently been a catastrophic eclipse in the Middle East of pro-Western feeling, British prestige and popularity in Jordan itself had risen greatly since 1957, when I was last there. Our paratroopers have been very well received by the Jordanians.* The reports of Cairo Radio about gallant resistance of Jordanian patriots to British imperialism, although perhaps widely believed outside Jordan, are now no more believed inside the country than the claims of Cairo Radio at the time of the landings in Port Said that these same paratroopers had all been killed by the Egyptian army. . . .

The second fact was that nothing could be further from the truth than the stories put about by Cairo and other hostile radio stations to the effect that the King is cowering in his palace for fear of being killed or torn to pieces by the mob. Unfortunately these stories are very widely believed in the Arab world, although in fact the King travels freely all over the country visiting the principal cities, the tribes and army units. . . . In fact he has gained considerable support from many of the waverers in Jordan, even among those in opposition and those on the West Bank who have often been hostile to him. More important, however, the Jordan army and especially the large bedouin element in it are believed to be very loyal to him. All this has helped to maintain confidence and made it possible for the ordinary person in Jordan to go about his business in the normal way, which is more than can be said at present for Beirut and Cyprus. . . .

In Cyprus, too, the Iraqi *coup d'état* had an incidental but no less important effect. One of the reasons for holding on to British sovereignty was to show the Nuri Said régime that Britain was fully committed to its support. A relinquishment of British sovereignty might

---

* King Hussein had appealed to the British for military help and a parachute brigade had been flown in from Cyprus.

have sapped Iraqi confidence. But this reason was now eliminated. Provided she could retain her military bases there, Britain had no further interest in the island and she eventually agreed to its independence.

Events in Iraq very soon bore out the predictions Billy had made in the House just after the *coup d'état*. During the first five months of the new régime Kassem survived two challenges to his power. The first came from Arif, his chief companion in the *coup*. Kassem arrested him and had him sentenced to death, but in the end allowed him to live as a retired officer. (Four years later, in February 1963, Arif repaid Kassem for his leniency by leading a *coup d'état* in which his benefactor was murdered and he himself was brought to power.) Rashid Ali, the old rebel of 1941, suffered the extreme penalty for foolishly indulging in a half-baked anti-Kassem plot. One after another, the principal figures of the old régime were likewise condemned to death, while the communists, Kassem's closest allies, pressed for more and more executions. The communists gained control of virtually all publicity media. The government radio and television plugged the communist line. The press was overwhelmingly communist in tone. The communists created the Popular Resistance Force, a paramilitary organisation which took control of the streets at night. The state security forces were undermined. The police were discredited. The morale of the army disintegrated. On 31 December 1958, at a New Year's party, a cousin of Kassem who presided over the People's Court shouted at the guests at midnight: 'I have a New Year present for you – twelve executions.'

Billy had every reason to be pessimistic about Iraq's future.

No one in his constituency could have criticised him for undue absence abroad during 1959. Apart from three weeks in February/March, which he spent in the Far East as a member of a parliamentary delegation to the Philippines, Vietnam, Laos and Cambodia, he devoted the whole of the first half of the year to Inverness and Westminster. At the end of August he flew out to Bangkok on another tour of the Far East, but had to return sooner than he had planned on hearing that the general election was to take place on 8 October. 'On 8 October,' he said in his election address, 'the choice before you is clear: whether you want a Socialist government deeply divided on the H-bomb and all the major issues of foreign affairs, and wedded to a policy of controls; or whether you prefer a strong Unionist government under the firm and wise leadership of Mr Macmillan, who has restored prosperity at home and confidence abroad and to whom the future of the nation can safely be entrusted.'

His supporters took the point, and returned him with an increased majority of 4075.

A week later he flew out to Tunis on the first of several visits to Africa. Soon after the New Year he made a tour through Egypt, the Sudan, Ethiopia, Kenya, Zanzibar, Tanganyika and the Federation of Rhodesia and Nyasaland, where he spent about a month. In a speech he gave on his return he said:

I flew straight out from London to Salisbury in Southern Rhodesia and it was interesting to find that this journey was easier, more comfortable and almost as quick as it is for me to travel from Westminster to attend a constituency meeting or cattle sale in Dunvegan on Skye.

I did not go to the Union of South Africa and would therefore hesitate to pass judgement upon what is happening there. I feel, however, that far too many ill-informed and prejudiced statements about South Africa have already been made by people in this country who have never been in the Union and know very little about conditions there. Statements of this kind can only do harm and make it more difficult for the people in the Union to work out their own problems for themselves.

I am bound to say, however, that I personally cannot accept the principle of apartheid because I feel it is, from the Christian point of view, morally wrong, and from the political point of view it is quite contrary to our British ideas and beliefs. It is also, I think, impractical and its application is often clumsy and sometimes unnecessarily brutal.

I do not, however, believe that the boycott of South African goods or the attempted boycott of the South African cricket team is appropriate or effective. In fact, if either achieved anything, it would be to infuriate almost all the white South Africans and to drive the moderates into the arms of the more extreme elements. I am therefore opposed to these attempted boycotts.

Another African country presently claimed Billy's attention. Within six days of being granted independence on 30 June 1960, the Belgian Congo plunged into anarchy and chaos. The new nation's president was Joseph Kasavubu; its first prime minister, Patrice Lumumba, a one-time postal clerk who had long been involved in left-wing politics and with whom the Belgian Communist Party had consolidated their influence, helping him with money and expert organisation to win the elections. His opening declaration to the Belgians was: 'From today we are no longer your monkeys.' Unsheathed blades presently flashed on the streets of Léopoldville; stones flew; black people spat at whites.

On 6 July the surly troops in the Congo Army's Camp Leopold II mutinied. Only Lumumba's hasty order expelling the Belgian officers and promoting all the Congolese by one rank saved Léopoldville from a bloodbath. Yet, even as these mutineers returned to camp, the Congolese garrison at Thysville rose against its Belgian officers and began to march on the capital. For two terror-filled days, 7 and 8 July, half-crazed Congolese soldiers roamed the city at will, threatening to massacre the whites and fighting with the Belgian paratroops who had been rushed in to protect them. Not until UN forces began moving in did a semblance of order return. Even then off-duty Congolese troops, uniforms in disarray, were to be seen lounging around bars and at street corners, swinging their belts at passing whites and fingering their bayonets.

On 11 July the province of Katanga, under its self-styled premier Moise Tshombe, declared itself independent of the central government and appealed for closer links with Belgium. The Katanga gendarmerie was reorganised under a Belgian officer, and Tshombe mobilised his forces to repel the UN troops should they attempt to move into his territory. He did not need them, he said; he did not want them, and he would not have them.

He had a good deal of justice on his side. Unlike the rest of the Congo, his province was at peace thanks to the presence of the Belgian troops he had requested. The mines were operating, the shops were open, people went about their business in safety. It was obvious, then, that if the UN were to intervene it would be for a purely political purpose: to end Katanga's secession. Tshombe knew that most of the UN Congo contingents, especially the Ghanaian, Moroccan, Guinean, Malian, Indonesian and Egyptian, were opposed to his declaration of independence; and so, of course, was the central government, who looked upon him as a Belgian stooge. His fear, he said, was that 'in the luggage' of the UN troops would come the Lumumbists, bringing with them 'anarchy, disorder, pillage, murder and misery'. He had a point. In the end he made the best of a bad bargain by accepting a token force of 237 Swedes; but a quick build-up followed and within a week there were more than 2000 UN troops in Katanga, and as they moved in the Belgians moved out.

The UN had neither the forces nor the stomach to maintain effective control in the bush. Inter-tribal fighting broke out and horrible atrocities occurred. Those who suffered most were members of the Katanga 'establishment', the educated, the prosperous, those associated politically with Tshombe and with the Church. Meanwhile

Lumumba took advantage of the situation to further his own ends. In his opinion the function of the UN in the Congo was to support him with its bayonets against Tshombe, and when this support seemed to him insufficient he illegally accepted aid from Russia. Inevitably he soon fell foul of Kasavubu, and at the beginning of September the latter went to the studios of Radio Léopoldville and announced: 'The prime minister has betrayed the task entrusted to him. I have therefore decided to dismiss the government.' Less than an hour afterwards Lumumba called his cabinet into late-night session and proceeded to dismiss Kasavubu. Thereupon Joseh Mobutu, the thirty-one-year-old chief-of-staff of the Congolese army, seized power. None of the three was prepared to move against either of the others. Kasavubu sulked in the presidential palace: Lumumba hid in the prime minister's residence under guard of Ghanaian UN troops, and Mobutu toiled manfully to keep the government going. Such was the situation when Billy flew out to the Congo in the autumn and which he described in an article commissioned by the *Daily Telegraph*.

I felt as if I had been to an unrehearsed comic opera of 'Alice in Wonderland' in which the Congolese leaders and the United Nations officials were the guests at the Mad Hatter's tea party. The other side of this comedy, however, is one of tragedy and suffering. For, in four short months, the once-prosperous Congo lies shattered in anarchy and bloodshed. . . .

The Congolese nationalist movement has now deteriorated into a series of savage tribal feuds frequently erupting into battles where the warriors and youths of the various tribes, inflamed by alcohol and drugs, slaughter each other without asking for quarter or giving it. The worst bloodbath so far has been the massacre of the Baluba of Kasai by their tribal rivals the Lulus, gleefully assisted by Lumumba's soldiers of the Force Publique specially flown to Luluabourg by the Russians in Ilyushin aircraft. . . .

By his erratic actions Mr Lumumba has, together with his communist friends, done more to discredit modern African nationalism in the eyes of the world than any other African before him. He has escaped arrest and trial only by the intervention of the United Nations authorities themselves. He is now trying, with the money he is still receiving from the Russians, to stage a comeback. . . .

In the general Congo chaos, Katanga alone shows signs of stability and gives a glimpse of hope for the future. . . . There is little immediate chance of the Katanga government being overthrown from within, although two months ago an attempted invasion by two battalions of Lumumba's Force Publique was a very real threat. There is, however, a new danger. The UN troops, by their intervention in Katanga, may themselves destroy the Tshombe régime. . . .

Whatever views one may have about Mr Tshombe's aim of independence for Katanga, surely no one can take real exception to his desire to preserve law and order and to his willingness to continue to work with Belgian and other technicians to ensure the healthy economy of his country and avoid mass unemployment for his people.

The decision to support or to destroy the law and order maintained by Mr Tshombe in most of Katanga now rests largely with the United Nations; but Britain should use her influence to ensure that the UN troops do not unjustifiably intervene. . . . We should also, of course, do what we can to encourage a reasonable and responsible Congolese government to emerge in Léopoldville. . . . In the meantime, however, we should give Mr Tshombe and his government all the moral and practical support we appropriately can.

After meeting Tshombe and various other ministers of the Katanga government, Billy flew on to Ethiopia as secretary of the Anglo-Ethiopian Parliamentary Group. On 14 December there was an attempted *coup d'état* against Haile Selassie's government (the Emperor himself was on a visit to Brazil at the time) to which Billy alluded a week later in another article for the *Telegraph*.

Why the attempted *coup d'état* in Addis Ababa should have taken place at this moment is not yet clear, nor what internal or external forces were behind it. And although the immediate danger has been overcome, a question has been raised that must be answered:

How can Ethiopia play her part in modern Africa, where the forces of extreme African nationalism and neo-communism are changing the pattern of social and family relationships; and at the same time preserve her own ancient Christian-Judaic traditions which are far more Byzantine, and thus more European, than African?

Until now Ethiopia has guarded her independence, with various degrees of success, for nearly 3000 years except for five years of Italian occupation. This has been due not only to her geographical remoteness and the inaccessibility of her great mountain plateau rising to an average height of nearly 8000 feet, but also to the warlike qualities of the Amhara and the political skill of their rulers.

These qualities have been sustained through periods of great adversity by the faith of the Amhara and Tigreans in monophysite Christianity and their respect for the Solomonic imperial tradition.

For, according to Ethiopian history, the ancestor of the present emperor was Menelik I, the son of Solomon and the Queen of Sheba, who founded the Ethiopian monarchy and converted the Ethiopians to Judaism, to which faith they held until the beginning of the fourth century, when St Frumentius converted them to Christianity.

Ever since then Ethiopia has stood like a rock of Christianity above the swamps of African paganism and amid the sea of Islam. Even in the 16th century, at the highest tide of Islam, when the Moslem Danakil and Somali tribes under Emir Ahmed Gran stormed the plateau, Ethiopia still managed to survive as an independent state with the aid, it is true, of 400 Portuguese knights under Christian da Gama, brother of Vasco da Gama.

But today, among the younger educated Ethiopians, there is a growing feeling that Ethiopia should identify herself more and more closely with Africa and African nationalism. It would, however, be a tragedy if Ethiopia, in doing this, were to be engulfed in the more extreme and irresponsible forms of African nationalism or communism, both of which are entirely alien to her own national traditions.

The tragedy that Billy feared eventually occurred.

By the end of the year events in the Congo had begun to bear out his gloomiest forebodings. Late in November Lumumba slipped out of his village and made a break for it. He was caught by Mobutu's troops, beaten up and brought back in chains. He died, still in custody, nine weeks later, in circumstances which suggested Tshombe might have been his killer, and Kasavubu and Mobutu accessories before the fact. His murder led to savage reprisals, which the UN troops were either unable or unwilling to prevent; they concentrated instead on putting an end to Tshombe's régime. On 21 February 1969 the Security Council passed a resolution calling for the withdrawal from Katanga of 'all Belgian and other military and paramilitary personnel' and authorising the use of 'force if necessary' to prevent civil war.

Tshombe's reaction to this was to call a meeting of every Congolese leader of importance to seek a solution to the country's political problems. The three-day conference wound up on 10 March and resulted in the following decisions: the present centralised structure was to be replaced by a 'Community of Congolese States', a loose confederation of nearly sovereign states. There was to be a central government at Léopoldville and Kasavubu was to remain president, serving on a 'Council of States' made up of the presidents of the member states.

What emerged was a compromise between partition and federation. It was not a perfect solution but it had much to recommend it, if only because it was a Congolese solution. Perhaps it was for this very reason that the UN contemptuously brushed it aside and, far from retracting the resolution authorising the use of force, flew in an additional contingent of 4700 Indian troops despite the protests of the Congolese leaders.

The situation deteriorated rapidly. There were several clashes between Katangan units and UN troops, and both sides suffered casualties. Worse, Kasavubu fell out with Tshombe and came to a private agreement with the UN. By 1 August the die was cast. Despite pious protests to the contrary, the central government and the UN were once again of one mind and had one purpose in view: the overthrow of Tshombe's régime and the reintegration of Katanga in the Congo.

On 28 August a task force of Indian and Swedish troops moved into Elizabethville before dawn and seized the airport, the radio station, the post office, the telephone exchange, army headquarters and several hospitals. Their objective: to arrest and deport all Europeans serving in the Katangan administration and armed forces. By 9 September more than 300 white officers had been rounded up and only 104 were unaccounted for. Four days later Gurkha troops supported by Irish armoured cars reinforced the UN force already in position, and the UN special representative in Katanga, Conor Cruise O'Brien, proclaimed the end of the province's secession. But Katanga's fourteen months of independence were not to be ended so easily. Heavy fighting continued and Tshombe issued a proclamation demanding 'total war' against the UN.

Billy commented on these developments in a speech he made in Inverness on 16 September:

The present armed intervention in the internal affairs of Katanga by the UN forces under Mr O'Brien on the flimsiest, indeed almost non-existent legal pretexts, is a cynical act of power politics which has shocked many of us here in Britain and is bringing grave discredit upon the United Nations. The UN representatives in the Congo have consistently tried to destroy Mr Tshombe and the law and order he has maintained in Katanga. They resent his being willing and able to work successfully with Belgians and other European technicians. . . .

The Soviet government and certain negative elements in the UN are opposed to Mr Tshombe because they seem determined at all costs to make it impossible for newly independent African countries to remain on friendly terms or work in co-operation with their former imperial rulers. They want to divide Europe from Africa economically, culturally and strategically. The Soviet government encourages and supports this policy because it will ensure that the new African nations would not be able to cope with their economic difficulties and would turn, they hope, toward communism and thus weaken the Free World.

The destruction of Mr Tshombe and his government in Katanga would be a great triumph for these people, and a tragic warning to other African leaders of the fate that might befall them if they were willing to co-operate on equal terms with us or other former imperial powers.

Both Mr O'Brien and Mr Hammarskjöld [UN Secretary-General] must bear direct and individual responsibility, because, by their prejudiced and ill-considered interpretation of the resolution, they are guilty of spreading into hitherto peaceful Katanga the anarchy, murder and bloodshed which engulf the rest of the Congo and which may now spill over into Northern Rhodesia as well unless the strongest possible counter-measures are taken.

The British government must now make their position clear by protesting in public at the United Nations in New York against the continuation of the present cynical, wicked and senseless UN policy towards Katanga. . . . In any case no more reinforcements of UN troops should be sent there to increase the intensity of the fighting. If, however, the present UN policy continues, Britain should immediately disassociate herself from it and refuse to pay her contribution of more than £300,000 per month towards the Congo special operation fund. . . . This money would be far better used for a fund to compensate the innocent victims of all races whose sufferings are being caused by the ill-considered and biased measures of the UN forces and representatives in Katanga.

Billy was not alone in criticising UN activity in the Congo. Important segments of world opinion were marshalling in condemnation of what appeared to be a clear violation of the UN's own charter. The UN had placed themselves in a position from which they could not extricate themselves. The only solution seemed to be a ceasefire. Hammarskjöld and Tshombe therefore agreed to meet on 17 September at Ndola, Northern Rhodesia, in an attempt to arrange a truce. Hammarskjöld failed to arrive. His plane crashed in a forest glade nine miles north-west of the rendezvous and no one on board survived. The tragedy resulted in the shift of at least a portion of world opinion against Tshombe, as if he personally were responsible for it.

In October Billy once again felt the lure of the Middle East and flew out to Beirut, 'to hear the latest gossip'. He found the situation in the Lebanon ostensibly unchanged – 'business as usual' seemed to be the watchword – but he detected more secret agents, terrorists and thugs than ever before. 'The pro-Nasser agents,' he reported, 'are trying hard to influence the outcome of the elections in Syria and also, I believe, to bring about the assassination of King Hussein of Jordan. The pro-Kassem and the anti-Kassem agents compete against each other, while a motley collection of Saudi Arabians and Kuwaitis spend their money on various intrigues, to the profit and delight of the Lebanese.'

He also had a definite impression that Arab nationalism was fragmenting and reverting to the traditional internecine strife that had existed almost for ever between the Middle Eastern states. Egypt was at loggerheads with Iraq, and Syria's secession from the United Arab Republic had not only nullified Nasser's claim to leadership but had also enhanced British prestige, Britain being widely believed to have engineered the coup. In consequence, Billy felt, the initiative in the Middle East once again lay in Britain's hands and he therefore advocated the adoption of a more constructive and positive policy instead of the defensive and delaying tactics Britain had been pursuing for the previous few years.

From Beirut he flew on to Kabul, where evidence of Russian activity struck him as soon as he landed. There, parked on the airfield, glistening white in the bright sunshine and clear air 6000 feet above sea level, were several Soviet jet airliners. The Russians were building another civil airfield just outside the capital which, together with the development of an oilfield and a number of other projects, formed part of the Soviet Union's contribution to Afghanistan's first five-year plan, amounting to the equivalent in roubles of about £75 million. They had already completed a large military airfield a few miles further north, another in northern Afghanistan, and a third was under construction near the Iranian border.

Soviet engineers were also at work on strategic highways linking these airfields to one another and to the railhead ports on the Russian side of the Oxus. Another road was being built across the Hindu Kush. It would therefore soon be possible for vehicles to pass from Russia, right through Afghanistan and into Pakistan, with comparative ease and speed. This, to Billy, was the most alarming result of Soviet aid to the country. For it meant that although the Russians at present had little direct political influence in its internal affairs, they could take it over, or at least control its transit facilities, whenever they wished.

He returned to London in time to attend an important debate

on 14 December, the motion being 'That this House supports the actions of Her Majesty's Government in making a formal request to the Secretary-General of the United Nations to secure an immediate cease-fire in Katanga in order to bring to an end the destruction of life and property resulting from the present fighting and thus create conditions in which, in a united Congo, a peaceful and just basis for co-operation may be negotiated.' Billy abstained on the vote of confidence because he felt, as he had said before, that Britain should refuse to give financial, moral or material support for operations which the Prime Minister himself had described in Parliament as 'a battle between the United Nations and the Katanga people'.

This description was an understatement. Since Hammarskjöld's death relations between Tshombe and the UN had gone from bad to worse. On 20 October central government troops had invaded Katanga and suffered heavy losses. Tshombe's military successes and his defiance raised the antagonism of the Afro-Asian bloc in the Security Council to an almost hysterical level, and U Thant, the new acting secretary-general, accepted a resolution to put an end to Katanga's secession by force. This amounted to a declaration of war, and from then on Tshombe's fate was sealed. But it was to take the UN almost two more years to get the better of him and force him to submit to the central government, persisting to the end in their refusal to recognise Katanga's right to self-determination.

Early in the new year, 1962, Billy had a long conversation in London with Ghazi Daghestani, commander of the division in which Kassem had been serving as a brigadier at the time of the 1958 *coup d'état* in Baghdad. The loyal Iraqi major-general, who had barely escaped with his life, was now living in exile; but he kept in touch with his native country and was a valuable source of information. He told Billy that Kassem was in a very weak position, engaged in a hard and bitter struggle against the Kurds, and that little would be needed to topple him. At present the Kurdish rebellion was aimed at establishing an independent Kurdistan, but this was doomed to failure, being opposed not only by the Iraqi government but by the Turkish and Iranian governments as well. If, however, the Kurds could be persuaded to concentrate instead on getting rid of Kassem, they might well receive support from Jordan and ultimately gain a privileged position, perhaps even a form of autonomy, within the new state of Iraq.

This was music to Billy's ears. He flew out to Amman at once to discuss the matter with King Hussein, who told him he would do all he could, and by military means if necessary, to restore a decent government in Iraq. Then he flew back to London for further discussions with Daghestani, and the two of them set to work on a plan of action to be put into practice in the event of Kassem's death or overthrow.

The plan that eventually took shape was for a Jordanian force of about 2000 men, disguised as Iraqis, to move into Kurdistan in support of the present rebellion. They would advance in three main columns: the first on Habbaniya to seize the airport and two strategic bridges on the Euphrates; the second on Nekhab, along the Saudi Arabia–Iraq border, to capture two large provincial towns further downstream; the third (operating, with the Shah's approval, from Iran) on Samarra, to cut the main Baghdad–Mosul road. All three would then converge on the capital and claim to be Iraqi army units in revolt.

But the problems of security, co-ordination and logistics proved insurmountable. The plan had to be abandoned, and Billy turned his attention to another field of action.

An agreement signed at Evian on 18 March 1962 brought to an end seven and a half years of savage war between Algerian nationalists fighting for their independence and French colonists trying in vain to hang on to a country which they had occupied for 132 years. The well-prepared and carefully synchronised revolt throughout Algeria had been launched on 1 November 1954 by a movement which called itself the National Liberation Front, better known by the initials FLN. Its nine founder leaders, all in their early or mid-thirties, included a strongly built young Arab called Ahmed Ben Bella who, together with a Kabyle colleague, Hocine Ait Ahmed, had in 1949 organised the first major revolutionary coup: an armed raid on the central post office of Oran.

French paratroops arrived to help restore law and order, but their repressive measures only strengthened the FLN's resolve and multiplied its adherents. The fighting intensified, and in March 1956 the rebels received an unexpected bonus with France's granting of independence to Morocco and Tunisia. From then on the FLN had friendly and open frontiers to east and west. Eight months later, on 22 October, while flying in an Air Maroc DC3 from the one neighbouring country to the other, Ben Bella and Ait Ahmed were kidnapped by the pilot, a Frenchman, who received radio orders in the name of the French Ministry of Defence to land them in Algiers instead of Tunis. They were promptly arrested and spent the remainder of the war in prison.

On their release they rejoined the leadership of the FLN, and Ben Bella became Vice-Prime Minister in the provisional Algerian government that had meanwhile been created in Tunis. Billy flew out there at the end of June 1962 and reported back to the *Daily Telegraph.*

> I found most of the provisional Algerian government offices and organisations in Tunis in some degree of chaos. Piles of paper were lying about, and harassed secretaries were explaining to their bosses why this or that file or document had been sent on to Algiers with the advance party to start up a new office. But the government itself and most of the FLN leaders are still in Tunis. They will move to Algiers after Sunday's referendum to start the campaign for the elections, which must then be held within three weeks.

The referendum was duly held on 1 July; two days later President de Gaulle recognised Algerian independence; and by the end of the summer Ben Bella had established his ascendancy and become independent Algeria's first president. Billy flew out again to report on the situation.

He was driving along the waterfront road near Algiers with three other foreign journalists, when bullets started whistling overhead. They had run into a gunfight between gendarmes and anti-government guerrillas. Leaving the car on the roadside, they took cover in a ditch and were pinned to the ground for almost an hour before police reinforcements arrived and put the gunmen to flight. Characteristically, Billy did not even mention this incident in his report but concentrated instead on the plight of the Europeans who had stayed on:

> Of the million Europeans living in Algeria before the Evian agreement, only 300,000 are still there. The rest have fled to France. The other day I visited Bab el Oued, once the crowded European working-class district of Algiers and the stronghold of the OAS.* I saw practically no Europeans in the streets, and almost all the shops, houses and apartments were filled with Moslems.
>
> Although law and order are now being restored, the Europeans are all gloomy about the future. The large landowners and business people can probably make their own arrangements, if not to stay on at least to obtain some compensation under the Evian agreement. But for the others it is a human tragedy. Some say, 'There's no place here any more for the likes of us'; others, that Algeria 'no longer pleased them', meaning, I presume, that they could not bring themselves to

---

* The Organisation Armée Secrète, composed of *ultras* whose ruthless anti-Muslim activities appalled even the hardened paratroopers.

live on as an ordinary minority group where once they had lorded it as masters.

Many of these *pieds-noirs** supported the OAS in their terrorist activities because they felt that this was the only chance to prevent France from giving independence to Algeria. They were prepared to go down fighting rather than quietly surrender, but when finally the OAS signed a cease-fire with the FLN they panicked and fled from what they thought would be a massacre of revenge. In fact there was no mass murder of Europeans. . . . In spite of all the torture and atrocities on both sides, I found surprisingly little bitterness between the European and the Moslem communities, and almost no animosity against France.

There was bitterness between Muslim and Muslim, however, and animosity within the country's leadership. It was not long before the FLN split into rival groups; Ben Bella and Ait Ahmed fell out; and, surprisingly but as a direct consequence of their quarrel, Billy found himself involved in an adventure requiring the combined gifts of a James Bond and a member of the League of the Scarlet Pimpernel.

* The nickname by which the European settlers were known, presumably because they wore black shoes instead of native slippers.

9 *McLean of the Yemen*

On 20 September 1962 Imam Ahmed of the Yemen died and was succeeded by his son, Mohammed al-Badr. Less than a week later a group of army officers headed by Colonel (instantly self-promoted to brigadier) Abdullah Sallal, opened fire with artillery on the royal palace in Sana and scored several direct hits. The rebels then announced that Imam al-Badr had been killed in the bombardment and they proclaimed a republic; and within four days Egyptian troops had been airlifted into the Yemen to support the new régime.

Nasser had been casting an avid eye on the Yemen for several years. If his ambition to impose an Egyptian hegemony on the Middle East was to be realised, he first had to transform the thousand-year-old imamate into a pliant ally or a puppet state. His initial step, in 1956, was to offer Imam Ahmed financial aid and to arrange for his son to visit Moscow. The visit resulted in closer ties with the Soviet Union, including a trade agreement, and laid the Yemen open to left-wing Arab nationalist penetration. An Egyptian military mission arrived in Sana; in exchange, young Yemeni officers were sent for training to Cairo; more and more Soviet arms poured into the country; and when, in 1958, Nasser invited the heads of other Arab states to associate themselves with the recent Egypt–Syria merger – the so-called United Arab Republic – the Imam shrewdly jumped on the bandwagon by joining it on a federal basis, in what became known as the United Arab States.

Disillusion followed. It soon became clear that Nasser's aim was not to achieve Arab unity but to extend his personal dominion over the Arab states and rule them as the Kremlin rules its satellites. When therefore Syria seceded from the United Arab Republic in September 1961, the Imam too broke with Egypt. But by then the damage was done. Nasser's agents had been at work and the ground was prepared for a *coup d'état*. It occurred just a year later, on the night of 26 September 1962.

At first it seemed to have succeeded. Brigadier Sallal's government was reinforced by the arrival of several 'progressive' leaders trained in Cairo; and more Egyptian troops, with tanks and armoured cars, landed at Hodeida and elsewhere on the coast. Meanwhile, Radio Sana tried to persuade a bewildered population that the death of Imam al-Badr and the establishment of a republic heralded the end of feudalism and the beginning of a new era. But Imam al-Badr was not dead. He had miraculously escaped from his ruined palace and, disguised as an ordinary soldier, made his way with a few loyal subjects to a secret headquarters in the north-west of the country. From there he announced that he was still alive and was forming a royalist government. The tribes at once started rallying to him.

At this point, three weeks after the coup, no one outside the Yemen knew exactly what was happening inside the country. Reports emanating from Sana, inevitably distorted by Sallal's propaganda, indicated that the republicans were in control of the capital, the main towns and the roads between them. No foreign correspondent or diplomat had been able to visit the areas held by the royalists, where conditions were for the time being as unknown to the Western world as they had been in the reign of the Queen of Sheba. At the instigation of King Hussein of Jordan, who was on a visit to London, Billy decided to fly out and see for himself.

After an overnight stop in Amman for further consultations with Hussein – during this visit he also made his will, not knowing what lay ahead – he flew on to Riyadh, where he spent the night of 23 October as the guest of King Saud, who received him in a marble summerhouse in the grounds of the royal palace. The King, he noted, wore dark glasses; his voice was deep; his gestures heavy and lethargic. His large yellow hands hung relaxed over the arms of his leopard-skin chair but, when he talked, shook like those of a man in the early stages of Parkinson's disease. He said he was in excellent health, however, apart from rheumatism in one leg; and his strong, deep laugh belied his somewhat languid appearance.

He told Billy that Nasser's intervention in the Yemen was the first phase of a much wider plot, in which the Russians were also involved, and that unless the Egyptians were checked, there would be an immediate and serious threat to security in the whole of the Arabian peninsula. Without the help of Egypt the rebels would be speedily destroyed, for, apart from the officers and others who had been trained in Cairo, Sallal had little popular backing; he had been

able to seize Sana and the others towns by surprise, and now held them
only by force. But in the Yemen it was the tribes that mattered, not the
towns. The Imam's main weakness was lack of aircraft to counteract the
Egyptian air force, which was bombing royalist-held villages without
opposition. But if Britain were to give him air support – openly if
possible, secretly if necessary – he would soon regain control of the
whole country.

From Riyadh Billy flew on to Aden, in those days still a Crown
colony, to make arrangements for entering the Yemen.

The most suitable approach was through Beihan, one of the
numerous little emirates and sultanates belonging to the Federation of
South Arabia, then under British protection. Sherif Hussein, Minister
of the Interior of the Federation, provided two Landrovers, an armed
escort and an interpreter; and on the afternoon of 27 October, Billy
reached Harib, the first village over the border and headquarters
of Ahmad al-Sayaghi, Deputy Prime Minister and Minister of the
Interior in the royalist government. His arrival was greeted by a
fusillade fired by several hundred tribesmen who had marched in
that very day to swear allegiance to the Imam. The place was a
hive of activity, with messengers scurrying to and fro, and, Billy
was most favourably impressed by al-Sayaghi, who told him that
there had recently been heavy fighting in the area, during which a
hundred Egyptian paratroopers had been killed or disarmed. Billy
himself met one of them, a wounded prisoner, who said that Nasser
had told him he was being sent to the Yemen 'to fight the British'.

Al-Sayaghi, a man of exceptional capacity both intellectually and
as an administrator, was the only commoner in the royalist leadership. All the other commanders, as Billy now learnt, were uncles or
cousins of Imam al-Badr. Many of them had lived abroad and picked
up liberal ideas, which did not endear them to al-Badr's father Ahmed;
but Ahmed's death and the subsequent coup reunited them at once
under the young Imam's banner. The oldest and most distinguished
of them, Prince Hassan, came hurrying back from New York where
he had been serving as the Yemeni delegate to the United Nations.
All the others recognised him as imam when they thought al-Badr
was dead; but when the truth came out he renounced the title
immediately and became prime minister and commander-in-chief.
Two of his sons, Hassan al-Hassan and Abdullah al-Hassan, had
likewise taken to the field, the latter as commander of the 2nd
Army operating closely with al-Sayaghi's 6th. The Imam's youngest
uncle, Prince Abdurrahman, in due course assumed command of the

5th Army, based on Sudah, but to begin with, being fluent in English and several other languages, he was indispensable as a sort of roving ambassador, handling royalist affairs in foreign countries on both sides of the Atlantic. Two more armies, the 3rd and the 4th, commanded by Prince Abdullah Hussein and Prince Mohammed Ismail respectively, were in action further north. Several other cousins were leading smaller units.

Thus the whole of east Yemen was firmly held by the tribes. But heavy fighting was still going on in the west and Billy had to make a detour of over 100 miles, travelling eighteen hours non-stop on foot and on camel, to reach Prince Hassan's headquarters in the mountains near Amlah, twenty miles to the east of Sada. The Prince, dressed in pale-blue nylon denims and looking older than his age – he was fifty-six – received him with great warmth but unfortunately refused to use an interpreter and insisted on talking in English, in which he was not at all fluent. Billy gathered, however, that although this area was solidly behind the Imam, lack of air support was a serious disadvantage. The thirty YAK fighter-bombers which the Russians had given the Yemen before the coup had been standing for years on the airfield, covered with tarpaulins, and the Prince said that if one looked inside 'mouses jumped out'. But he maintained that, with the help of more bazookas and mortars, as well as some air support to counteract the Egyptian raids, the tribes would rise *en masse* and the fighting would be over.

At the end of three days Billy made his way back across the border to Najran, where a Saudi aeroplane picked him up and took him to Riyadh for another audience with the King. From there he sent a telegram to the Foreign Secretary, Lord Home, strongly advising the government not to recognise Sallal, at least until he could stand on his own feet without having to rely on Egyptian troops and aeroplanes to keep him in power.

This telegram was of crucial importance and arrived in the nick of time. Lord Home had been under strong pressure from Washington to approve the Nasserite adventure in the Yemen; he now stood firm and his refusal to recognise the rebels kept the way open toward diplomatic reconciliation with Saudi Arabia, which had broken off relations with Britain during the Suez crisis six years before. Since then relations between Saudi Arabia and Egypt had in their turn deteriorated; on 6 November they were broken off altogether and Saudi guns and gold began to flow over the border to the Yemeni royalists.

*   *   *

On that very day, in London, Prince Abdurrahman, who had come to England to plead the royalist cause, outlined the situation in a press conference at the Connaught Rooms:

> The purpose of this conference is for me to lay before you certain facts about the recent rebellion in the Yemen. This is necessary because much of the information coming from there has been based on propaganda put out by the rebel forces. For example, the report that the Imam had been killed was a deliberate lie designed to demoralise the people of my country.
>
> First of all, I should like to stress that this is not a popular revolt. It must be made clear that the leaders of the rebellion have taken ruthless advantage of the crisis created by the death of the late Imam. The rebellion has prevented His Majesty, the present Imam, from carrying out the reforms he so much desired. I will not deny that these reforms were needed. Neither His Majesty nor the rest of our family were content with the rule and conditions of the last fourteen years. The present Imam is a very progressive man, who for many years was against the strictness of his father's rule. Indeed, the very day he came to power, his first act was to release political prisoners and introduce a programme of much needed social reforms. But before he had a chance to take positive steps to carry them out, the traitors struck.
>
> Now let us look at the character of the self-appointed leader of the rebellion. Sallal is an uneducated malcontent who failed in Officer's School. Through guile he insinuated himself into His Majesty's trust when His Majesty was still Crown Prince,* and through ambition betrayed him at the first possible opportunity. But Sallal is only the front man of a far more dangerous character. I refer, of course, to al-Baidani.§ Al-Baidani, far from being a patriot, is not even a Yemeni. His father is Indian, his mother Egyptian, and he was born in Egypt which even now is his real home. He has spent less than one year of his life in the Yemen. He is no more nor less than a tool of Nasser and it was he who brought the Egyptian troops

---

* Imprisoned in the mid-fifties by Imam Ahmed on suspicion of being implicated in subversive activities, Sallal owed his release to the Crown Prince, who intervened on his behalf in the belief that he was a genuine reformer who wanted to do what was best for his country. No sooner had he gained the Crown Prince's confidence than he started plotting against him.

§ Abdurrahman al-Baidani, chairman of the Free Yemenis, a subversive organisation supported by Nasser, based in Cairo and operating also in Aden, arrived in Sana from Cairo four days after the coup to become Deputy Premier in Sallal's régime.

who with their tanks, guns and aeroplanes are brutally suppressing my people.

We like the ordinary people of Egypt, but have no wish that their master should be ours. But this is exactly the aim of Sallal and al-Baidani. At this very moment Cairo and Moscow are plotting the future of my country . . . I need not warn you of the very serious consequences for the entire Arabian peninsula should they succeed in their schemes.

Billy issued a similar warning a week later from the floor of the House of Commons.

What is the reason for the Egyptian intervention in the Yemen? After all, the Yemen is a poor, rather barren and mountainous country with a warlike and unruly population, and there does not seem to be a great deal of profit therefrom for the Egyptians. We may rule out the idea that Colonel Nasser would be prepared to send troops and incur the expense of fighting in a distant country for the sake of altruistic ideals. It is far more likely that he had a very good reason for going there. Apart from the obvious one – that by establishing his puppets in the Yemen he can overcome the loss of prestige which he suffered from the breakaway of Syria – he believes that if he can establish himself in the Yemen it would give him an excellent base from which to extend the Arab socialist revolution into Saudi Arabia, perhaps through a military *coup d'état* there, and then perhaps later into Jordan and the Persian Gulf. Also he would be in a position to turn the heat on us in Aden. . . . In the end, I believe that he will be thrown out of the Yemen. But in the meantime he could do immense harm in that part of the Arabian peninsula.

Less than a month later Billy flew back to the Yemen, as a guest of the Imam himself. Once again he stopped off in Amman, spending two days with King Hussein, and also in Riyadh where the Prime Minister, Prince Feisal, arranged the onward stages of his journey; and on 4 December he flew by special plane to Jizan, a small port on the Red Sea, whose governor provided two Landrovers to take him to the Imam's headquarters in Jebel Qara, forty miles south-west of Sada, which he reached in the middle of the night after a four-hour drive. He was shown into the tent which had been prepared for him, and woke at dawn to find himself in a large untidy camp sprawling at the foot of a lofty range of mountains crowned with medieval castles and fortified villages. Kilted and turbaned tribesmen, festooned with bandoliers, pistols and hand-grenades, and with enormous curved daggers stuck in their belts, swarmed round the Imam's tent, chanting battle songs and firing salvoes from their rifles, while a couple of anti-aircraft guns fired occasional bursts into the air to ward off the buzzards circling overhead in search of offal.

Later in the day Billy had his first of several audiences with the Imam, an amiable young man of thirty-five, and was charmed by his friendly, easygoing manner. 'He laughs a lot,' he noted, 'and enjoys a joke, even a joke against himself. My own impression is that he has courage and guts in times of crisis or war, but lacks the ability to apply himself seriously to any task other than political plots or personal intrigues.' The Imam said he was determined to fight to the end, with or without British help, but he could not understand why Britain and the rest of the Western world remained aloof while Egyptian aeroplanes destroyed Yemeni villages and killed Yemeni women and children. Surely the British government was not indifferent to the establishment of Egyptian military and political power in Arabia, when Nasser had made it clear that one of his major aims was to chase the British out of Aden and the Persian Gulf? Billy found it difficult to answer these questions, especially since a delegation of British MPs had recently visited Sana and been received by Sallal.

That evening the Imam took him into his confidence and told him how, when he was Crown Prince, he had been utterly seduced by Nasser's charm and had succumbed completely to his influence. He had even lent an ear to an Egyptian proposal that he should carry out a *coup d'état* against his father, Imam Ahmed, for which he was promised £50,000 sterling, £25,000 in Egyptian currency, and two cases of pistols. He had of course refused but had kept in close touch with Nasser and continued, at his instigation, to have dealings with Russia and other communist countries. On his own initiative he had persuaded the Soviet Union to construct port facilities at Hodeida, and talked the Chinese into building a motor road from Hodeida to Sana. His father's blunt refusal to pay for either, when the builders presented their bills, did not lessen the usefulness that both port and road afforded to Nasser's troops when they landed in the Yemen a few years later.

Most of the royal family had disapproved of the Crown Prince's left-wing proclivities as strongly as they resented his father's feudal rule and, even after the young man had learnt his lesson and mended his ways, they felt apprehensive and tried to make sure he would not repeat his mistakes or go from one extreme to the other once he had succeeded to the throne. This was the first time, he now said, that he had mentioned the subject to a stranger, but, far from swearing Billy to secrecy, he asked him to repeat what he had told him to the British Prime Minister, in the hope that the past might be forgotten and a new chapter opened in the relations between Britain and the Yemen, which had not always been altogether happy.

After three days at the Imam's camp Billy was driven back to Jizan and then flew on to Najran, where he conferred with Prince Mohammed Hussein, Minister of Communications and Director-General of the Imam's armed forces, a typical young revolutionary firebrand in manner, dress and appearance, who, though rabidly anti-communist, reminded him of the partisan leaders he had met in Albania. The Prince provided a couple of Ford pick-ups to take him and his escort to Prince Hassan's headquarters, and early next morning they drove off. The road skirted the edge of the desert before petering out, at the end of four hours, in a wadi in the foothills. There they transferred to camels for the rest of the journey, which was to take four hours more.

Since Billy's previous visit, Prince Hassan's forces had occupied the town of Sada and captured the airfield before being driven back again by an Egyptian relief column advancing up the road from Sana. But his forward troops were still entrenched only three kilometres from the town, which was being supplied by air. The republicans had reinforced several other garrisons in the area and threatened to cut the Prince's lines of communication with Najran; but he seemed to be more concerned about the plight of the villagers who had fled, destitute, to the mountains after their houses and crops had been destroyed by Egyptian bombers, and again he stressed the desperate need for air support.

Billy found him as friendly and courteous as ever, but rather confused and indecisive. His thinking seemed to be done for him by a secretary–adviser named Ibrahim al-Kibsy, who, though still a student in Beirut at the time of the coup, had been one of the first to rally to the Imam's colours. A short, wiry, thin-faced young man, he was clearly very bright, spoke excellent English, and had vowed not to shave or cut his hair till the last Egyptian had been killed or driven out from the Yemen.

Next morning Billy and his escort rode back to the wadi where they had left their vehicles, and motored for the rest of the day along the edge of the Empty Quarter without seeing another living soul. But, as often happens in the desert, no sooner had they halted than a bedouin appeared from nowhere and joined them at the campfire. He told them that one of the tribes through whose territory they had to pass to reach their destination – Prince Abdullah Hussein's headquarters in the arid region of the Jauf – had just gone over to the republicans; so they had to make a long detour and drive all through the night before they arrived at the Prince's camp, tucked away in a wadi and well concealed from the air. After eighteen hours' non-stop travelling Billy was so tired that he fell asleep at once, to be woken only a couple of hours later by the flies and the heat.

Prince Abdullah Hussein was obviously the intellectual of the royal family. A slim, softly spoken young man, he had spent the previous four years reading philosophy at the American University in Beirut. But his quiet manner and composure concealed ardent patriotism and passionate hatred of the Egyptians. His headquarters were efficiently run and he handled his tribesmen with patience and skill. His army, about 2700 strong, had fought several successful actions along the Sana–Sada road, killing over 250 of the enemy. He told Billy he urgently needed more rifles and ammunition, as well as anti-tank and anti-aircraft weapons.

Billy and his escort left Abdullah Hussein's camp on the evening of the following day and drove through the night until they reached Marib, once the capital of the great Sabaean empire but abandoned since AD 570, when the final ruination of its celebrated dam, built in the eighth century BC, made it uninhabitable. The ruins were now littered with the remains of six Egyptian armoured cars which had recently been ambushed by the tribesmen. Here they were forced to spend the rest of the day, pinned down by artillery fire and dive-bombing, before creeping out under cover of darkness and heading in the direction of Sirwah, which was still held by the republicans. When they reached the outskirts of the town, Billy's Saudi escort and interpreter decided to go home; they had no wish to expose themselves to more air attacks and gunfire. But Billy was eager to press on to Prince Abdullah al-Hassan's headquarters at Al Urush, so he set off on a camel provided by the local commander, accompanied by four tribesmen who spoke no foreign tongue – and Billy's Arabic, on his own admission, was no better than Prince Hassan's English – and after journeying non-stop for almost twenty-four hours, reached his destination at the top of a great escarpment in time to witness a bombing attack by two Ilyushin-28s on a nearby village. Further along the road, while taking photographs of some Egyptians lying dead in the positions they had tried to defend, he was machine-gunned by a helicopter and spent five uncomfortable minutes crouching in the open on a completely exposed hillock. A little later he had to run for cover as an armoured car advanced towards him; luckily it proved to be a captured vehicle manned by Egyptian prisoners.

Prince Abdullah al-Hassan was an unlikely looking guerrilla leader; he had the aquiline features and large sloe eyes of a Byzantine icon. But he was extremely intelligent and energetic, and the tribesmen respected him for his bravery. At one moment when Billy was talking to him, two Ilyushin bombers overflew the camp. He made no move to take cover and showed no sign of fear. His army at present was some 6000 strong, but he said he could call up twice that number if he had the weapons for them; for all the tribesmen round Sana were eager to join him in an attack on the capital only forty kilometres away. What he needed most of all, apart from arms and ammunition, was wireless communication to keep in touch with other royalist commands and enable him to co-ordinate his activities with theirs. As things were, he was entirely on his own.

Billy was surprised to find two other foreigners in Al Urush – Patrick Seale, an Oxford postgraduate who was acting as special correspondent for *The Economist*, and a remarkable American who called himself Abdurrahman Condé and claimed descent from Louis XIV's famous general; he had become a Muslim, been naturalised Yemeni, had once been employed as adviser on stamp design by the Yemeni postmaster-general, and was now acting as Prince Abdullah's aide-de-camp. Since they were about to set off for Marib, Billy decided to go back with them. Their eighteen-hour march was constantly interrupted by enemy air activity, which forced them to take cover several times; but from Marib they were able to go on by truck and, after a non-stop drive of twelve hours, they reached Harib, the first Yemeni village that Billy had visited on his previous mission in October. In the afternoon of 16 December he motored across the border to Beihan, from where he flew to Aden, and then on to London the same evening. It had been an exhausting visit, lasting exactly twelve days.

Back home he reported again to the Foreign Secretary, advocating immediate British aid to the Imam and again stressing the importance of not recognising Sallal. Even in his own country, Billy explained, Sallal would never be universally accepted, and for a very good reason: he was a townsman, the son of a charcoal-seller, and no self-respecting tribesman, were he ever so poor and humble, would accept the suzerainty of an urban upstart. In fact Sallal had about as much chance of persuading the natural aristocrats of the desert that he was a worthy substitute for the Imam, a descendant of the Prophet and 'Prince of the Faith', as had Perkin Warbeck of convincing the nobles of fifteenth-century England that he was the last of the Plantagenets. Unable to win over the tribes, he had tried bribery, putting a price of 10,000 Maria Theresa dollars (about £3000) on the head of any member of the royal family, dead or alive; but not one of the Imam's relatives had been betrayed.

Till then foreign recognition of the rebel Yemeni régime had been limited. As was to be expected, every communist state had declared itself in favour of Sallal the moment Cairo had described the coup as 'a revolution of the people'. So had Syria and Iraq. So, but only for a very special reason – to forestall the establishment of diplomatic relations between Egypt and East Germany – had West Germany. And on 19 December, three days after Billy's return, the United States followed suit. Nasser had persuaded the American ambassador in Cairo that peace in the Yemen depended solely upon a decision from Washington: if the United States recognised Sallal, the Western European powers were bound in their turn to do so; republican rule would then no longer need support from outside and the Egyptians would forthwith be withdrawn. President Kennedy had risen to the bait; it remained to be seen if Nasser would keep his promise. Billy personally doubted it, and he turned out to be right. When he flew out again to the Yemen in the following spring, he found the number of Egyptian troops there had been increased from 15,000 to 20,000.

But while he was in London two important things had happened. Thanks partly to his own friendly relations with King Saud, diplomatic relations between Saudi Arabia and Britain had been resumed. Billy himself was responsible for the choice of the Saudi envoy to the Court of St James. He suggested the appointment of Sheikh Hafiz Wahba, a former governor of Mecca, who had already served as Saudi ambassador in London for several years before the war. Billy had not yet met him, but had a letter of introduction to him from Julian Amery. Wahba was duly elected and became a close friend, acting not only as Saud's representative in the United Kingdom but also as Billy's own direct link with the Saudi court – a nice example of personal diplomacy. At the same time, on the strength of Billy's report, several million pounds' worth of light weapons had been secretly flown out from an RAF station in Wiltshire for onward transportation to the Yemeni royalists via Beihan. This operation was not repeated, but Beihan remained open for Saudi-financed convoys and also for Western mercenaries.

Billy flew out to the Yemen for the third time on 1 March 1963. By then his itinerary was well established. Once again he stopped off at Amman and Riyadh, and was immediately struck by the change of atmosphere in the Jordanian capital since his previous visit. King Hussein, with whom he stayed for a week, seemed extremely worried and appeared to have scaled down his active support for the Imam, mainly because of American pressure. Intrigue and conspiracy were in the air, and the King himself was the target of a whispering campaign which he believed to have been initiated by officers and other personalities in close touch with the US embassy. It was the same at Riyadh, where Billy stayed overnight as Prince Feisal's guest. The Prince told him that he too had been under American pressure to discontinue his support for the Imam, but he had not given in to it and did not intend to do so. As far as Billy could see, he was popular enough with the people, but his relations with his elder half-brother, King Saud, seemed more strained than ever, and the atmosphere was consequently tense.

Also staying in Riyadh were several Yemeni leaders who had gathered there for a conference. Those taking part were Prince Abdurrahman, Prince Abdullah Hussein, al-Sayaghi, and the Foreign Minister Ahmed al-Shamy. They were eager for Billy to fly down to Najran and visit Prince Hassan in his headquarters, and then fly across to Jizan and visit the Imam in his. So he took off in a Saudi air force Dakota which the Minister of Defence put at his disposal. Since a heavy sandstorm prevented him from landing at Najran, he decided to fly straight on to Jizan where the Yemeni leaders were to join him. But almost at once he noticed that the aircraft was heading over the coast and out to sea – in the direction of Egypt. Not knowing what to make of this, but preparing himself for the worst, he took his pistol out of his bag, cocked it and slipped it into his pocket. He did not have to use it, however. The plane presently started circling back and landed him safe and sound, and also slightly ashamed of his alarm and suspicion.

At Jizan he spent four idle and uncomfortable days in the guest-house until his Yemeni friends arrived from Riyadh, and then set off with them for the Imam's headquarters, travelling in a convoy of trucks. The Imam had moved from the camp where Billy had last seen him – driven out by a heavy air attack in which hundreds of his men had been killed and wounded – and was now living in a cave, on the side of a steep valley at Shadda, near Hijla, in considerable squalor but in comparative safety. He said that the military and political situation in north and west Yemen was better than ever and the morale of the tribes remained high. But there had been some reverses in the central sector: Prince Abdullah al-Hassan's headquarters had been cut off and could no longer be reached from Beihan or from Najran as the routes were blocked by the Egyptians and republicans. Billy was eager to visit the Prince, however, and resolved to slip through the enemy lines from the south-east. So he flew back to Saudi Arabia, then down to Aden and up to Beihan, where he persuaded the Emir to provide an escort and a dozen riding camels; with the roads closed, there was no hope of travelling by motor as he had done on his first entry into the Yemen.

The little caravan set off in the evening of 26 March and rode all through the night. From time to time deep sand-dunes forced them to dismount and struggle along on foot; and Billy kept nodding off from exhaustion, more than once waking with a start to find himself on the point of falling from his mount. At one point a quarrel broke out among his escort, which was composed of members of two different tribes. There was a cry of 'Let's fight it out!' and both sides dismounted, cocked their rifles and took up firing positions, leaving Billy alone and helpless on his camel, with the cord that served as a leading rein hanging limp from the animal's mouth and out of reach. Fortunately the dispute was settled without a shot being fired. At dawn they halted for the day in a wadi on the edge of the Empty Quarter; and at dusk, in a hubbub of human cries and animal grunts and gurgles, set off on another night's march. At daybreak they halted again, in a deep ravine five miles south-west of Sirwah, and again waited for darkness to fall before creeping past the enemy garrison, so close that they could hear the sentries calling to one another. At the end of the third day's march, after climbing a steep escarpment, they reached the comparative safety and relative shelter of a royalist stronghold high up on the Al Urush plateau. It consisted of a large isolated bothy containing several mortars and machine-guns. Ammunition cases spread with camel-hair mattresses served as bunks, on which dozens of warriors reclined cheek by jowl chewing *quat*,* smoking cigarettes, and casually dropping the butts on to the floor or into the boxes of explosives and shells. Billy wisely chose to sleep outside with the camels.

By this time he was used to discomfort, but still could not stomach the local food. On the march he managed well enough. The staple dish was a sort of porridge moistened with sesame oil or rancid butter. Coffee was made from the husks of the beans and sometimes spiced with ginger to make it more palatable. A dough of unleavened flour, wrapped round a stone and roasted in the embers of an open fire, made do for bread. But in camp this diet was supplemented by more sophisticated fare: boiled sheep, usually lukewarm and always tough and greasy. Luckily he had brought with him some bouillon cubes and raw onions which, weighing next to nothing and occupying very little space, not only sufficed for his personal needs but also served – since

---

* The dried leaf of the shrub *Catha edulia*, used as a stimulant and to appease hunger.

the etiquette of the road demanded that all shared their rations – as his daily contribution to the common pot.

Another day's march brought him at last to Abdullah al-Hassan's new camp tucked away in some caves above the village of Sukh-al Ahud, about sixteen miles from Sana. He found the Prince in a very precarious position. Since early February his lines of supply had been cut and his tribesmen were so short of ammunition and money that he had been forced to agree to an unofficial truce with the Egyptians, nominally for the purpose of exchanging prisoners. The agreement, whereby he would be allowed to withdraw from the area under safe conduct, was due to come into effect in four days' time. But now, he said, he would be able to gain at least two weeks' grace by leaking the news of Billy's arrival in such a way as to give the impression that the escort's camels were laden with ammunition and gold.

Billy realised the need for immediate action if the Prince was actually to be supplied in time. He set off at once on his return journey, with an escort commanded by the Prince's Californian-born ADC Abdurrahman Condé, using the same route and taking the same number of days to get back to Beihan. His mission had been arduous and hazardous, but not in vain. It had proved that despite the break-down in communications it was possible even for a much larger convoy of camels than his – possible, for a great part of the way, even for jeeps – to get through to the beleaguered sector. From Beihan he flew down to Aden, where he was able to send a telegram to the British Foreign Secretary reporting Abdullah al-Hassan's situation and stressing the dangers – a collapse of the central front, a reinforcement of the Egyptian positions in east Yemen, and a drop in royalist morale throughout the country – in the event of the Prince being forced to withdraw in accordance with the truce. Then, on 16 April, he flew up to Jeddah and on to Riyadh for a conference with Prince Feisal.

Feisal told him he had concluded an agreement with Nasser whereby the Egyptian troops would be withdrawn from the Yemen on condition that Saudi Arabia ceased to send aid to the royalists; United Nations observers were to arrive very shortly to see that these terms were kept. This altered the whole situation. For although Nasser had already broken the spirit of the agreement – it was meant to be secret, but he had at once proclaimed it in Cairo as a personal triumph – the Yemenis now had a chance of settling their own affairs without foreign interference. Billy was thus able to announce to the press, on his return to London two days later, that all being well he would not be returning to the Yemen in the near future.

All was not well. The disengagement agreement came into effect at the end of April, and it soon became clear that neither Nasser nor Feisal intended to honour the terms. The Saudis continued, though on a small scale, to supply the royalists with arms, ammunition and money (thereby, to Billy's satisfaction, enabling Prince Abdullah al-Hassan to fight on). The Egyptians withdrew a couple of weakened divisions, only to replace them with full-strength ones. And the UN observer force proved to be too undermanned and ill-equipped to do anything about it. Billy realised he would have to resume his own investigations after all, and flew to Jeddah, then straight on to Jizan, on 30 June.

Next day, after buying some Arab clothes and stocking up with bouillon cubes and onions, he set off by truck across the border and drove throughout the night as far as a royalist stronghold tucked away at the foot of a steep hill. Conditions there were unusually luxurious. A waterfall above the camp provided running water and a pool for bathing. Electricity was laid on, and Billy was surprised to find his tent equipped with a refrigerator and even air-conditioning. The food, too, was perfectly decent: Egyptian tinned beans for breakfast, roast mutton with curried vegetables and rice for the midday meal and supper. During the day a reconnaissance plane circled overhead, trying without success to locate the camp, and the four-engined TU-16s that followed dropped their bombs harmlessly in the valley below. But there was talk of other bombs that had fallen six weeks before on the village of Al Kowma, some three hours' march away, where many of the inhabitants had died not from explosion but from fumes and smoke. Could the Egyptians be resorting to chemical warfare? It sounded very much as though they were, but Billy could not be sure until he had more evidence. Arrangements were made for a court of enquiry to be held on the spot, and he set off on the steep climb to Al Kowma with the official who was to conduct it.

At the entrance to the village they were greeted by the headman, who guided them to the place where the bombs had been dropped, and, as they approached, Billy noticed an unusual and unpleasant smell – something like a mixture of chloroform and geranium leaves – which, though it had rained in the intervening time, still emanated from the pitted and discoloured earth. The enquiry established that six children had died within a short time of the raid, some after four days, others after only two hours, and all had shown the same symptoms: vomiting of blood, black spots on the skin which when scratched festered into sores, severe coughs and swollen faces. Billy was present throughout the proceedings, which lasted two hours, and, though unable to grasp every word, he was convinced that the witnesses had spoken the truth. Besides, he had the evidence of his own eyes: the survivors, some of whom he was able to photograph, still suffered from after-effects and complained of skin irritation, bronchial trouble and loss of sight. All these symptoms pointed to some sort of poison gas.

Billy found similar conditions in many other villages where such bombs had fallen and which he visited in the course of the next three weeks, and his findings formed the most telling part of the report he drafted when he returned to England at the beginning of August. Now, on moral as well as military and political grounds, he was more than ever convinced of the need to give the royalists effective support. In his first report he had advised the British government not to recognise Sallal; in his latest he recommended positive action. Feisal, he said, should be discouraged from extending the disengagement agreement and be urged instead to increase the flow of Saudi arms across the northern border; and Britain herself should send more supplies, openly or secretly, through the southern route from Beihan which he had personally reconnoitred. In a further memorandum he suggested that unattributable aircraft should drop supplies by parachute to those royalist commanders who would otherwise continue to be virtually isolated. Western mercenaries expert in the use of mortars, field artillery and explosives should also be infiltrated into the Yemen to raise the level of the royalists' tactics, and a number of British observers should be attached to the various princely headquarters. All these suggestions were eventually adopted.

As a matter of fact Billy had already made arrangements for at least one observer – none other than his old friend and brother-in-arms, David Smiley – to enter the Yemen in the guise of *Daily Telegraph* correspondent. Since the abortive Albanian operation in 1949 David had returned to regular soldiering and for three years had commanded his regiment in Germany. From 1955 to 1958 he had been military attaché in Stockholm and had then served as commander of the Sultan of Oman's armed forces* – his last appointment before retiring from the army in 1961. He was later to command all the mercenaries in the Yemen, who at the height of their activity never numbered more than forty-eight. They were mostly Frenchmen and Belgians, but Billy meanwhile set up an office in London to recruit British volunteers as well. In view of the odium attached to the word 'mercenary' David's own view on the subject, which Billy shared, is worth quoting here:

* The first half of his enthralling book *Arabian Assignment* (Cooper, 1975) is devoted to his three years' service in this capacity; the second half deals with his activity in the Yemen.

'A hired soldier in foreign service' is the *Oxford Dictionary*'s definition of the term, and so it must include such fine infantrymen as the Gurkhas and such distinguished British soldiers as General Gordon and, in our own day, Glubb Pasha. I am very happy to be in such company. Although mercenary excesses in the Congo brought discredit to our calling, I maintain that it can still be an honourable one – with the important provisos that the mercenary's own conduct is honourable, and that what he is doing is in the interest of his own country or in the defence of his own ideals. Speaking for myself, I was – and am – certain that what we were trying to do was in the interest of Britain.

Billy had been back in England no more than two weeks when his father died. The old man – he was eighty-two – had suffered an attack of pneumonia at the beginning of June, from which he never fully recovered. His financial situation had been none too healthy either, as Billy now discovered. Some years before, for the sake of economy, he and his wife had moved to Jersey. Latterly they had been spending just under £10,000 a year – not a large sum compared to the rate at which they had previously lived – but Mrs McLean's lifelong extravagance had whittled down their income to little more than £2000, so that there was an annual deficit of more than £7000. Doctors', nurses' and hospital fees accounted for over half this sum, which also included an allowance to Billy of £1000 a year.

Billy had never been concerned with financial problems, but now he had to face them, for his mother was incapable of dealing with them herself – she too had been ill, suffering from diabetes and from hardening of the arteries, which was beginning to affect her brain though she was only seventy years old. His first move was to forego his allowance – he had been shocked to find what a strain it must have imposed on his parents' unimaginably reduced circumstances – and then he made arrangements to realise enough assets to pay off the overdraft and keep his mother in reasonable comfort. Fortunately even she seemed to be aware of the need for economy, and agreed to the house being sold so long as she could retain her own furniture and treasures. These were put into store and the house eventually fetched £26,000, which enabled her to move into a hotel until she found a more settled abode.

All this occupied much of Billy's time, and it was not until June 1964 that he was able to return to the Yemen. On the way there he stopped at Jeddah and called on Ibraham al-Kibsy, Prince Hassan's former private secretary who had been appointed consul-general some months before.

Al-Kibsy also served as a special agent and, since his appointment, all movements between the Yemen and Saudi Arabia had been handled with greater speed and efficiency.

There were several other Yemenis in Jeddah. A committee headed by Ahmed al-Shamy had been working there with a group of Saudis to produce the draft of the new constitution. Prince Feisal had approved it except for one or two clauses that he found too progressive for the Saudis; and Prince Hassan and Prince Mohammed Hussein had objected to some others as being too revolutionary. It catered for an elected Imam with a cabinet system, an independent judiciary and an elected legislative assembly. Government was to be based on human rights and evolutionary progress, and the Imam was bound by the pursuit of social justice and evolutionary reform in accordance with the standards of progressive countries but in keeping with Islamic principles. All those Billy talked to agreed on the need for the new constitution, though they had sometimes differed over the details; at one moment Prince Mohammed Hussein, who was not on good terms with al-Shamy, had even issued his own version of it. As for al-Shamy himself, he had refused to go to the Imam and present him with the draft because he feared this might antagonise some of the other princes and place him in mortal danger. He recalled that the last constitution he had helped to draw up – in 1948, after the murder of Imam Yahya, al-Badr's grandfather – had nearly cost him his life and had earned him two years in the dungeons of Hajja castle.

Following his usual itinerary, Billy flew from Jeddah to Aden, then on to Beihan, where he found he could still reach the Jauf and Najran by truck, despite a recent build-up of Egyptian troops on the eastern front. So he was able to enter the Yemen again by the route he had pioneered.

It took him thirty-six hours, travelling more or less non-stop, to reach Prince Mohammed Hussein's headquarters to the east of Sada. Prince Mohammed had assumed command of the whole of the eastern sector, taking over from Prince Hassan, who now devoted himself to mainly political matters since the Imam was in poor health. He told Billy that the royalists' position was extremely precarious owing to an acute shortage of ammunition, although a number of successful parachute drops (carried out by unmarked aircraft operating from 'somewhere in Africa') had for a time boosted morale. But if fresh supplies were not quickly made available, there was a risk of his losing the support of his tribes. He and Billy sat up most of the night discussing the situation, and at dawn made their way on foot to Prince Hassan's headquarters, about three hours' march away.

Hassan confirmed all that Mohammed Hussein had said about the precariousness of the royalist military position. He also described the narrow escape he had had ten days before, when some tribesmen in Egyptian pay had raided his camp after exhorting his personal body-guard to mutiny and seize him at a given signal. Fortunately the two men detailed to arrest him warned him instead and he was able to escape, leaving behind all his possessions. The mutineers had then begun to destroy the arms dump, including a large quantity of heavy ammunition which was badly needed at the front. In the nick of time Prince Mohammed had turned up with 200 men and a detachment of mortars. He had bombarded the mutineers, most of whom had then fled, and those unable to escape had their ears cut off by loyal tribesmen and were now awaiting trial.

Billy also discussed the political situation with the two princes, in particular the recent emergence of a so-called Third Force, composed of certain republicans who advocated an end to all foreign aid to either side and were in favour of the Yemenis negotiating their own peace settlement among themselves. He suspected their motives, and on his return to England he continued to press the government for further aid to the royalists.

This time he stayed at home for several months, occupied with constituency affairs. In October there was a general election, at which the Inverness Unionist Association exhorted the electorate to vote for 'the right McLean' – a play on words designed to distinguish Billy from the Labour candidate, who had the same surname. Neither of them was returned. Billy lost his seat to the Liberal, who gained a majority of 2136; and the election resulted in a Labour government. Billy's frequent absences abroad no doubt contributed to his defeat; for domestic issues were the main concern of most of his constituents, who felt perhaps that he should have spent more time on them.

A month after Billy lost his seat King Saud of Saudi Arabia lost his throne, deposed by the ruling family, who appointed Prince Feisal in his place. It was thus as a private citizen, and at the invitation of a new monarch, that Billy stopped off at Riyadh on his way back to the Yemen in January 1965. Here he learnt of an important event that had taken place while he was in England. At Erkwit, on the Red Sea coast of the Sudan, under Feisal's auspices, a Yemeni royalist delegation, headed by Ahmed al-Shamy, and a similarly representative group of republicans had met in secret and agreed on a ceasefire, which would come into effect on 8 November. But hostilities had since resumed, as Billy was shortly to see for himself.

During his talks with Feisal the Third Force came under discussion.

Billy believed that any neutralist group of this sort would be more interested in strengthening its own position against the royalists than in fighting the Egyptians and the republicans. Backing it might indeed lead to the end of the present hostilities but only, he feared, at the risk of a civil war breaking out instead. He was therefore much relieved when the King told him that he himself had no intention of supporting anyone but the Yemeni royal family. Armed with this reassurance, Billy flew down to Jizan on his way to the Imam's headquarters and, twenty-four hours later, accompanied by Prince Abdurrahman, who was now Deputy Prime Minister, he set off by truck across the border.

On the way, after driving all night, they saw an Ilyushin-28 drop two large bombs on a target some distance ahead, and when they reached the spot where the bombs had landed they found two huge craters. Luckily no damage had been done to persons or to property, but the bombing was in blatant contravention of the Erkwit agreement, which neither side had yet repudiated. In the early afternoon they arrived at the foot of the mountain below the Imam's new camp, which they reached after a thirty-minute climb. They were then shown into the guest cave where they dined separately, before being admitted to the Imam's personal cave nearby.

The Imam said that royalist morale was higher than ever, and next morning Billy had ample evidence of marked improvement in the military situation. There had recently been heavy fighting in the area, and a tour on foot of the battlefields revealed the extent of the republican casualties, the unburied corpses still littering the ground. There was progress on the other fronts as well, thanks in part to the Western mercenary instructors and wireless operators attached to the princely commanders. Billy visited each headquarters in turn, travelling on foot or by camel, and always by night to avoid being spotted by Egyptian reconnaissance planes. Lying up during the day, he and his escort were often within range of the enemy positions and at one point they had to run for cover when shells came whistling overhead.

He had been on the move for almost two months when his tour was interrupted by a minor accident. While mounting his camel one evening he stumbled and fell, giving his elbow a slight knock. He thought nothing of it and rode on, but presently his arm became so painful that he had to stop. He spent the rest of the night alternately shivering and sweating, and drinking cup after cup of tea to assuage the intolerable thirst which a mounting fever had induced. Next morning he was no better; the very thought of food revolted him and the nausea was accompanied by a blinding headache. But there was nothing for it but to press on, keeping himself going with frequent and copious draughts of tea. He was in very poor shape indeed when he reached the Red Cross hospital in Uqd, near the Saudi border; he had made a further all-night march and a final truck drive of seven hours. But he was up and about again in less than two weeks.

Although King Feisal himself still backed the Imam, other key figures in the war had risen to the bait of the Third Force. Among them was Sherif Hussein of Beihan who, much to the concern of the Yemeni princes, had withdrawn his support for the royalists and was toying with the idea of opening a new front independently of them. Billy's offer to act as an intermediary was eagerly accepted and so, as soon as he was fit enough to travel, he set off by truck for the south. It was an exhausting drive across the desert – several times the vehicle was stuck in sand-dunes and had to be dug out – but he was rewarded, at the very moment he reached the frontier, by the sight of two RAF Hunter jets zooming over on one of their routine patrols from Aden. After weeks of seeing nothing but Russian aircraft in the sky, this evidence of British air power elated him all the more. 'I had not had this feeling,' he recorded, 'since 1943, when I watched, on a moonlit night from a cave on the Albanian coast, two British destroyers sweep through the Corfu Channel on their way to Valona.'

Sherif Hussein, who had previously been so helpful, now turned out to be extremely tricky. He began by complaining about the Yemeni royal family, criticising their lack of leadership and their disunity; support, he said, should be given to anyone else who was willing to fight the Egyptians. But three days later, after Billy had pointed out that without the royal family there would be no national resistance at all – the tribes would not accept the overall leadership of anyone else and no tribal leader would have any influence outside his own area – the Sherif changed his tune and said that he loved the Imam and the princes as his own family. Billy was justifiably suspicious of this volte-face, but for the time being there was little he could do. He therefore flew down to Aden for consultations with the High Commissioner; also to buy several cases of whisky, gin, brandy and beer to take back to the Western mercenaries in the Yemen. The next few weeks were spent continuing his tour of the fronts, and on 15 May he flew back to London. His mission had lasted exactly four months.

Nineteen sixty-five marked a turning-point in the war. The royalists continued to advance on all fronts. Isolated in the towns or strung out along the roads, the Egyptian troops were in constant danger of being encircled. Unable to extricate himself from his rash adventure, Nasser bitterly referred to the Yemen as 'my Vietnam'. Like Hitler in 1938, he declared that his patience was exhausted. He even threatened to invade the Saudi frontier zone through which the royalists received their supplies. But his sabre-rattling had no effect. He had to swallow his pride and sue for peace; and on 25 August he signed an agreement with Feisal, undertaking to withdraw all his troops from the Yemen within ten months on the condition that Saudi aid to the royalists ceased. Billy again suspected Nasser's motives – 'We still do not know,' he said in a lecture he gave to the Royal United Services Institute on 20 October, 'whether he will keep his word and leave the Yemen, or whether he will use the time he has gained to try to find another way out of his predicament' – and again his suspicions proved to be well founded.

On 22 February 1966 the Labour government announced that British forces would be withdrawn from Aden by 1968, and Nasser, having only a few months before declared his intention of pulling out his troops from the Yemen, now declared that they would stay on there for five or even ten years if need be. In an article in the *Glasgow Herald* on 7 March, Billy denounced the government's decision as 'dishonourable, ill-timed and foolish. . . . Dishonourable, because it breaks a solemn pledge made by the [Conservative] government in 1964 to protect the South Arabian Federation. . . . Ill-timed, because Nasser's army of 70,000 soldiers with Russian aeroplanes, tanks and guns, and aided by some Chinese technicians, still occupy the Yemen. . . . Foolish, because Nasser himself is now in real trouble in the Yemen. . . . . His troops are bogged down in a long and costly war against the Yemeni royalists whom he cannot defeat. . . . At the same time he hesitates to take his army back to Egypt, for fear that his soldiers might mutiny against him and overthrow his régime at home.' As it turned out, Nasser merely pulled back his troops from the outlying districts and concentrated them along the coast and in the triangle formed by Sana, Taiz and Hodeida, leaving the rest of the country to the royalists.

In 1967 the Egyptians resorted once again to chemical warfare, using a more effective type of gas bomb received from the Russians. The biggest and most devastating attack, against the village of Kitaf, occurred on 5 January, and Billy prepared a careful report on it, compiled from all available sources:

The raid started with two MiGs each dropping one smoke bomb. Nine Ilyushin-28s then dropped the gas, three aircraft at a time, three bombs per aircraft, upwind of the village. The bombs made a crater three feet deep and six feet wide, and released the gas in a grey-green cloud which drifted with the wind over the village. All but 5% of the people within two kilometres downwind of the bombs' impact point have died or, in the opinion of the International Red Cross mission sent to the spot, are likely to die. Deaths now total well over 200. All animals in the area also perished, and crops and vegetation turned brown. Until the following morning the grey-green cloud of gas hung low over the village. Those unfortunate enough to breathe it compared its smell to fresh yeast or fresh fruit. Most of the victims were dead within 10 to 50 minutes of the attack. They died with blood emerging from mouth and nose, but without any mark on their skin. Affected survivors have no blisters or skin injury, but have difficulty breathing and cough continuously.

Billy now found himself spending more time in the Middle East than in England, repeatedly visiting not only the Yemen but also Saudi Arabia and Jordan. Consultations with King Feisal and King Hussein confirmed his own view that the stalemate in the war that had followed the 1965 Feisal–Nasser agreement was all in the latter's favour; for the Egyptian troops, no longer engaged in active hostilities, could be re-equipped and reorganised so as to be able to move southwards at a moment's notice and occupy any territory vacated by the British, while the Egyptian air force continued to raid royalist-held villages and even increased its use of poison gas. This situation might have gone on indefinitely had it not been for Nasser's ignominious defeat by the Israelis in the Six-Day War of June 1967. From then on his position in the Yemen was untenable and he had no choice but to start withdrawing his troops. The evacuation took three months, and even before it was completed President Sallal was deposed while on an official visit to Iraq. As Billy had maintained all along, the charcoal-seller's son could never have remained in power without Egyptian support; once this was withheld his downfall was inevitable.

In the meantime the gas raids continued, however, as David Smiley wrote in a letter to *The Times* on 14 July:

> After their defeat by Israel the Egyptians transferred most of their aircraft from the Yemen back to Egypt, and the Yemenis secured a respite of three weeks from bombing attacks. Now, however, the bombers have returned, and bombing raids have been almost a daily occurrence. . . .
>
> Last week Mr Brown, the Foreign Secretary, stated in the House of Commons that he considered it was not for the United Kingdom to raise the matter at the United Nations, but that it should be

raised by one of the Arab countries. Saudi Arabia has, on more than one occasion, informed the United Nations of the Egyptian poison gas attacks in the Yemen, and no action has resulted. It is most unlikely that any Arab country would now raise a subject to embarrass Egypt at a time when they are all demonstrating solidarity against Israel.

I returned from the Yemen a few days ago, where I have seen the surviving victims of poison gas bombs. I have been continually asked by Yemenis why the United Nations choose to ignore these attacks, while Israel and the United States are criticised for their attacks with conventional weapons.*

The use of poison gas is forbidden under the Geneva Convention. One would have thought that the more voices raised at the United Nations in condemnation of this type of warfare, the more chance there would be of world opinion forcing Egypt to abandon this inhumane method of killing innocent Yemeni civilians.

But not enough voices were raised, and the issue was quickly forgotten in the world's press and at the United Nations. Billy thought there was a conspiracy of silence on the subject. Duncan Sandys, the former Conservative Minister of Colonial Affairs, asked why Britain had not taken the lead in censuring Egypt. 'To raise the matter now would be counter-productive,' was the Labour Foreign Secretary's reply.

Sallal's downfall might have brought about the end of the war. Deserted by Nasser and governed by a provisional presidential council, the republicans found themselves both militarily and politically in disarray. Now if ever was the moment for the royalists to exploit their advantage in the field. They had encircled Sana; they had cut the road to Hodeida; they were bombarding the principal airfield of the capital. But the commander-in-chief, Prince Mohammed Hussein, still hesitated to launch an all-out attack. His position, already weakened by disunity among the royal family, was further compromised by Britain's evacuation of Aden at the end of November, when the Federation of South Arabia degenerated into the People's Democratic Republic of Yemen, dominated by a communist-minded National Liberation Front. NLF troops had in fact already been airlifted up from the south to strengthen the republican lines by the time Billy flew out again and joined Prince Mohammed on the Sana front.

On this visit he was accompanied by the distinguished traveller

* On 5 and 6 June Egypt had complained to the United Nations of Israeli air attacks on herself, yet on those very days her own bombers were dropping poison gas on Yemeni villagers.

and author Wilfred Thesiger, an old friend and comrade-in-arms in
the Abyssinian campaign. Thesiger had spent many years in Arabia;
he had twice crossed the Empty Quarter; he had also travelled in the
Karakoram and the Hindu Kush, the mountains of Kurdistan and the
marshlands of Iraq; he was therefore inured to hardship. Yet he found
conditions in the Yemen more strenuous than in any of these places:
more strenuous, and also more dangerous. Air raids and artillery
bombardments were daily events and once, when he and Billy took
cover in a shallow watercourse, a shell splinter nicked the back of his
neck. Billy's reaction was typical. 'Damn it, Wilfred, look what you've
done now!' he said, ruefully contemplating the blood-spattered box of
cigars he had brought with him for safekeeping.

A little later another raid destroyed all his notebooks and sketch
maps.

He spent the best part of three months observing the encirclement
of the capital, sometimes at a distance of only three kilometres from
the town walls. The royalists made several raids on enemy outposts,
set up ambushes and engaged in skirmishes; but these activities did
not amount to much and by the end of January 1968 it was clear that
Prince Mohammed had lost his chance. A strong republican relief
column of armoured vehicles and tanks, backed by fighter aircraft
piloted by Russians and by Soviet-trained Yemenis, advanced from
Hodeida and, on 8 February, broke the royalist cordon. The siege of
Sana was over and Billy flew back to England to report.

As he saw it, everything now depended on the Yemeni royal
family presenting a united front. But this was easier said than
done. The Imam, ill and exhausted, had for several months been
living almost permanently in Taif, near Mecca. He was thus out of
touch with his own country and, to make matters worse, in open
conflict with Prince Mohammed Hussein, who had taken to styling
himself the 'Deputy Imam'. Many of the other princes were likewise
at loggerheads. Nevertheless Billy believed that the only solution was
for the Imam to return to the Yemen and assume overall command,
and with this end in view he flew out to Jeddah at the beginning of
April to consult the Imam himself.

His mission turned out to be fruitless. King Feisal was now
anxious to end the costly and inconclusive war and negotiate some
sort of peace. This would inevitably entail sacrificing the imamate
in favour of an Islamic state of Yemen or, at the worst, an Islamic
republic which the Saudis could more or less control or financially
influence. The Imam himself seemed reconciled to this policy; during
his talks with Billy he said more than once, 'I resign.' But then he

added, 'Don't worry, I know how to deal with all these problems and these people. I set myself up as Imam and no one is going to dislodge me except myself. I shall certainly not do that until the war is won. Then I may consider the matter.'

But the war was never won. Neither the royalists nor the republicans were able to achieve a decisive victory. Another stalemate set in, with the country more or less equally divided between the two sides. In March 1969 the Saudis cut off their supplies to the royalists. In May the republicans claimed that the war was over, but later in the year the royalists attacked once more. This proved to be their last throw, for, since they were no longer being paid to fight, the tribesmen saw no point in continuing and simply drifted away, some to their homes, others to join the republicans. Deserted by their followers, many of the princes left the country; Prince Mohammed Hussein himself abandoned the royalist cause and retired to Saudi Arabia. Prince Abdullah Hassan died in action. In March 1970 King Feisal, who had no wish to see the Russians take Nasser's place in the Yemen, arranged a meeting between the republican prime minister and senior royalist leaders, excluding the royal family who were thus doomed to perpetual exile. The outcome was a coalition government of republicans and royalists. The imamate had come to an end, to be reborn as the Yemen Arab Republic, now more commonly called North Yemen.

This was a fair compromise, and North Yemen today is at least sympathetic towards the West. But for Billy's efforts, it might well have gone the way of its neighbour, the People's Republic of South Yemen, which itself might have been spared its Marxist régime had Billy's warning as to the dangers of abandoning Aden been heeded. Saving North Yemen for the West was supremely Billy's achievement. Without him there would have been no mercenary support for the royalists. Without him the Saudis would not have given anything like as much aid as they did. Like T. E. Lawrence's, his name became a household word in the desert. Duncan Sandys, who accompanied him on one of his missions, recalls how tribesmen coming upon him in the middle of nowhere would cry 'McLean!' as they recognised him, and dismount from their trucks or their camels to embrace him. They still remembered him years later. Hugh Astor, travelling with him along the edge of the Empty Quarter long after the war was over, witnessed the same reaction, and likewise recalls delighted cries of 'Colonel Billy!' as turbaned veterans re-encountered their former comrade-in-arms.

10 *The Scarlet Pimpernel*

Though the Yemen was Billy's crowning achievement, other matters also occupied him throughout those years. While he was still an MP, constituency affairs made a constant claim on his attention and never-ending demands on his time and energy. There were social commitments he could not avoid, functions he had to attend, duties he had to perform, hospitality he had to return. Thanks to Daška, he acquitted himself in style. She lent an exotic note to Inches House, the successor to Nairnside, and created an atmosphere of sophisticated well-being. The reports of 'champagne and canoustie up at the manse' were not exaggerated; they were borne out by the facts; and even the rumour of the house being full of 'Russkies' turned out to be true, when she and Billy found themselves acting as hosts to a delegation of Soviet VIPs.

It was at the request of Julian Amery who, as Minister of Aviation, had been lavishly entertained in Moscow a few weeks before by his Russian counterpart, Pietr Dementyev. He felt such hospitality deserved more than a mere official visit in return, so he invited Dementyev and his colleagues to a tour of the Highlands and asked Billy to make the arrangements.

Billy rose to the occasion. Rather than put them all up in a nondescript Inverness hotel, he housed the most important visitors at Inches and, knowing the secret weakness of communists for the aristocracy, billeted the rest on Lord and Lady Lovat at Beaufort Castle and on other noble friends with seats nearby. The only drawback to their being separated in this way was that none of them had his own luggage, their belongings being packed into suitcases shared by the group as a whole. So it was only by coincidence that any toothbrush, bedroom slipper or spare shirt turned up under the same roof as its owner. But careful liaison with his fellow hosts, and a discreet and speedy ferry service between one house and another, enabled Billy to sort out the muddle in time to forestall the suspicion of its being a capitalist plot.

Apart from the aviation minister, the fourteen-strong delegation included S. V. Ilyushin, Russia's leading aircraft designer; Arten Mikoyan, brother of the deputy premier; and Sergei Krushchev, son of the premier himself. Billy organised various excursions for them: to the battlefield of Culloden, where he told them how the Duke of Cumberland's victorious troops massacred the Young Pretender's wounded Highlanders; to Loch Ness, where he apologised to them for the non-appearance of the famous monster; to the RAF depot at Fort George, where he treated them to a slap-up banquet. He spoke to them through an interpreter attached to the party, his own Russian being rather rusty and the visitors' English non-existent – or so it appeared until Daška discovered that one of them at least was not entirely ignorant of the language.

Her three guests at Inches were Dementyev, his personal interpreter, and young Khrushchev. One morning she came down to find the latter alone at the breakfast table, the other two having gone out for a stroll. She tried to make herself understood in a Russified sort of Serbian, and to her astonishment – for till then she had heard him speak nothing but Russian – he replied in perfectly adequate English. But the gift of tongues seemed to desert him as soon as his compatriots returned. In their presence he reverted to his native language and was careful to conceal his knowledge of any other.

'Splendid!' said Billy when Daška told him about it. Soviet obsession with secrecy, especially such a grotesque and blatant example of it, never ceased to amaze and amuse him.

The Russian visit was the last big function over which he presided as an MP. Six months later he lost his seat, at the general election of October 1964. He regretted it deeply, and so did Daška. With nothing to keep them in Inverness any longer, they packed up and went back to live in London.

Leaving the Highlands was a wrench for them both. Billy missed his constituency; on the other hand, he was now able to devote himself entirely to the Yemen and Middle Eastern affairs. For Daška, however, there was no such compensation. She now saw less of Billy than before. Even when he was back in England more often than not he lunched at one of his clubs, or else at the Amerys' where a political discussion might last from the first pre-prandial glass of champagne to the last drop of port from the decanter, and sometimes even longer – Julian often came home after an afternoon at the House to find Billy and Catherine still thrashing out a topic they had broached before he left, both of them inspired by a second or third decanter which they had opened after his departure.

Billy would then nip back across the square in time to change for dinner. Whether he and Daška were dining with friends or entertaining at home, it was often an official or semi-official function or else a large family party. So an evening on their own was something of an occasion.They hardly ever went to the theatre, because it did not fit in with his timetable, and though they occasionally sampled a restaurant together they much preferred eating in, especially when Billy took over the kitchen and produced some extravagant or recherché dish, heedless of its cost and calorie content and of his own expanding waistline and incipient double chin.

Knowing the delicate nature of some of his activities, Daška never enquired into them too closely, although he on the contrary, and much to her amusement, always questioned her in detail as to how she spent her time. When he was away she had no news of him at all, because he never put pen to paper. Well might she point out that David Smiley always managed to write home to *his* wife, she still received no word from him nor did he try to excuse himself or even apologise: the leopard cannot change his spots.

In June 1965 the Iranian ambassador in London arranged for Billy and Daška to spend a week's holiday in Iran. They were met at the airport by a representative of the Foreign Office and an official from SAVAK, the state security organisation, who escorted them to their suite at the Hilton Hotel. A car and chauffeur were put at their disposal and they were thus able to visit Isfahan and tour the Caspian coast in luxury and style. For Billy, however, sightseeing was only a secondary consideration. He had long wanted to contact the Kurdish leader Mullah Mustafa Barzani, whom he had tried to meet at Mahabad, once the capital of the short-lived Kurdish republic, eighteen years before. Here was his chance, provided he could persuade the Iranian authorities to infiltrate him over the border into the Kurdish-held part of Iraq. And so, when Daška flew back to London, he stayed on to make the necessary arrangements.

After many delays and much prevarication SAVAK granted his request, but insisted on the strictest secrecy, and from then on he was under close observation. A SAVAK official flew with him to Kermanshah, where another accompanied him by car to Sanandaj; here a third official lodged him in a small and rather primitive hotel. Next morning, accompanied by yet another SAVAK official, he was driven up to Khane, the last outpost in Iranian territory. His arrival there was deliberately delayed until after dark, when he was hustled straight into the hospital, at the back of which SAVAK had a secret guest-house. There, after a hasty meal, he was joined by an officer with an interpreter and two armed soldiers, who had been sent from Tehran to escort him over the border. They set off in a Land-rover shortly after 10 p.m. and after half an hour's drive passed through the Iranian frontier post without incident. Then, after another quarter of an hour, they were stopped at a road block by a posse of *peshmargas*.*

When Barzani was forced to withdraw from Iran in the spring of 1947, he had led his men north-westward into the Iraq mountains. For fifty-two days they had struggled through deep snow, eluding the Iraqi troops who were out to intercept them, then, after crossing into Turkey and dodging the Turkish army, they moved back into Iran, where they would have been cut off by the Iranian forces had they not raced for refuge across the Soviet frontier, covering the last 220 miles in fourteen days. They remained in exile for the next eleven years.

The Russians were impressed by Barzani and groomed him as the leader of a Kurdish nationalist movement. Their plan was to create an independent pro-Soviet Kurdistan out of the Kurdish districts of Iran, Turkey and Iraq. But with the overthrow of the Hashemite monarchy in 1958, Russian policy changed. Kassem, the new ruler of Iraq, had strong Soviet leanings and was a better Trojan horse for breaking into the Middle East. Russia therefore dropped her support of Kurdish independence and instead persuaded the Mullah to return to Iraq and open negotiations with the Baghdad government. He flew back in September, leaving his 500 men to follow him by sea. But Kassem's military dictatorship failed to fulfil Kurdish aspirations, and relations between him and Barzani steadily worsened until, on 11 September 1961, the Iraqi army launched a full-scale attack on Kurdistan. The war that ensued was still going on. Kassem had since come to a bad end, murdered by the fawning Nasserite Abdel Salam Arif. Arif was determined to bring the Kurds to heel once and for all; but he had been no more successful than his predecessor and Barzani still controlled most of the Iraq–Iran frontier area with a force that had swollen to an estimated strength of 25,000 *peshmargas* permanently under arms.

Billy had kept abreast of these events and had followed Barzani's career. His immediate personal impression was favourable – 'a strong, clear-minded and realistic man of medium height, very powerfully built, with a strong and aggressive head'. Barzani on his side seemed delighted to receive a British visitor, though Billy emphasised that he held no official position and was merely an individual observer interested in

* Literally, 'those ready to die', the Kurdish equivalent of *nos morituri*, but applied not to gladiators but to freedom fighters.

the Middle East. They conversed for nearly five hours, during which Barzani said nothing that suggested a communist or Marxist bias. His only purpose in fighting, he claimed, was to defend his people against the oppression of successive Arab governments in Baghdad. At present his forces were tying down five divisions of the Iraqi army, about 50,000 men all told, as well as about 20,000 Kurdish levies; these were the notorious Sawaran Sallahuddin or 'Cavalry of Saladin', more commonly called *josh*, or 'donkeys'. If he was to maintain this pressure, however, he would need help from outside, preferably from the West; and if the West denied him support, he would accept it from Soviet Russia or from any other source.

But, as Billy knew, Russia dared not back the Kurds for fear of weakening Arif's government and arousing Nasser's resentment. It was on Great Britain, therefore, that Barzani pinned his hopes, and he asked Billy to transmit his friendly greetings (as well as a list of his arms requirements) to Her Majesty's Government. Billy did so when he got back to London two days later.

Bad news of his mother awaited him. His lawyer in Jersey had written to say that she showed symptoms of senile decay and could no longer look after herself. A week earlier she had gone to Liechtenstein, accompanied by a member of the St John Ambulance detailed to see that she arrived safely. A few days later she was found wandering in the streets of Zurich, with no idea where she was or where she was staying. Luckily someone alerted the British consulate, who repatriated her in the care of the Red Cross, and her lawyer had found her a room in a nursing home in Rottingdean. He was anxious to keep her out of Jersey, at least until her financial situation had been settled. Her present income was about £1500 a year, barely enough to cover the storage and insurance of her furniture, which was therefore being put up for sale. She had consented to this, but her lawyer was afraid she might change her mind at the last minute. Billy accordingly arranged for her to move into a service flat in London, with three nurses working in shifts to look after her.

Billy had been interested in Algeria ever since going there to report on the country's newly won independence. The Algerian revolution, like many other prolonged revolutions, had consumed its own. The FLN had begun to split into rival groups even before the French flag was lowered, and mutual recrimination among the Muslim leaders was even worse than it had been between the rebels and the French. One by one Ben Bella's former colleagues fell away or were purged. In April 1963 Mohammed Khider, Ait Ahmed's brother-in-law, resigned from the post of Secretary General of the FLN. At almost the same time Ben Bella's Foreign Secretary was mysteriously assassinated outside the National Assembly. In June another of the nine founder leaders was arrested on Ben Bella's orders, and the following month Ait Ahmed himself announced he was going into opposition and withdrew to his Kabyle stronghold. In September 1964, supported by Khider, he led an armed revolt against the Ben Bella régime. It was quickly suppressed, and he was arrested and imprisoned; and Khider fled to Switzerland, taking with him the FLN 'war treasury' amounting to some £6 million. In June 1965 Ben Bella in his turn was arrested and imprisoned, in a military *coup d'état* led by Houari Boumédienne, one-time commander of the rebel army. But those who had fallen foul of Ben Bella were no less opposed to the new Algerian dictator, and he in return declared them outlaws. So Khider remained in Europe, and Ait Ahmed in jail.

Exactly how and when, and where and why Billy made contact with the Algerian opposition in exile, remains a secret. He never spoke of his connection with it, neither at the time nor later, not even to his closest friends. All that can be known for certain is that by the end of the year, with support from the FLN treasury, and presumably with Khider's approval, he had undertaken to rescue Ait Ahmed from his cell in the Maison Carrée, the old Turkish fort just outside Algiers. That he was willing to interrupt his activities in the Yemen shows the importance he attached to the undertaking, though it is not clear what he hoped it would achieve apart from boosting the opposition's morale and holding Boumédienne up to ridicule. This by itself might have been sufficient inducement, or else perhaps he merely found himself unable to resist the adventure.

By the new year his plans were laid. His first move was to charter a yacht from his mother-in-law's company in Monte Carlo. Called *Deo Juvante*, it had once belonged to Prince Rainier of Monaco, but after buying it from him Mrs Banac had renamed it after her daughter. Billy arranged for *Daška* to leave Monte Carlo at noon on 7 January and sail for Valencia, where he and Daška would join her, ostensibly for a pleasure cruise with a couple of friends, his old comrade-in-arms Peter Kemp and a young barrister called Simon Courtauld. But she was still in harbour at noon on the following day, and also on the day after that, unable to move, according to her captain, because an American ship was blocking the harbour entrance. It was not until the evening of 13 January that she reached Valencia, and Billy and his party went aboard.

Next morning they set sail, and it was clear straight away that the captain was not keen on the voyage. First of all he complained of a leak, then of engine trouble, which sent him scuttling for the haven of Alicante. From there he refused to go any further. Somehow, as Billy now discovered, he had got wind of the real purpose of the 'cruise' and wished to have no part of it, but would not come clean and admit to his fear. So there was nothing for it but to look for another boat.

Billy knew where to turn for help. King Leka of the Albanians, who had succeeded his father five years before, was then living in Madrid. Billy had kept in touch with the Albanian royal family and had followed the young monarch's development closely. Knowing he could rely on Leka's discretion and courage, he rang him up and explained what he wanted and why. Leka told him he had no suitable boat of his own, but knew of one that was captained by a friend of his called Peter Winter. Winter was in England just then, but the boat, *Startide*, was moored at Altea, only fifty kilometres up the coast from Alicante, where she could be inspected at any time.

Billy drove up to Altea at once, had a look at *Startide*, decided she would do, and took the first train to Madrid to make the final arrangements. Leka not only undertook to get Winter back to his boat as soon as possible but also insisted on joining the expedition, explaining that he could not allow any friend of his, let alone the sole member of the crew, a nineteen-year-old girl who also did the cooking, to take a risk that he himself was not prepared to face. So Billy revised his plans, sending Daška back to England for safety's sake, and Simon in advance to Algiers, while he himself drove back to Altea with Leka and Peter Kemp.

At this point Peter Winter takes up the story:

> I received a telephone call from Leka saying, 'Do you want a charter?' I asked, 'Where to?' and he said he couldn't tell me. I said, 'Well, for how long?' 'Minimum five days, maximum ten,' he said, 'but if you want it you'll have to start for Altea at once.'
>
> I thought it over for a minute or two and finally decided yes. Then I went round to Cookie's. She was just about to go to the hairdresser's, but I told her she could forget that and pack her bags instead. An hour and a half after Leka's call we were on the cross-Channel ferry.
>
> Snow was lying heavily in France and it was a rotten drive. In order to arrive on time in Altea we had to go non-stop; and non-stop we went. On arrival we drove down to the port, past *Startide*. She looked awful, lying on her four winter anchors and with rust marks down her side. We didn't go on board at once; we thought we'd go into town first to buy some stores for supper, and then try to tidy up and wait for our visitors. Out in the street the local telegraph man gave me a whistle and came over and said, 'Captain, I have a telegram for

you.' I opened it and I well remember its contents: 'Imperative we leave tonight. Arriving this afternoon.'

This was a bit of a headache, because I was feeling damn tired and rather sick after the non-stop driving. We bought our stores and went back to the harbour, and there, opposite the boat, we saw three figures, one of whom, almost seven foot tall, was unmistakably Leka. He introduced us to the other two.

We started to load their luggage onto a dinghy to take it out to *Startide*, where Billy was going to brief us. Peter Kemp said he wasn't a sailor and wouldn't be coming anyhow, so couldn't we have our little talk on shore? But no, Billy bundled him into the dinghy together with the rest of the luggage. Leka had brought with him a suitcase, something that looked like a golf bag, and various other bits and pieces.

Once on board, I was allowed to know our plan of action. I told Billy it was quite impossible to leave that night because there was a full gale blowing. I also said we needed the relevant charts. Leka had thought of this and had brought some with him and also an Admiralty Sailing Directorate. I looked at them and saw that they were indeed what we wanted for the Algerian coast, but there was no Western Mediterranean chart to take us across the sea. We also had to fuel up, and this couldn't be done at night in a little port like Altea. So we decided to take off next day.

That evening Leka drove me into Alicante, where I scrounged around some friends in the port and managed to find the chart we needed. But when I unfolded it I saw it was marked 'cancelled'. Still, it was all we had, so it would damn well have to do. We went out to dinner and I ordered a steak. But I just couldn't eat it, I was feeling so sick. On the way back I had to ask Leka to stop, and actually was sick. I was sick again several times during the night and again in the morning. The smell of the diesel as we fuelled up didn't help; I had to lean over the side and was sick again twice, much to Billy's astonishment. I learnt later that he had taken Leka aside and remarked: 'I thought you said the captain was a staunch fellow, but he's chucked up three times already and we haven't even left harbour.'

Peter Kemp saw us off, then disappeared to make whatever telephone calls he had to make announcing our departure. It was not until we were actually under way that I was told the details of our plan. We were to sail for the little port of La Pérouse, about fifteen miles east of Algiers and that much closer to the prison where Ait Ahmed was being held: a total distance of 189 miles, which at cruising speed would take us eighteen hours or so. But for obvious reasons we couldn't sail straight there, having told all and sundry – in other words the local fishermen; there was no one else around –

that we were off for a jolly weekend in Majorca. I got a weather forecast over the radio which didn't do much to raise our morale. It was a sou'westerly gale 8. And since we had to set course first of all to Majorca, I allowed twenty hours for us to get to La Pérouse.

The boat itself didn't have any stabilisers. She was sixty-eight foot but had only a three-foot draught, because she was designed with tunnel transmission which enabled her to be run up on the beach on a kedge anchor and then be pulled off after whatever had to be done to her was finished. A three-foot draught in an 8-force gale is not the sort of thing you want. But we didn't have anything else, so that was that.

Leka succumbed almost at once and retired to his cabin. After a couple of hours I went down to see how he was. He looked absolutely green and couldn't move. Billy, on the other hand, was fine. The sea didn't seem to upset him at all and he asked if he could be of any use. I said yes, the day tanks had to be pumped up with fuel every two hours and the pair of pumps had to be oiled. He said he thought he could do this, though he knew nothing about engines, and offered to take over the duty for the rest of the trip.

On his first shift I took a look at him through the hatch, and I must say it was the most wonderful sight. He was taking the job extremely seriously. He would start pumping, then look to see if the gauge was full, decide that it wasn't and conscientiously set to work again. Much later he told me he enjoyed every moment in the engine-room; the two big Gardeners thumping away gave him enormous confidence, and he was happier down there on his own than up on the bridge with me.

The weather got steadily worse. Our course didn't help the movement of the boat, because we had this damned gale right on our starboard beam. At one stage an eighteen-foot wave hit us broadside. Luckily I had asked my passengers to put on their life-jackets. As soon as *Startide* had come back up again after rolling damn near over, Leka's head popped out of a hatch aft and I heard him say, 'Are we the right way up, chaps?' It would have been too bad if we hadn't been, because he had already inflated his jacket and was quite incapable of getting through the hatch.

I had been thinking about what we were going to say to the port authorities on our arrival. We obviously had to have some sort of excuse for turning up at La Pérouse at this time of the year. So, when we were still about six miles off, I stopped the boat and put her slow astern. We had been towing a water-log at the end of a fifty-foot length of rope to measure the distance we had travelled. Now, most yachtsmen in their day have gone astern and accidentally wrapped this thing round their propeller. It was only too easy. But doing it on purpose was a very different matter. I pulled in the damned contraption and dangled it over the stern for a good twenty minutes. Nothing doing. But in the end I managed to get it wound round the starboard propeller, and we limped into port on one engine.

The officials came on board as soon as we had docked. They asked what we were doing there and we explained that with the sea running as it was, and with one engine out of action, we had had to find shelter where we could. We also asked them for a diver to disentangle our prop. In fact we had a couple of diving bottles on board and could have done it ourselves. But we chose not to. The diver appeared very quickly and set to work. The job should have taken him no more than five minutes, but he spent over half an hour under the boat. We could hear him moving around from bow to stern, probing here and there, just to see what he could find.

Then came the paperwork. As captain, I had to fill in any amount of forms. I also had to show them my passport. Luckily they didn't ask the others for theirs, as it might have been quite a business to explain what the King of the Albanians was doing on board.

Billy was anxious to contact Simon, and asked if he could borrow Cookie. 'What for?' I said. 'Well, as soon as I get ashore,' he said, 'there's bound to be someone tailing me, and I want Cookie to come along and draw him off.' I wasn't too happy about this, but she was all for it and said, 'Oh, please, Skipper, let me.' What was I to do? 'All right, Cookie,' I said, 'but if you get into trouble go straight to the British Consul.' Billy looked at me with a broad grin and said, 'We have no diplomatic relations with Algeria, so there isn't any British Consul.' But he went on to explain that the Swiss were looking after our interests. And off they went.

While *Startide* was at sea, Simon had been busy on land. Billy's instructions to him had been explicit. He was to contact a red-headed Scottish schoolteacher called Maggie, who was in touch with an uncle of Ait Ahmed called Sayed. Sayed was in the habit of visiting his nephew in jail every day with several female relatives, and if Maggie were to dress as they did, in a head-to-foot white *haik*, he would be able to pass her off as one of them. The plan was for her to enter the prison wearing a second *haik* over her own for Ait Ahmed to put on, and bringing with her a wig for him to wear. When his visitors left he would walk out with them – the guards would never notice one more white-robed figure in the group – drive out with Simon to La Pérouse, jump on board *Startide*, and sail for Majorca.

Simon's first rendezvous with Maggie was in the bar of the Hotel Aletti. She seemed extremely nervous and drew attention to a couple

of men sitting within earshot. To frustrate these two tails, they moved
to a nearby restaurant where they could not be so easily overheard.
He told her that the boat they were expecting would be late, and
discussed the timing of the operation in view of this delay. After
lunch she went off to report to Sayed and to arrange a meeting with
him for that evening. The tails were on duty again before dinner, but
she and Simon shook them off by jumping into a taxi, stopping it in a
side street, and slipping off on foot to a café Sayed had designated.
There they discussed further details of the plan, and she agreed to
rehearse her part by accompanying Sayed on his visit to the prison
next day.

The dress rehearsal augured well for the opening night. Maggie,
who spoke no Arabic, could hardly have been word perfect; but her
bearing and demeanour, so long as she kept silent, enabled her to enter
and leave the prison without betraying herself or rousing suspicion. She
was also able to boost Ait Ahmed's morale and give him the latest
information. But there were still several details that had to be settled
if the operation was to succeed.

Next morning Simon received a telephone call from Billy announcing *Startide*'s arrival. Thanks to Cookie, Billy had managed to shake
off his tail by the time he reached the Aletti, and he and Simon were
able to discuss the operation while walking up and down outside. They
had lunch together in a restaurant, then Billy went back to the boat
and Simon back to the hotel. In the afternoon Leka rang Simon up and
reported unusual activity on the quayside at La Pérouse. Apart from
the police sergeant who had been detailed to keep an eye on the boat
from the very beginning, two police cars had now been parked, one on
either side of the harbour, to serve as observation- and guard-posts.
After passing on this news to Maggie, Simon drove down to La Pérouse
to see for himself what was happening. He went on board *Startide* and
found Billy and his companions entertaining a man in civilian clothes
whom they introduced as the Chief of Police.

But he was only on a jaunt, not on duty. At least that is what he
said. They had seen him strolling along the quay and were wondering
who he was, when the sergeant guarding *Startide* recognised him and
told them. They invited him on board for a drink and, as he entered
the saloon, Cookie noticed Leka's pistol (a good Albanian never travels
unarmed) lying on one of the benches. She barely had time to slip it
under the cushion before their guest sat down, right on top of it. If
he pondered at all on the nature of the object he could feel through
the thin foam rubber, he made no comment, and his only sign of
discomfort was to shift every now and then from one buttock to the

other. In due course he got up and left, and they all breathed a sigh of relief. They spent the rest of the evening studying the situation yet again in the light of these new developments. What did the presence of the two police cars really portend? Was the visit from the Chief of Police as fortuitous as he had made out? There was no means of knowing.

Next morning they woke to find two machine-gun nests established at the end of the pier and a helicopter flying overhead, and when Leka drove into Algiers later in the day he saw half a dozen Soviet gunboats in the harbour. On his return to La Pérouse he noticed a strange greyish flow from *Startide*'s side. Billy was taking no chances. He had burned all his incriminating papers in a bucket, diluted the ashes with water, and flushed the mixture down the lavatory. Simon, in the meantime, was desperately trying to get in touch with Maggie, whose boy-friend, an American journalist, had arrived unannounced from Tunis the day before. When at last he contacted her, she had bad news for him; she had just called on Sayed; he was not at home; there was no sign of his servants, or of the caretaker; even his dog was nowhere to be seen; and the house was not only locked and bolted but also boarded up, as though no one had lived there recently or planned ever to return.

The game was up, obviously, but there was no time to ponder how or why. The first thing was to get word to Ait Ahmed and tell him what had happened. This, Maggie undertook to do. She even brought a message back from him, advising Billy to call the whole thing off and clear out at once.

Simon drove back to La Pérouse for further instructions. Billy told him that now he was on board, he had better stay there and sail with the rest of them. 'I couldn't possibly do that,' Simon objected. 'I haven't paid my hotel bill. Besides, I've left my dinner jacket in my room.' So he went back to the Aletti next morning and flew to Majorca on his own, and Billy and his shipmates put to sea.

A police boat escorted *Startide* out of La Pérouse, while the helicopter that had appeared earlier again hovered overhead, and the six Russian gunboats that Leka had seen in Algiers left harbour on a parallel course. As there was still a risk of being intercepted and boarded, Billy prepared to dispose of his notebook – he had not had the heart to burn it – by tying it to a heavy shackle which could be dropped overboard should the need arise. Leka, too, was prepared for an emergency, as he now revealed by opening his golf-bag. It contained not mashies and niblicks, but a couple of submachine-guns. He had another surprise up his sleeve. Each of the tins he had brought with him to supplement the boat's stores turned out to contain not soup or salmon, but an anti-personnel hand-grenade. It was just as well, Peter Winter reflected, after toying with the idea of tossing the monarch over the side, that so far there had been no occasion to use them.

The voyage back was uneventful and Billy had plenty of time to ponder on what had gone wrong. That the authorities had got wind of the operation was obvious from their recent activity. But how? And what explanation was there for Sayed's dramatic disappearance? Had he been betrayed and arrested? If so, who was the traitor? Or had he just taken fright and fled? These and many other questions remained unanswered, until Billy's subsequent enquiries threw a glimmer of light on the mystery. Maggie's boy-friend, he learnt, was a CIA man as well as a journalist, and had wanted the United States to take the kudos for springing Ait Ahmed from jail. So he had somehow got Sayed out of the way, or persuaded him to lie low, until such time as the rescue could take place according to the original plan but under American auspices.

Less than four months after the abortive operation, Hocine Ait Ahmed, wearing a *haik* and a wig that had been smuggled into his cell in the Maison Carrée, walked out of prison in a group of other white-robed figures, boarded a waiting yacht, and sailed for Europe.*

In April Billy flew out to Ethiopia, at Haile Selassie's invitation, to attend the twenty-fifth anniversary of the Emperor's return to Addis Ababa and the victory over the Italian invaders. The celebrations lasted three days. There were military parades at which units of the imperial army and bodyguard, parachutists and territorials marched past with modern tanks, guns, mortars and mechanical transport. For Billy, however, the most moving display was provided by a contingent of veteran patriots, many of whom he recognised, proudly wearing their British and Ethiopian war medals, shouting their war cries and re-enacting in their tribal manner the feats of valour they had performed a quarter of a century before. While the Emperor took the salute, his small, slim, erect figure in field-marshal's uniform seemed little changed since the day, twenty-five years before, when he had marched into Addis Ababa at the head of these same ill-clad and poorly armed warriors.

Billy had kept in touch with his old comrades-in-arms, many of whom now held important positions in the government and were able to give him first-hand information about the political

* He is still alive and living in Switzerland. His cousin Khider was assassinated in Madrid in 1967.

and economic situation in the country. They all voiced their alarm at Nasser's intervention in the Yemen, and their dismay at Britain's decision to withdraw from Aden. Ras Asserate Kassa, the newly appointed Governor-General of Eritrea, was particularly concerned, pointing out that unless the Americans filled the vacuum created by the evacuation of the British, Egyptian forces would almost certainly walk into Aden unopposed and, once established there, would try to drive the Ethiopians out of Eritrea so as to seize control of both sides of the Red Sea. This would create a fundamental shift in the balance of power not only in Aden but also in the Persian Gulf, the Red Sea and the African seaboard of the Indian Ocean as well, and represent a serious threat to Ethiopia's independence.

These were prophetic words. Within eight years rebel soldiers had overthrown the monarchy and murdered Ras Asserate and fifty other members of the aristocracy, and declared Ethiopia a communist state.

11 *The Unofficial Under-Secretary*

Billy's mother died on 21 April 1969. It was a merciful release. She had been ill and unhappy for many years, and her mental faculties were deteriorating steadily. Persecution mania turned the nurses who looked after her into spies and fiends. She gave them the slip whenever she could, and would then march into the local police station to report that they were 'out to get her'. Billy was her sole heir, but she had precious little to leave: the remains of her furniture, a few pieces of jewellery, any number of dresses, and 250 pairs of shoes. He had long before inherited her expensive tastes.

These, thanks to Daška, he could afford to indulge. He had no financial worries and had never had to earn his living. It was not for material gain that he had entered Parliament. His MP's salary covered only a small fraction of his expenditure, so that losing his seat entailed a barely noticeable pecuniary loss. His style of life remained unchanged. And even if he regretted his defeat at the polls, being deprived of an official position did not lessen his reputation as an expert in many fields. In the Yemen, to cite but once instance, his transition from MP to private citizen detracted not at all from the influence he wielded or the respect and affection he commanded.

At home, too, his opinion was no less highly regarded for being expressed in personal reports instead of voiced on the floor of the House. He continued to have the ear of the powers that be, who appreciated the value of an experienced and independent observer with no axe to grind and no ambition to fulfil. Foreign heads of state would often speak to him more freely than to an accredited ambassador, knowing that whatever message they wanted to convey would be delivered with discretion and without recourse to diplomatic channels which were inevitably less direct. His role, in short, was that of an unofficial under-secretary for foreign affairs, unpaid and supplementary to the establishment.

In this capacity he continued to show the clarity of mind and

170

purpose that had informed his political career and dictated his policy. Though Britain was no longer a world power, he believed that she still represented a force for good in the world and that her imperial system, for all its faults, was preferable even now to the alternative. It was not a question of jingoism and flag-waving, but of facing facts and taking appropriate action. Either Britain still had vital interests east of Suez, or she did not. If she did, there might be room for practical compromises imposed by lack of sufficient strength at any one time or place. But there was no cause for indecision or confusion about objectives.

Though anything but a cynic, he understood the realities of power and diplomacy. It was just because he saw the world as it is, that he prized with such profound affection the traditions of the British, the amenities of parliamentary democracy, the gentleness and *douceur de vivre* that still distinguished European civilisation. What dictated his political stance was not a blind regard for convention and precedent, but a firm belief that the future can be built only on the foundations of the past and must take full account of the character of the nation or community concerned. Britain, undisturbed by revolution for some 300 years, had more reason than most to beware of violent changes and to rely instead on evolution. This was the doctrine she had to preach, this the example she had to set.

With Billy away so often, and her children growing up and marrying and leaving home, Daška came to rely more and more for family affection on her only other close relation, her brother Vane. His shipping business kept him in London, where he also held the post of Consul-General of Monaco, but he spent every summer in Majorca, on the coast near Formentor, which reminded him of his childhood in Dalmatia. Here he had built himself a house and a little harbour for the boat he used for underwater fishing, a sport in which he delighted and excelled. He transmitted his enthusiasm to Billy and the two of them spent many happy days together, goggled, flipper-shod and armed with spears, reconnoitring the submarine landscape, diving after their prey, and surfacing to clear their breathing-tubes like a couple of whales releasing twin jets through their blow-holes.

Daška, too, revelled in the sea and loved staying with her brother and sister-in-law. But she also enjoyed her independence, and so decided to build a house of her own. The site she chose was spectacular: the edge of a cliff on the opposite side of the bay from Vane's. It overlooked a little cove protected by an encircling rampart of rock and accessible only from the sea, until flights of steps were cunningly contrived to zigzag down the sheer cliff-face. Colonnades, terraces, guest wings and servants' quarters eventually materialised, and lawns and pine trees provided an appropriate setting for the architectural jewel Daška had in mind. La Guarda, as it came to be called, was a pleasure-dome for children, for grandchildren both present and to come, and for friends and relations by the score. It was also a haven where Billy could drop anchor between one odyssey and the next.

No longer occupied with the Yemen, he was able to extend his field of activities. A visit to Morocco, from 27 January to 12 March 1970, was enough for him to recognise the potentially excellent access it provided, via discreet lateral portals, to most of the Arab countries and to the more interesting French-speaking African states. Gibraltar–Tangier–Rabat was to become one of his regular itineraries.

For the Easter holidays he and Daška went to Iran again as guests of the Iranian Foreign Minister. They arrived in Tehran on the last Friday of Muharram, the initial month of the Muslim calendar and, for the Shiites, a time of mourning to commemorate the martyrdom of Hassan and Hussein, the sons of Ali and Mohammed's daughter Fatima. The celebration overlapped that year with the pre-Islamic Zoroastrian spring festival, Nawroz, and the Shah decreed the latter of less significance. So instead of attending the usual Nawroz parades in the capital, he and the entire cabinet had moved to Meshed, in the far north-east of the country, to pray at the shrine of Reza, the eighth Imam, regarded by the Iranians as particularly holy. In consequence Billy was reduced to sightseeing – never his favourite pastime – until Muharram was over and he was able to have talks with ministers and other officials on their return.

The main topic was the forthcoming withdrawal of British troops from the Gulf, announced by the Labour government three years before, and the subsequent ending of the old treaty relationship with the nine emirates there under British protection. The politicians he consulted seemed relatively unconcerned about this latest British retreat in the Middle East, which could only lead to increased Soviet influence in the area. In fact they appeared to be so reconciled to it that he even suspected the Shah of having come to some secret understanding with the Russians about the future of the territories after the British had gone. This understanding would presumably allow for a 'neutral' Gulf under a certain degree of Iranian influence: a policy which Iraq was bound to find unacceptable but which the Russians could abandon whenever they wished, in favour of renewed support for the forces of Arab revolution. There was said to be tension already between Iraq and Iran, but the only signs of it that Billy saw when he flew down to the southernmost part of the border were numerous Iranian machine-gun and artillery posts along the banks of the Shatt al Arab and in the neighbouring palm groves.

He also discussed the effects of the Kurd–Iraq agreement that had come into force a few weeks earlier. For the time being it had put an end to the fighting, but no Iranian he spoke to believed it would last. So it was much to his surprise that Mustafa Barzani's local representative, whom he knew quite well, declared himself on the contrary extremely optimistic and told him there were several secret clauses in the treaty, in addition to those made public on 11 March, whereby almost every Kurdish demand was satisfied. Billy felt this was only wishful thinking – his informant, though a loyal Kurd, was married to an Iranian and lived comfortably in town, miles from any fighting – and subsequent events confirmed this opinion.*

What interested Billy most of all during this visit was the new harbour under construction at Bandar Abbas, on the Strait of Hormuz. It was connected by an excellent road to the copper-mining town of Karman. This road was being extended up to Meshed and across the Afghan border to Herat. The Russians had already built a highway into Afghanistan from the north, and so they would soon have access to the Gulf.

There were tremors of unrest elsewhere in the Middle East. For some time tension had been building up in Jordan between King Hussein and the *fedayeen*, who had lately taken over the Palestine Liberation Organisation. These fanatical guerrilla units were the creation of Syria, just as the PLO itself had been invented by Egypt's Nasser and founded under his auspices. Hussein was opposed to both organisations, but circumstances had forced him to accept them.

In 1947, when the British mandate came to an end, a partition plan was proposed for Palestine. There was to be a Jewish state and an Arab Palestinian state. The Jews accepted it; the Arabs rejected it. They wanted all or nothing. In consequence, after the establishment of Israel in 1948, what remained of the territory was effectively partitioned between three neighbouring countries: Syria seized the small town of al-Hamma in the north of Galilee; Egypt occupied the Gaza Strip; and Abdullah of Transjordan annexed the ancient biblical lands of Judaea and Samaria lying on the opposite side of the river from his emirate, which came to be known as 'the

---

* The Iraqi Government and the Kurds never came to terms and fighting between them broke out again four years later.

West Bank'. Both banks were then united to create the Hashemite
Kingdom of Jordan.

Israel gave full rights of citizenship to those Palestinian Arabs
who remained within her borders, but in the rest of the territory some
700,000 had fled from their homes and, though most of them settled
on the West Bank, hundreds of thousands of them were deliberately
kept by their fellow Arabs in a condition of homelessness. Arab leaders
would not allow them a country of their own, nor would they allow
them to become integrated citizens of the Arab states. It was this
homelessness and enforced separateness from other Arabs that turned
the Palestinians into a nation.

The Palestinian cause revived Nasser's dream of a united Arab
world under the hegemony of Egypt. The humiliation of the conquest
of Palestine by the Jews was shared by all the Arab states, and the
potency of that common emotion was what he hoped to draw into
his hands by creating a 'representative' Palestinian organisation. In
January 1964, at an Arab summit conference in Cairo, he proposed
the establishment of the PLO, and the proposal was approved. King
Hussein could hardly fail to see the PLO for what it was. The granting
of separate representation to the Palestinians, most of whom lived in
Jordan, was a threat to his government's authority. He and his kingdom
would be the first target of Nasser's new instrument designed to bring
every Arab state into Egypt's dominion. But, as a member of the Arab
League, he had no choice but to give the organisation his blessing.

Nasser, however, did not have it all his own way. The Syrians,
unwilling to let Egypt steal a march on them, began to build up a
rival organisation and recruited Palestinians in the refugee camps in
Lebanon to be trained as *fedayeen* (fighters willing to sacrifice themselves for the cause). They then established camps on the West Bank
and started launching raids into Israel. Meanwhile Nasser was using
the PLO to subvert the Jordanian government, and Hussein found
himself in a dilemma. In a speech to the nation on 13 May 1965 he
said that 'ever since the union of both banks of the Jordan, the two
people have integrated: Palestine has become Jordan, and Jordan
Palestine.' But this argument did not help; for if the inseparability of
the two 'nations' proved that the Jordanian government had authority
over Palestinians, it also proved that the PLO had authority over
Jordanians. The PLO multiplied its demands for a Palestinian army
to be stationed in Jordanian territory and, when this was refused, a
stream of anti-Hussein propaganda poured out of Egypt. The Jordanian
government saw no recourse but to break off relations with the PLO,
which it did in July 1966.

The Syrian-sponsored *fedayeen* raids and Nasser's incessant sabre-rattling inevitably led to war between Israel and her Arab neighbours. Lebanon stayed out of it, but the three others formed a sudden and uneasy alliance. Israel made short work of them. In June 1967, in the space of six days, she took the whole of the Sinai Peninsula from Egypt, the Golan Heights from Syria, and the whole of the West Bank from Jordan. Hussein's kingdom was thus reduced in area to his grandfather's original Transjordanian emirate, and more refugees (about 130,000 in the first wave alone) moved across the river to temporary camps on the East Bank.

Hussein now had no choice but to allow the *fedayeen* to have bases in Jordan. He was afraid of rousing their antagonism, even though their activity prejudiced the security of his realm and threatened his own sovereignty. They ignored the law of the land, defied the Jordanian army and police, and gradually created what amounted to a state within a state. By the end of 1968, backed by other Arab countries, they were coming close to sharing power with the government. Under the leadership of Yasser Arafat they were also in the process of taking over the PLO, Nasser having given up direct control of the sacred cause. As time went on, they encroached even further on the state's prerogative. Hussein had reason to fear that his power was being usurped and his government destroyed. But it was not until two attempts had been made on his life that he decided to take action. On 17 September 1970 he launched his army against the *fedayeen* camps.

In spite of being supported by Syrian and Iraqi troops advancing from the north, the *fedayeen* were soon on the run. Within ten days they had been driven out of the capital and all the other big towns, some of them fleeing over the border into Syria, others making their way to the banks of the Jordan in the hope of giving themselves up to the Israelis rather than face Hussein's bedouin soldiers. But they were still holding out in their last strongholds, and 18,000 Iraqi troops still remained in Jordan, when Nasser persuaded Hussein to agree to a ceasefire. It was the Egyptian leader's last achievement. He died the next day.

This was the situation Billy found when he flew out to Amman at Hussein's invitation towards the end of October.

The King told him how disappointed he had been by Britain's attitude during the recent crisis. Communication between London and Amman, he complained, had not been regular enough, nor had the British reply to Jordan's urgent request for help been sufficiently prompt. Then he added – 'with a charming, rather sorrowful smile', Billy recalled – that perhaps he was being too severe; however, he *did*

want to stress the importance of maintaining the closest ties between
the two countries. Now that Nasser was dead, he went on, there was a
golden opportunity for a pro-Western country to assume leadership in
the Middle East. And what Middle Eastern country was more friendly
to the West than Jordan? But first she would have to repair the damage caused by the fighting, and reconstruct and reorganise the state
machine; and this she could do only with Britain's help and support.

Billy noted the extent of the war damage when he visited the
town of Zarqa, recently evacuated by the Iraqi troops who were
still hanging about a few miles up the road, uncomfortably close to
the capital itself. The area commander, a brigadier, told him that the
fedayeen plan for Zarqa had been well prepared. They had selected
and occupied almost all the key positions in and around the town,
and laid anti-tank and anti-personnel mines on all the approaches.
There were many Europeans in their ranks, as well as Arabs from
Syria, Iraq and Algeria, acting as advisers and technicians; and their
arms included Chinese, Russian and Czech submachine-guns. But their
fighting spirit was poor, and their discipline weak – fortunately; for they
had heavily outnumbered the Jordanian troops, and the brigadier had
had to supplement his strength with tanks from the local training school
and with cadets from the Zarqa military college. These youngsters were
still carrying out patrols and road checks in the town, and Billy found
them alarmingly trigger-happy. But the brigadier said he had not the
heart to disarm and disband them after they had done so well in the
fighting, which they had enjoyed and were still enjoying as a change
from school routine.

Billy also toured the northern border area, travelling by helicopter
with Crown Prince Hassan. On this front the fighting was against the
Syrian troops, who had since returned to their own country with a
bloody nose. Their Russian-built T45 and T55 tanks had been no
match for Jordan's British-built Centurions. A Jordanian tank commander gleefully described how his 105-mm gun had hit the turret of
a Syrian tank and 'sent it flying twenty metres through the air'. Not
that the Centurions were by any means perfect. Their gear-pins often
broke when they were crossing rough and rocky ground. They used
petrol and had to be refuelled three times a day, whereas the T45s and
T55s, run on diesel, needed only one refuelling daily. They also lacked
infra-red sights. Billy made a note of all these shortcomings to include
in his report on Jordan's military requirements.

He also listed the country's civil needs, starting with a more powerful
radio station in Amman to compete against hostile neighbours. The
electricity system too would have to be renovated, and the water and

telephone systems as well. Another project was the construction of a new airport; irrigation schemes were likewise high on the agenda. If all these enterprises were to be realised, Britain would have to provide not only technical assistance but also financial backing. Billy felt it was in her interests to do so, and this was the policy he advocated on his return to London.

Like many people who are capable of extreme physical exertion when it is absolutely necessary, Billy did not believe in exercise for its own sake. He had never enjoyed games or athletics, and had long ago given up hunting and riding. Underwater fishing was his most strenuous activity, shooting his favourite sport. But he refused to take it too seriously and was anything but a huntin'-shootin'-fishin' stereotype. He behaved absent-mindedly at the butts. He would sometimes turn up without cartridges, and once, on being reminded in advance, he brought with him two cardboard boxes, which were indeed marked 'cartridges' but turned out to contain four volumes of a history of the Chisholms of Cromlix. Like his friend Sir Iain Moncreiffe of that Ilk, he would often be carried away by his own conversation and let the partridges fly over unheeded while he discussed Middle Eastern problems with the neighbouring guns or outlined a tactical manoeuvre to his loader.

His relatively sedentary existence (much of it spent in aeroplane seats) was aggravated by habitual self-indulgence in food and drink. He was a gourmet rather than a gourmand and, though no one had ever seen him even remotely drunk (except for his youthful performance in the Greys' sergeants' mess on the eve of his departure for Abyssinia) he drank regularly and what milksops might call heavily. Exotic dishes and sweet liqueurs began to take their toll and in 1971 he developed gout – fortunately a mild case, confined to one wrist – for which he was treated for the rest of his life. This was followed in the summer of 1974 by diabetes, for which he also received light but lifelong treatment, and later that year he suffered cardiac failure. And as though these tribulations were not enough to contend with, news from Addis Ababa dealt him another painful blow.

Discontent and unrest had been simmering in Ethiopia since the beginning of the year. Rising prices were largely to blame, and the people who felt the pinch most were the emerging middle classes. The teachers and the armed forces had other causes for complaint, and the students, from force of habit more than for any particular reason, were soon on the rampage. Two weeks of public disorder and army mutinies ended with the resignation of the entire government. A new cabinet was sworn in and the Emperor announced a revision of the constitution, whereby more power would devolve on Parliament and the people. But by then the country's radicals had taken the initiative.

Industrial unrest and military rebellion continued throughout the summer. A self-styled 'Armed Forces Co-ordinating Committee', composed of left-wing elements, gradually assumed control of the capital and started arresting members of the ruling class and senior officials. Among them was Billy's friend Ras Asserate Kassa, a quiet, dignified and brilliant man, and as much a 'royal' as the Emperor himself, his father having at least as great a claim to the throne as Haile Selassie. But, for the time being, the Dergue (the term by which the Armed Forces Co-ordinating Committee came to be known) continued to declare its loyalty to the Emperor. It was not until 12 September that a group of officers went to the palace just after 6 a.m., summoned the elderly monarch, and informed him that he was now deposed. Then they led him away to 'a place of safety'. He was to die, of circulatory failure, almost exactly a year later.

But a natural death was not to be vouchsafed to Ras Asserate Kassa or to fifty-nine other leading officials detained with him in the main civil prison. During the night of 23–24 November they were lined up against a wall in the courtyard and shot, without trial, 'for crimes against the Ethiopian people'.

Billy remembered with poignant clarity what Ras Asserate had told him when they had met eight years before. They had both foreseen the possible loss of Ethiopia's independence as a result of Britain's withdrawal from Aden, and Billy had even envisaged the consequent overthrow of the imperial régime; but never had he imagined that this might also entail his friend's untimely and violent death. He regarded it as an evil augury for the country as a whole, but for the time being he was too ill to feel anything but personal sorrow.

His heart failure had been heralded by bouts of fever and chronic shortage of breath. The fever could have been malarial or symptomatic of some other tropical disorder; or it could have been due to a condition known as sub acute bacterial endocarditis (SABE for short), in which one of the aortic valves becomes infected and small clumps of bacteria break off and travel to other parts of the body in the circulation. Billy was subjected to various tests to identify these bacteria and for the appropriate antibiotic to be administered. But the tests proved negative. So early in the new year he was admitted to King Edward VII Hospital for a more detailed examination.

His liver first came under suspicion, because of two previous attacks of infectious hepatitis on his travels and also because of his breakdown in 1955. A biopsy was performed under a local anaesthetic – a procedure which upset him more than all the other indignities he was to suffer in the ensuing months – and the result showed some cirrhosis, but though this might have caused his fever it was not enough to account for his overall condition. SABE then seemed to be the most likely culprit and treatment for this was carried out in the National Heart Hospital, to which he was transferred so as to be under closer surveillance and more rigorous discipline.

After the King Edward VII, where he had taught the chef to make a decent omelette and where Daška could spend all day with him in his private room, the National Heart seemed unnecessarily austere. He was given a bed in a private ward but he found the food uneatable, so Daška cooked at home for him and brought him lunch and dinner every day: a considerable feat seeing that the inflexible meal times did not coincide with the equally inflexible visiting hours. But for his privileged diet he would have lost even more weight than he did. As it was, Daška was shocked by his appearance: he looked like a proper 'hospital case' as he shuffled down the corridor to the lavatory, making his own way, on doctor's orders, despite being attached by his forearm to a drip. At the end of four weeks, however, he felt better; his fever disappeared; the infection had halted. But the aortic valve was damaged and now leaked. So he was re-admitted to hospital for catheterisation. A hollow tube was passed into his heart for samples to be taken from each of its compartments and to study the pressure and the oxygen content of each sample. This test confirmed the diagnosis, quantified it, and made it abundantly clear that surgery was the only option.

On 11 July Billy had his damaged aortic valve replaced and the mitral valve repaired: an operation that had only recently been able to be performed. Had he been in the same medical condition a few years earlier, he would certainly not have survived. As it was, he nearly died; and he remembered the experience in detail. He seemed to become detached from his physical body, to slip away from the straitjacket of his flesh and hover painlessly and calmly above it. At the same time he felt he was passing from a world of darkness into a kingdom of light, which filled him with what he could describe only as 'ecstasy'. Regaining consciousness was an anti-climax, but he found that he could never again be frightened of dying.

He left hospital on 8 August and went off to convalesce at La Guarda. The cardiologist and his own doctor, David Hay, had given him precise instructions as to what he could and could not do in the way of physical exercise. He could bathe, they told him, but not swim. 'What about snorkelling?' he asked, with a perfectly straight face.

Sense of humour, natural stamina and sheer determination contributed to a marked improvement in his health, and he returned
to England in November. But he was worried that a pain in his
breastbone, which had been cut to give access to his heart, might
affect his shooting or put a stop to it altogether. It so happened that
Dr Hay, who was also fond of shooting, had developed bursitis in his
shoulder and was wondering how it might affect his swing. So the two of
them went to the Holland & Holland shooting school at Northwood and
shot alternate clays – 100 between them – which the doctor considered
quite a feat for someone who had had major open-heart surgery only
three months before. 'It was one of the most enjoyable consultations
of my life,' he recalled.

Billy refused to behave or to be treated like an invalid. He was
impatient of anyone overconcerned with matters of health and he
dismissed hypochondriacs and valetudinarians as 'wet' – on *his* lips,
an epithet of supreme contempt. He rose above his own ailments by
disregarding them. His consumption of port and liqueurs remained
undiminished and he would never resist a delicacy which he knew
to be forbidden. Dr Hay's wife once caught him coming out of the
Lebanese food centre in Chelsea with a parcel of 'something special'.
He swore her to secrecy.

In London he continued to be a focal point for Albanian exiles,
Ukrainian refugees and Kurdish freedom fighters. To these were now
added survivors from the Ethiopian massacre. He had been too ill to
attend the memorial service in St Margaret's, Westminster for Ras
Asserate and his fellow victims – Daška had made a point of going
in his stead – and he was angry and ashamed that Britain's pusillani-
mous Labour government had not sent a single representative to it,
presumably for fear of offending Ethiopia's new rulers. His immediate concern was for the victims' widows and the female members of
the Emperor's family held prisoner in Addis Ababa. There were fifty
of them, herded together in two rooms of what used to be a prison
clinic; they had not been charged with any offence, and there were no
apparent arrangements for bringing them to trial. Billy started lobbying
for their release, and never relaxed his efforts.

He also continued to travel, for pleasure as well as in duty
bound. He had always gone abroad whenever he had time to spare,
either slipping off on his own and on the spur of the moment, 'to get
away from it all', or else embarking on a longer and more organised
journey with Daška and the children. He had introduced the twins to
Constantinople, and under his guidance they had discovered the glory

of Byzantine architecture and also, since man cannot live by culture alone, the excellence of Turkish cooking. He took them to a different restaurant for every meal and made sure that neither ordered the same dish as the other or that either had ordered before. He urged them to sample every variety of *loukoum* at his favourite confectioner's and to assess the respective merits of *kadin gobegi* ('lady's navel'), *bülbül yuvasi* ('nightingale's nest') and the many other syrupy concoctions at his favourite pastrycook's.

(He had always encouraged the young to appreciate good food and drink, and expected them to have his own capacity for both, forgetting that if a schoolgirl's appetite could sometimes match his own, a schoolboy's head for alcohol was weaker than an adult's. Leo Amery, Julian's son, had been a case in point. When he told his father he wanted to leave Eton before his time there was up, Julian was against it but, not wishing to lay down the law, asked Billy to have a word with the boy instead. Billy agreed that a man-to-man talk might make him change his mind, and asked him to dinner. He entertained him as he would have done any friend of his own age, with the result that young Leo reeled home at four in the morning aflame with Dutch courage and deaf to the voice of reason, and Julian had to lay down the law after all.)

Each of the children had benefited from Billy's wanderlust; it was now the grandchildren's turn. They were well travelled even as infants, being taken by their parents to spend part of every summer at La Guarda, and as their numbers increased Billy sometimes felt suffocated by the nursery atmosphere. 'It's not the babies I mind as much as the mothers,' he would say, and would then take off at a moment's notice for some undeclared destination and for an unspecified length of time. In due course Daška would receive a dozen orchids by way of apology, and once or twice even a postcard from wherever he happened to be.

As her grandchildren grew older, she undertook to take each of them for a holiday abroad, one after another, and Billy would then organise their journey as he had done when their mothers were that age. Thus a second generation derived pleasure and instruction from his enthusiasm and experience. Tessa's eldest son, Damian, even had the honour of travelling with him on his own, motoring across Bosnia and Hercegovina while Daška stayed behind at Dubrovnik. What impressed the young man was not the mosques and monasteries they visited, or even the pitchers of wine they shared at lunchtime every day; it was the compliment Billy paid him by letting him do all the driving, aware that he was barely old enough to hold a licence, yet confident of his being able to hold his liquor.

A visit to Peking with Julian Amery in January 1977 afforded Billy an insight into China's attitude toward the Soviet Union and the United States, and also a glimpse into the Chinese official mind. 'There is great disorder under heaven,' Foreign Minister Huang Hua told his two guests, 'and it is becoming greater.' It was due, he said, to the rivalry between the two superpowers, a rivalry that was absolute and irreconcilable. The United States had been weakened by Vietnam, Watergate and the world economic crisis, while the Soviet Union had become more adventurous – witness the Russian 'invasion' of Angola. This should never have been allowed to happen, the Minister went on, but it had at least opened the eyes of the world to Russia's imperialist policies. He hoped that more and more people in Europe would recognise the extent of the Soviet threat and unite to support and strengthen the European Community. Having said this, he declared that the Soviets, as a superpower, were contemptible and by no means invulnerable; on the contrary, they were increasingly isolated and their imperialist designs increasingly exposed; 'therefore, though there is a great disorder under heaven, the present situation is excellent.' To Billy's amusement, Julian made no comment on these contradictions and merely complimented his host on the sweet-sour sauce with which he had eaten his words.

Meanwhile Ethiopia had drifted into anarchy. The so-called government – the Dergue – under Colonel Mengistu Haile Mariam, faced rebellion from every quarter. The northern province of Eritrea was in the hands of the ELF, the Eritrean Liberation Front; in the north-west the EDU, or Ethiopian Democratic Union, controlled most of Begemder; other resistance forces, backed by Somalia, were active in the south and east of the country. Nearly 100,000 Eritrean and Ethiopian refugees were living in camps in the Sudan after fleeing in terror from Mengistu's atrocities. Surprisingly, his régime had been supported by the Americans, and when they cut off supplies in March 1977 he turned openly to the Russians for arms and other aid. Billy, as usual, wanted to see for himself what was happening. So against doctor's orders and all other advice, and despite an anxious warning from Ras Asserate's eldest son, Asfa Wossen, who knew Mengistu had assassination squads stationed in the Sudan, he flew out to Khartum to make plans for crossing the border.

It was easier than he expected. The Dergue was so hard pressed that it could not even control the frontier. The tribes of the border regions crossed it at will. The nomads on one side of it visited relatives and fellow tribesmen on the other, and cattle-rustlers and smugglers took no more notice of it than if it had never been. Billy drove across without any fuss in a Sudanese security force Landrover, and soon he was back in his old wartime haunts, among patriots who might have been the sons and grandsons of the very men he had commanded more than thirty years before. 'They certainly looked much the same,' he recorded, 'in their torn and motley rags, with a wide assortment of rifles, machine-guns, mortars and bazookas.'

There was the same shortage, too, of money and ammunition, and a complete lack of medical supplies. Some of the units Billy saw were well equipped and disciplined, but many of them consisted of very young boys and even girls armed with wooden imitation rifles. They left him in no doubt, however, about their morale and their keenness to fight, the Dergue having alienated almost every region, race and class. Most of the troops were local peasants and farmers; some had fled from the tyranny of the Dergue in the towns; and all were determined to overthrow the Marxist dictatorship with its hated militia and armed communist vigilantes. But Billy felt this was easier said than done. The arrival of Russian arms and Cuban advisers was bound to strengthen Mengistu's hand, and also increase the danger to neighbouring Sudan with her thousand miles and more of common frontier with Ethiopia. Somalia, another neighbour, was already under Russian influence, and had for many years laid claim to Ethiopia's Ogaden district inhabited largely by Somali nomads. The Ethiopians, on the other hand, maintained that the present frontier was inviolable. This dispute had given rise to periodic conflicts, which Russian intervention was bound to aggravate. In this, too, Billy recognised a potential danger, which he outlined in an article for the *Daily Telegraph* and for which he suggested a solution:

No doubt the chaos in Ethiopia and the conflicting interests of Ethiopia and Somalia, and of the various other groups in the Horn of Africa and the Red Sea, may prove a very tricky hand for the Russians to play. But no more difficult than Turkey and Greece are for NATO. It is high time the free countries of the area – especially Saudi Arabia and Egypt, as well as the Sudan – and the Free World in general wake up to the dangers.

The continuation of the present anarchy in Ethiopia under a Marxist pro-Soviet régime gives the Russians their main opportunity to intervene further there and thus to gain the initiative in the Horn of Africa. Therefore support for the EDU – the only real alternative government to the Dergue – seems at present the only way to end the chaos and bring to power a reasonable and friendly government in Addis Ababa. At the same time it would put a stop to any further deterioration in the situation in the Horn of Africa and the mouth of the Red Sea.

Billy's words went unheeded, but events were soon to bear him out. In August, less than four months after his visit, the Somalis made a pre-emptive bid in the Ogaden, turning the region into a battlefield; and in November they expelled the 2000 Russian advisers stationed in Mogadishu and elsewhere in Somalia. It was a strange situation, and in February 1978 Billy flew out there to see what he could make of it.

President Challe Siad Barre told him how it had come about, starting with the Soviet plan, established during the period of Somali-Russian co-operation, for the take-over of the Horn and all the strategic ports at the mouth of the Red Sea. The Somalis were to be the main instrument for the first steps to destabilise the neighbouring countries prior to the setting up of Soviet hegemony over the Horn. In turn for their help they would be allowed to unite with the Somali population of the Ogaden. The Somalis, the President asserted, felt no particular friendship for the Russians and certainly no sympathy with communism, but they saw in the alliance with Russia the best chance to achieve their ambition.

When the Dergue came to power, however, the situation changed. The Russians saw an opportunity to penetrate Ethiopia. They hoped to establish themselves there and at the same time maintain their position in Somalia, and tried to establish a *pax Sovietica* over the Horn comprising both countries. But the Somalis, who pride themselves on being the Irish of Africa, would not fit into the pattern the Russians had designed for them. They refused to listen either to the Kremlin or to Fidel Castro, who tried to persuade them to continue their role in helping to established Soviet hegemony over the Horn. They were furious when the Soviets refused to allow them to occupy the Ogaden, which they had been promised as their reward. So they took the initiative, hoping to achieve a *fait accompli* before the Russians and Cubans arrived in Ethiopia in strength. The Russians were obviously unable to support both Somalia and Ethiopia and, not surprisingly, they opted for the latter with its 30 million population in preference to the 2 million of the former. So the Somalis got rid of their Soviet advisers. They hoped, and perhaps indeed were encouraged to hope (by Saudi Arabia and other states in the area), that the Americans and the West would support them in their stand against the Russians. But the Americans and the West had failed them and now they found themselves in a desperately isolated position, fighting against a much larger Ethiopia backed by massive Soviet military support.

Billy summed up the situation in an article for the *Spectator*.

> The Somali leaders say they will not surrender or voluntarily abandon the Ogaden because they fear, with good reason, that the Soviet-Ethiopian-Cuban forces will carry out a police of genocide on the local Somali population. . . . The Russians have two immediate aims. The first is to consolidate their position in Ethiopia and then obtain control of the ports in the mouth of the Red Sea; and at the same time they want to punish Siad Barre and Somalia and make an example of them to other states in Arabia and Africa who might be so foolish as to oppose the Soviet Union and rely upon the West for help. They seem at present well set to achieve these two objectives. They have played for high stakes in Ethiopia, gambling on the unlikelihood of the West's reacting with sufficient force, if at all. If they have calculated correctly, they are more than likely to win. There are, however, inherent contradictions, difficulties and weaknesses in their plans for the area, which could trip them up and create for them their own Vietnam. But the hour is late and, unless the West stirs soon, there is little hope for the Horn.

A crisis was also building up in Iran.

The last time Billy had been there, in 1970, he had found a rather unsettled situation caused by the decision of Britain's Labour government to end its military commitments east of Suez in the following year. Since then things had become clearer. With British and American approval, Iran had assumed Britain's role as the policeman of the Gulf and the Shah had begun to acquire armaments in the quantities he had always craved. With the price of oil hoisted by some 400 per cent in the aftermath of the 1973 Yom Kippur War, he could well afford them. At the same time he had embarked on an ambitious programme of industrial expansion and social reform, whereby he hoped to raise Iran's living standards to the level of Japan's. By the end of 1977 the Americans were so pleased with him and his achievements that President Carter asserted: 'There is no leader for whom I have a deeper sense of personal friendship and gratitude,' and he referred to Iran as 'an island of stability in one of the more troubled areas of the world.'

But this was just another example of Carter's naïvety and wishful thinking. That the situation was not so rosy as he appeared to believe was proved only nine days later, when an event occurred that opened

a whole wellspring of bitterness against the Shah's régime and pre-
cipitated a spring-and-summer-long cycle of protests and killings. On
9 January 1978 theology students in the holy city of Qom demonstrated
against the publication of an article by the Minister of Information
attacking the exiled Ayatollah Khomeini; police fired on the crowd
and there were several casualties. In February hundreds of people
were killed and injured during two days of rioting in Tabriz, and
another wave of protests broke out there at the end of March. The
army had to deploy tanks against demonstrations in Tehran on 11
May, and for the first time shouts of 'Down with the Shah!' were
heard in the capital's main streets. On 31 May 2000 students rioted at
Tehran University. In July it was Meshed's turn. The biggest outbreak
of violence began in Isfahan on 11 August, and within twenty-four
hours that city, and Shiraz, Ahvaz and Tabriz as well, were under
dusk-to-dawn curfews. At six in the morning of 7 September a large
rally converged on Tehran's Jaleh Square. Most of the marchers were
probably unaware of the imposition of martial law a few hours earlier.
When they refused to disperse, the army opened fire and mowed down
over a thousand of them.

By this time it was clear that the country was beginning to collapse.
One strike after another erupted over economic and political issues.
There was panic buying and widespread hoarding of goods. To stem
the unrest, the Shah conceded billions of dollars in wage settlements
and, to appease the mullahs, he closed all theatres and gambling halls.
He even released a number of political prisoners. Yet he remained as
unpopular as ever and the unrest continued. So what had gone wrong?
Billy flew out to Tehran at the end of October to find out, and this is
what he discovered:

The mid-seventies oil boom had caused a massive influx into the
cities, resulting in a rootless and discontented proletariat. Far from
raising living standards nationwide, the Shah's petrodollars had spread
chaos and disappointment among his subjects, while offering golden
opportunities of corruption to the court and to the royal family. There
was no confidence between the government and the governed; more
and more use had to be made of coercion and control; and the state
had become increasingly dependent on SAVAK, the secret police.
The Shah's reforming zeal had declined and he had become remote
and autocratic. Surrounded by sycophants, he was isolated from the
people and they therefore turned to their traditional leaders, the Shiite
Muslim clergy, headed by Ayatollah Khomeini.

Khomeini had always opposed Western-style reforms since they con-
flicted with Islamic tradition, and in 1964 he had gone so far as to exhort

the army to rise up against the government. The Shah's advisers had advocated death for the 'louse-ridden mullah'; but leniency prevailed and Khomeini was merely banished, first to Turkey and then to Iraq, from where he continued to rail against Iran's 'satanic' régime and to deride the Shah as a 'servant of the dollar'. At this stage the nation was divided into two more or less equal camps. Some favoured the Shah as an enlightened despot pursuing liberal policies in the face of dogmatic reaction. Others saw the Ayatollah as a saintly old man determined to introduce more democratic measures and more spiritual values. Opposition to the Shah had since increased, but at the time of Billy's visit to Tehran the crisis had not yet come to a head. Two things he noticed at once, however, and both were significant: the women, as though rejecting the emancipation the Shah had granted them, had abandoned Western dress and were all wearing the mournful black *chador* which their grandmothers had worn; and the big black Mercedes cars used by SAVAK were conspicuous by their absence.

Billy's main source of information was Amir Abbas Hoveyda, a former prime minister, who had resigned in the face of the economic difficulties. Billy met him in his flat where he appeared to be under house arrest, though the police guarding the premises might conceivably have been there to protect him. Hoveyda told him that only the Shah could save the situation, by coming forward and taking a firm line. Though he had renounced absolute power he still had the army behind him and enjoyed considerable prestige. But unfortunately he seemed too depressed and irresolute to take any decisive action.* He had personally ordered his troops to avoid bloodshed and practise restraint, but this had merely resulted, as Billy had seen for himself, in the soldiers on patrol in the streets being mocked and taunted by the crowd with impunity. Though the Carter administration still refrained from public criticism of the Shah, it did nothing to encourage or uphold him. Nor did the British government, and Billy was full of foreboding when he flew back to London at the end of four days.

He had reason to be. While he was still in Tehran, the Iranian government had made a silly mistake. It put pressure on Iraq to expel Khomeini, who promptly found refuge in France. From then on all the world's press had unfettered access to him and he became an international celebrity. This strengthened his hand and he grew increasingly intransigent, preaching revolution and Islamic

---

* There was a reason for this indecision, though it was a closely guarded secret at the time. Since April 1974 the Shah had been suffering from cancer, which made him progressively more listless and fatalistic.

fundamentalism as the only means of cleansing Iran. 'No gradualism, no waiting,' he insisted. 'We must not lose a day, not a minute. It's now or never.' In November, after three days of serious rioting in Tehran – including the burning of all cinemas, many banks, and the British embassy – the Shah appointed a martial-law government. This was about the last card he had to play. He didn't know what to do next, and the only advice he received from Washington was to accept a constitutional monarchy. But it was too late: the country had already begun to lurch into chaos. At the end of December the 'big push' – an all-out attempt to bring down the régime – was heralded by a day of gunfire and lawlessness. Trucks and cars burned in the streets, which echoed to the sound of sirens, rifle shots and exploding tear-gas grenades. Merchants shut up shop and carried off their stocks to hide them. Nervous troops opened fire on a funeral procession for a demonstrator killed the day before, and the crowds chanted: 'Carter gives the guns, the Shah kills the people.' By the new year it was clear that the Shah's position was no longer tenable, and on 16 January he left Iran, never to return.

On the very same day, by an odd coincidence, Billy had been asked by the Monday Club to give a talk on the Iranian crisis. To an audience composed of traditional Tories he was able to unburden himself more freely than he could in an article intended for the general public.

What had happened in Iran, he said, was a major defeat for the West. Apart from being an important oil producer herself, Iran also controlled the Strait of Hormuz through which 70 per cent of Western Europe's imports from other oil-producing states had to pass. Yet the West had done nothing to prevent the downfall of the Shah, whom Billy described as 'a great friend of Britain'. Of course he was not perfect, he went on, and had long been criticised for his lack of democratic fervour. But this did not excuse, nor did he deserve, the stream of hostile propaganda emanating from certain Western sources under the influence of communists and so-called progressives who had no real understanding of the issue. The media in particular were to blame, and not least the BBC. His father, the late Shah Reza, would have dealt with the crisis in a more decisive and maybe brutal way. It might not have gone down well with Western liberals, but it would probably have saved the situation. The present Shah had yielded in order to avoid bloodshed. But sometimes, unfortunately, it was necessary to shed blood in order to survive.

What, then, did his critics hold against him? That he had spent too much on arms? But Britain had encouraged, almost forced, him to do so. Because of the frivolous irresponsibility of a Labour government, Britain first abandoned Aden, then the Gulf, and left the Shah to defend the area for it. What else could he do but build up his armed forces? Furthermore he did defend the area, more than once. He sent his aeroplanes and troops to support the Sultan of Oman's army against the guerrillas of the Aden-sponsored Popular Front for the Liberation of the Occupied Arab Gulf, and he also helped the royalists in North Yemen.

Of course he had made mistakes. In his anxiety to improve his subjects' standard of living, he had concentrated on economic development and industrialisation at the expense of agriculture, which was the mainstay of the country. But his greatest mistake was to underrate the power of the religious leaders. The mullahs and ayatollahs were traditionally opposed to the monarchy in Iran. They set themselves up as the mouthpiece of the people and skilfully exploited the xenophobia of the uneducated classes. They even allied themselves, when it suited them, with the communists – the illegal Tudeh Party – who for obvious reasons were hostile to the Shah. This combination of religious and political fanaticism was enough to shake the throne. All that was needed to overthrow it was a nudge from the left-wing media and anti-Western press.

Billy went on to discuss the probable effect of the Shah's downfall on the other Middle Eastern rulers who were friendly to the West. 'They must be shivering in their shoes,' he said. 'We may not approve of everything these rulers do, or what they stand for, but they are on our side and are trying to keep their countries out of Soviet control. For this reason alone we should give them all the support we can.'

Though gunboat diplomacy was out of date, he concluded, there was something to be said for it still. The Russians repeatedly resorted to it, and got away with murder. Our only hope was to fight them with their own weapons. But for this to happen there would have to be a change of heart in Britain – a change of heart which, in view of Labour's lamentable record, could be brought about only by a change of government.

As though in answer to his prayer, the Conservatives under Margaret Thatcher were returned a few weeks later at the general election of 28 March. It remained to be seen whether the new government would live up to his expectations.

With the Conservatives in power again, Billy's position as an unofficial link between the government and foreign heads of state was appreciated all the more. He and Julian Amery were of one mind on most political issues, and they often travelled together. Considering the anti-Nasser sentiments they had both frequently expressed, they were surprised to receive an invitation from President Anwar Sadat to visit him in Egypt.

Sadat had held a variety of posts under his predecessor, and his docile loyalty had led colleagues to dub him 'Nasser's poodle'. Indeed, he had been one of Nasser's leading anti-Western propagandists and it was to him, as a member of the United Arab Republic's Revolutionary Command Council, that Nasser had delegated Yemeni policy. On his shoulders, therefore, rested most of the blame for Egypt's pro-Sallal intervention. Since then, however, he had performed an extraordinary volte-face. When he took office, the Soviet Union had been more deeply entrenched in Egypt than ever; but less than three years afterwards he had abruptly abandoned Egypt's long-standing alliance with Moscow and expelled some 17,000 Russian military advisers from the country. He had then made the historic leap of imagination that sent him to Jerusalem with an olive branch and ultimately produced a peace treaty with Israel: the famous Camp David accord.

Julian had not been in Egypt since 1955, when Nasser had said to him: 'Mr Amery, if you had been an Egyptian you would have been with me. And if I had been an Englishman I would probably have been a member of your Suez Group!' But the banter masked hostility. This time, October 1979, things were very different. Sadat's cordiality was manifestly genuine; the visitors felt they were talking to a friend, perhaps even an ally, of the West, and they found themselves in almost total agreement with him.

He had had no trouble, he told them, in getting rid of Egypt's Soviet advisers; he had given them a week to get out and they had gone like lambs. People still did not understand that if you stood up to the Russians they usually retreated. Elsewhere in Africa Soviet expansion was in full swing. The Russians had established two belts of influence on the continent: the first in the north, across Libya and Algeria, which they were trying to connect with Ethiopia and the Horn; the second further south, across Angola and Mozambique. But the Americans seemed unable to grasp the situation or to respond to it appropriately. They had also made a big mistake in not arming the Somalis at the time of the Ogaden war. The Soviets, the President concluded, were a very cautious people and if the West put up the slightest resistance they would soon climb down. Given American and European support, the free countries still had the upper hand.

Sadat's mention of a Soviet belt of influence stretching across Libya and Algeria prompted Billy to go and have a look at that area, especially the Western Sahara, which had been a Spanish colony until 1975.

Negotiations between Spain, Morocco and Mauritania in November of that year had resulted in an agreement under which Spain would withdraw her troops by February 1976 and cede the territory to the two other signatories. The implied partition was strongly contested by Algeria, which backed the Polisario Front, a native movement favouring independence and taking its name from the Frente Popular para la Liberación de Saguia el Hamra y Rio de Oro: the Popular Front for the Liberation of the two provinces of Saguia el Hamra and Rio de Oro, which together made up what was known as Spanish Sahara. There was trouble as soon as the handover was completed and formal partition took place. The Polisario proclaimed the Saharan Arab Democratic Republic (SADR), to which Algeria pledged political, moral and material support, at the same time securing a similar pledge from Libya. The guerrilla force that came into being then went into action against the Moroccan and Mauritanian occupying armies.

The Polisario concentrated on knocking out Mauritania, the weaker of its foes, and after three years of sporadic fighting this was achieved. In August 1979 Mauritania renounced its alliance with its northern neighbour, sued for peace and agreed to evacuate that portion of the former Spanish colony which had fallen to its share. The fighting intensified. Supplied by Libya with new weapons and missiles, the Polisario guerrillas were often superior in fire-power to the Moroccan army; but in November King Hassan despatched sufficient reinforcements to contain the enemy and to cause a lull in the fighting. This was the situation when Billy flew out to Rabat three days before Christmas.

It was not easy for foreigners to enter Western Sahara – special permission was required from the King – but, thanks to the contacts he had made on previous visits to Morocco, Billy obtained it without any trouble. Before setting off he had a meeting with Prime Minister Maati ben Abid, who was about to visit London and was hoping to reach an understanding with Mrs Thatcher about the increasing danger to Morocco, and to the other free countries in Africa and the Middle East, from the aggressive and successful advance of the Arab and African socialist states led by Soviet Russia. He was disillusioned with America, distrusted France, and desperately wanted a meeting of minds with the British government under its present leadership, which he felt was more suited and better placed than that of any other country to advise Morocco's European and American friends on the right course to follow.

Two days after Christmas Billy drove down to Casablanca and

from there took the regular Royal Air Maroc plane to El Aaiún, the principal town and port of Western Sahara, through which phosphate used to be exported from the nearby mines at Boukra, until these were closed down because of a glut of the product on the world market. After a night in the only hotel he flew on, in a military plane packed with troops, to Dakhla. Here, in the capital of Western Sahara's southernmost province, Rio de Oro, where the vast sandy desert meets the ocean, he stayed with the governor and met the local military and police commanders, 'a tough and competent bunch of thugs'. The morale of the troops seemed excellent – they were all on double pay – but he had no means of judging their fighting capacity, as he was not allowed to accompany a patrol or to observe any operation.

As a matter of fact there was little action of any kind just then, apart from occasional raids by Polisario columns consisting of a thousand men and more, based on Tindouf, in distant Algeria. It was hard to stop them from entering Western Sahara or even Morocco proper, because the Moroccans lacked the equipment to guard nearly 2000 miles of frontier. The interior was almost totally unpopulated. Most of the nomads had left the desert and settled in the four small towns; others had fled to Algeria and Mauritania. They had eaten all their camels, kept only a few goats, and had lost all traces of nomadic life, being supported by various welfare schemes or employed in local development projects. Those who had chosen Algeria were press-ganged into the Polisario units, joining forces with other refugees from the desert and with mercenaries from other countries.

A week's stay was enough to convince Billy that Morocco was fighting at a disadvantage, with little or no support from America or from the free countries of Europe, Asia and Africa; and on his return early in the new year he stressed the urgency of a closer relationship between the British and Moroccan governments.

The threat of Soviet imperialism continued to be Billy's main preoccupation. The Palestinian problem, as Julian Amery so vividly put it, was still the maypole around which the power struggle for the Middle East was being danced. Everyone in the area paid lip-service to the principle of Palestinian self-determination; yet no one wanted to see a Palestinian state, at least not one with the normal attributes of statehood. The general attitude seemed to be: 'We must go on talking about it, but for God's sake don't let's do anything about it.' The PLO leaders themselves were divided. So it was not on this issue that the struggle for the Middle East would be decided;

it was much more likely to turn on the apparent balance of military power.

The West still enjoyed naval and air superiority in the Mediterranean; with the support of Morocco, Turkey and Egypt, it commanded all the approaches to the inland sea. But the threat of Soviet military power, based on the Soviet Union itself and on Aden and the Horn of Africa, hung heavily over the Persian Gulf and the Red Sea. South of the Gulf the Soviets were entrenched in Aden as strongly as Britain once was. Across the water from Aden they controlled Ethiopia through the puppet Mengistu régime, backed by some 15,000 Cuban troops as well as smaller Soviet and East German forces. In Libya, on Egypt's western flank, they had set up a vast stockpile of weapons. Further west their influence was strong in Algeria and had been growing steadily with the Sahara war, in which the Polisario was fighting Morocco with the help of Soviet arms. Soviet influence predominated in Syria, and Iraq was linked to Moscow by treaty and depended on the Soviets for most of its tanks and aircraft. The latest Soviet incursion, into Afghanistan, had brought Russian troops to within 300 miles of the Strait of Hormuz, through which the overwhelming bulk of Persian Gulf oil had to pass on its way to the West. Afghanistan could also serve as a Soviet base for destabilising Pakistan. Billy was able to study this possibility more closely when he and Julian flew out to Islamabad at the end of July, at the invitation of President Zia ul-Haq.

Zia himself felt that Pakistan's position was extremely exposed and precarious. To the east it was confronted by an unfriendly if not openly hostile India; to the west by a disintegrating Iran; to the north by the Soviet army in Afghanistan. With Russian troops less than 300 miles from the Indian border, the Indians were in no position to risk serious differences with the Soviets. Instead, by collaborating with them, they might secure increased security against China and important gains at Pakistan's expense. Some two-thirds of the Indian army was concentrated on the Pakistan frontier, and their equipment was far superior to that of the Pakistan forces. Much of the latest Soviet–India arms deal consisted of tanks and other weapon systems which would hardly be suitable for a war with China. So what did the Indians want those weapons for, and against whom? As for the Soviets, if they chose to promote an independent Baluchistan under their aegis, the Baluchis of Pakistan would almost certainly join. The partition of Pakistan between India and the Soviet Union would then be complete.

What Pakistan needed, Zia concluded, was to modernise its army and build up a Western presence in the area as quickly as possible. At the same time the West should give maximum aid to the Afghan resistance, and in particular provide it with anti-tank and anti-aircraft capabilities, with the object of making Afghanistan as uncomfortable as possible for the Soviets and so perhaps delay its use as a base for further advances. Billy and Julian transmitted these recommendations to Mrs Thatcher on their return to London, together with Zia's warmest good wishes. He was deeply impressed, he said, by the difference between the British leader's reaction to the present world crisis and that of other Western leaders he had met recently. All of them, as he put it in his blunt soldierly way, seemed 'shit-scared' by comparison.

Soviet imperialism was again on the agenda when Billy and Julian flew out to Cairo in November 1981, at the invitation of the Egyptian Foreign Minister. President Sadat had been assassinated by Muslim fanatics only six weeks before, and his successor, Hosni Mubarak, was still feeling his way. The country was under martial law; press restrictions were in force; a number of people had been arrested and were awaiting interrogation. But the authorities were confident that as Sadat's murder was an entirely Egyptian affair, with no international ramifications, the situation would soon return to normal. Meanwhile, Mubarak assured his two British visitors, resistance to Soviet imperialism remained his prime objective and he saw close co-operation with the United States as the best way of organising it. In fact he would like to see the United States build up an extensive military stockpile and servicing facilities in Egypt itself as well as in the Gulf.

He went on to discuss the PLO. Their leaders, he said, did not have an interest in peace, since their fellow Arabs gave them a great deal of money to carry on as they were. If a Palestinian state were to be established, that state would receive the money instead of the PLO leaders, to the detriment of the latter's Swiss bank accounts. The PLO consisted of a number of factions, the largest of which was controlled by the Syrians and therefore, ultimately, the Russians. The PLO would negotiate only if the Russians and the Syrians 'gave them the green light'. The PLO would do anything for money. The Egyptians, on the other hand, accepted the principle of Palestinian self-determination. But they did not believe that the moderates in the PLO could decide PLO policy so long as the Syrians remained in Lebanon, with the main body of the PLO under their physical control.

As a result of their talks with President Mubarak, Billy and Julian felt that as far as Britain was concerned the Palestinian problem could be shelved for the time being. They also felt that the British government should pay more attention to Egypt than it had in the recent past, and they said so to Mrs Thatcher on their return.

12 *The Unrepentant Patriot*

While Billy continued to view Soviet imperialism as a threat to the free world, he was equally preoccupied by the problem of international terrorism. To his mind, the one and the other were related. He believed that the totalitarian origins of terrorism were rooted in Marxist-Leninism and that liberal democracies, being an affront to that philosophy, were therefore its perennial targets. The figures bore out his contention: of a total number of 6700 terrorist incidents that had occurred between 1968 and 1980, only sixty-two were recorded from within the Soviet bloc.

The ideological underpinning of terrorism by the Soviet Union, he argued, was based on the principle that violence was permissible – indeed legitimate – against non-communist societies in the name of counter-oppression, liberation or anything else that fitted the local context. In 1967 this principle had received a regrettable boost when a committee of the International Red Cross at Geneva voted to extend prisoner-of-war status to captured terrorists. Britain, together with Israel and Brazil, voted against; but the United States, the Soviet Union and sixty-three other countries endorsed the principle, thereby endowing terrorism with a semblance of political legitimacy. As a result, many sections of society seemed no longer able or willing to distinguish between a soldier who might be forced to kill, in self-defence or to protect others, and a mass-murderer calling himself a liberationist.

Billy was appalled by this. He regarded terrorism as common criminality and he deplored the tendency of the mass media to play it up, with headlines and photographs focused on the criminals, while neglecting the plight of the victims. Such publicity, he thought, so glamourised the terrorist as to incite anyone with equally pernicious instincts to emulate him in the hope of becoming a comparable 'anti-hero' and achieving similar notoriety.

It was not only the hijacker and political assassin that the popular

196

press acclaimed. It also laid emphasis on the 'rights' of ordinary felons – muggers and the like – whom it tended to excuse on the grounds of 'economic disadvantage' and 'educational deprivation'. To Billy, this was so much emotional claptrap. He believed that crime should be punished, not condoned; rehabilitation of the criminal was all very well, but what about the safety of his victims? He also believed that the punishment should fit the crime, and therefore advocated the death penalty for murder. He was aware this might occasionally lead to the execution of an innocent person, but felt it was a relatively small price to pay for saving the lives of many more equally innocent people. To the claim that the death penalty had never been a deterrent, since murders had continued to be committed notwithstanding it, he countered that no one could possibly know how many would-be killers it had deterred, since the murders they consequently did not commit had never been enumerated.

Meekness, indecision and appeasement were alien to Billy's nature and he saw no reason why bullies and blackmailers, any more than kidnappers and fanatics, should be handled with kid gloves just to satisfy some ill-defined concept of 'democratic freedom'. Men and women had rights, granted. But they also had duties, to their neighbours and hence to society as a whole, and the former could be gained and retained only by the performance of the latter.

The doctrine of *laissez-faire*, which stresses man's rights at the expense of his duties, was inherently dangerous; if not checked it led to anarchy. But the opposite tenet, which exaggerates the claims of the community at the expense of the individual, was even more disastrous; in communist states it had led to slavery. Billy therefore continued to preach against both these extremes, and to advocate a middle course aimed at combining freedom with order and social justice. His allegiance to the Tory party remained unshaken, as did his loyalty to Queen and Country. He firmly believed that Conservatism was best for Britain, and that what was best for Britain was best for the world. In this respect he was an unrepentant patriot.

During the opening years of the eighties, which coincided with the closing years of his life, Billy was constantly on the move. Semi-official visits to heads of state took him to Israel more than once, to Jordan several times, to China, to Turkey and to South Africa. In April 1982, combining business with pleasure, he called on King Leka of the Albanians, who had recently moved from Madrid to Johannesburg. They discussed the situation in Albania, and this is what Leka had to say:

Though the country was still totally isolated from both East and West, and indeed from every other part of the world, there was a certain amount of clandestine traffic across the poorly guarded frontiers. In the autonomous province of Kosovo, in the south-east of Serbia, 90 per cent of the inhabitants were Albanian and they were in regular contact with their compatriots on the other side of the border. The Kosovo Albanians had for some years been in open rebellion against the Yugoslav government, establishing guerrilla groups in the mountains and organising large-scale uprisings in the towns. There seemed to be no stopping the Kosovars' nationalist aspirations but, unless properly directed, they were not in the interests of a free Albania. On the contrary, it was in free Albania's interest to support Yugoslavia, since chaos or anarchy of any kind was bound to lead to Soviet intervention, which in turn would end all hopes of liberation from the Hoxha régime. The Kosovars should therefore be encouraged to direct their activities against the Albanian, not the Yugoslav, government.

Surprisingly, in view of what had happened in 1949, when Britain and the US had tried – and dismally failed – to regain Albania for the West, Leka was all in favour of making another attempt. The moment was ripe for an uprising, he said. The manpower (a discontented population) was available; the motive (liberation from a cruel dictatorship) was all the stronger after forty years; the political situation in the Balkans seemed favourable, and so did the world situation. Furthermore, a lesson had been learnt from the previous mistakes. This time small groups would not be infiltrated into the country one by one; instead, there would be a concerted move from within, fomented by clandestine communications and propaganda, and supported in due course by a strike force operating from an external base. Leka reckoned it would take two years, and from $25 to $30 million, for a plan to be put into action; meanwhile he personally would need $1 million, to organise himself and pay off his debts. But first of all the British government would have to remove the 'block' on aid for him from Saudi Arabia and the United Arab Emirates.

Billy undertook to transmit these proposals and requests, though he did not expect anything to come of them. Nothing did.

A visit to Istanbul late in the year brought him into contact with a group of Central Asian refugees from Eastern Turkestan. Among them was an old man of eighty, Jusef Alpetkin, whom he had met in Urumchi in 1946. At that time Alpetkin was helping to set up a provincial government in Sinkiang under the auspices of Chiang

Kai-shek's personal representative in north-west China, but when the Chinese People's Liberation Army marched in he had had to take flight. Since then nearly half a million of his countrymen had also fled, to avoid the persecution that ensued during the Cultural Revolution. Most of them had found asylum in Alma Ata, the capital of the Kazak Soviet Socialist Republic, but 50,000 had settled in a little township a short distance up the Ankara road. To remind himself of the happy time he had spent in their homeland, Billy drove out there to see them.

No sooner had he entered the place than he felt completely at home. The quilted coats, huge turbans and high-heeled knee-boots he remembered from Kashgar were no longer in evidence – cloth caps, three-piece reach-me-downs and townee shoes, as decreed by Kemal Atatürk, had taken their place – but the familiar features and bearing of the inhabitants revealed at a glance that they were indeed, for all their proletarian dress, the same people that had fired his imagination when he read about them at school and had lived up to all his expectations when he eventually met them in the flesh.

Lunch at the headman's house was another reminder of the Central Asia he had known. He could not make out if the first course was *suyug ash* ('watery meat') or *etli su* ('meaty water') – what's in a name? he reflected; a stew by any other name would taste as thin. Then came heavy dumplings stuffed with minced meat, and a pyramid of rice and mutton accompanied by greasy, leaden bread. There was water to drink. But the primitive fare suited his mood; a delicate meal would have been inappropriate.

Apart from fellow guests assembled with him round the table, other members of the community came to greet him in relays throughout the afternoon. Each had a tale to tell of the adventures that had befallen him on his long trek to freedom and of the oppression at home that had prompted him to flee. These individual sagas gave Billy some idea of general conditions in Sinkiang. But as usual he wanted to see for himself, and so flew out to Peking a few weeks later.

The only means of visiting his old haunts was to join a three-week guided tour, something he had never done before and, having done, was firmly resolved never to do again. It allowed him only four days in and around Urumchi; the rest of the time he spent on the move, travelling by coach, air, and train with his fellow sightseers from one tourist 'must' to another. There was no sitting back and drinking in the atmosphere, no sauntering down the street and taking the pulse of the place, no chatting with locals in tea-shops, no chaffering with merchants in bazaars. All that he brought back with him from China were a couple of suits and half a dozen shirts made to measure on the cheap in Hong Kong – and no more knowledge of conditions in Sinkiang than if he had never left England.

But he was compensated for this disappointing and uncharacteristic trip by his next eastern venture, in the late summer of 1983, when he accompanied Julian Amery on a fact-finding tour of Pakistan and retraced part of the route he had travelled on his way to Kashgar in 1945. How could he then have imagined, after trekking for several weeks by pony and on foot to get from Rawalpindi to Gilgit, that he would one day cover the distance by car (along the Karakoram high-way) in less than forty-eight hours; or that he would be able to leave Gilgit after daybreak and still reach Baltit in time for breakfast (to be entertained, as before, by the Mir of Hunza) and drive even further on, right up to the frontier of China, crossing *en route* the Batura glacier in a matter of minutes, a passage that had once taken him the best part of a day? All this, and much more, was made possible by their friend General Shahid Hamid, the Pakistan Minister of Culture, Sports and Tourism, who worked out their itinerary, laid on their transport, acted as their guide, and went out of his way – on many occasions literally – to make their tour as profitable and pleasurable as it triumphantly turned out to be.

Their main purpose was to study the situation on Pakistan's border with Afghanistan, where Russian troops had been stationed ever since the Soviet invasion in 1980. Their presence constituted a serious threat to Pakistan – a pessimist might have said that it looked as if Moscow had all but won the Great Game – but, so long as the Afghan resistance kept fighting, the Soviets would be denied a stable base for any drive south towards the warm waters of the Gulf and the Indian Ocean. President Zia attached the highest importance to strengthening the Afghan guerrilla forces, and discussed the matter with Julian and Billy; and in the report they subsequently submitted to Mrs Thatcher they made various suggestions as to how Britain could help.

They recalled the contribution British mercenaries had made to Nasser's defeat in the Yemen and believed there would be no lack of volunteers to lend similar support in Afghanistan. With 100,000 Red Army troops in the country, Moscow could hardly complain if a handful of Tommies exercised what Lord Salisbury, as prime minister, had called 'an Englishman's right to get his throat cut where and when he likes', and public opinion at home would be more likely to cheer them on than condemn. Britain could also help by organising the use of Soviet defectors for black propaganda or other subversive activities. In the early days of the resistance the Afghans killed all the Russians they captured, even those who deserted of their own accord. Since then they had come to see the point of taking prisoners and encouraging defection: a few Russians had actually joined their ranks. President Zia would not allow a prisoner-of-war camp to be established in Pakistan, but he told Julian and Billy that he would tolerate the passage of defectors through his country provided this was accomplished swiftly and secretly. It would be up to Britain to accept them, and to resettle them once they had served their purpose.

The Soviets stationed in Wakhan, the narrow strip of Afghan territory stretching into China and separating Pakistan from the USSR, were within striking distance of the Karakoram highway, that miracle of engineering and symbol of Sino-Pakistan co-operation, running all the way from Islamabad to Kashgar through some of the wildest country in the world, with mountains rising on both sides to over 20,000 feet and with passes seldom lower than 12,000. But the road could be easily sabotaged, as Julian and Billy saw for themselves when they drove along it and later overflew it in a helicopter: natural landslides already blocked it at frequent intervals.

The helicopter, by courtesy of General Hamid, turned their tour into a busman's holiday. It enabled them to obtain a bird's-eye view of the upland pastures and snowbound lakes on the Roof of the World, reminding Billy of the exhilaration he had felt on reaching them after that suffocating ascent from the Indus valley thirty-eight years before. It deposited them for picnics in spots as remote as the fictional Shangri-La and landed them one night at an actual Shangri-La, a holiday resort of that name, with cherry trees and apricots and peaches and an aviary of pheasants as resplendent as peacocks. It dropped them in on a brigade headquarters in an upland valley for an excellent breakfast of devilled chicken, curry puffs and the blackest of tea, then on to another unit for a second breakfast identical to the first but supplemented by delicious pink trout from a nearby lake. It took them to within easy driving distance of the Khunjerab pass, where they celebrated with drinks and mutual snapshots, just as though they had climbed under their own steam to this height of 16,000 feet; and brought them back to Islamabad and a reception at the Yemen embassy, where the ambassador toasted Billy and asked the other guests to greet 'a benefactor of my country, without whose assistance we should not have survived.'

The tour had been such a success that General Hamid suggested a repeat performance in the following year. Julian and Billy readily agreed. But when the time came Billy was not well enough to take part.

* * *

Though he had been under treatment for diabetes and gout for over eight years, he still refused to consider himself an invalid. He followed doctor's orders, but with characteristic levity, submitting at regular intervals to liver-function tests and then grading the result on an imaginary scale based on the average individual intake at the bar of White's. He had got over his respiratory trouble and, the last time he was in Majorca, had found no difficulty in climbing the 118 steps leading up to La Guarda from the sea. But on his return from Pakistan he began to suffer again from breathlessness. There were signs, too, of the arteries to the heart furring up. In fact he had a mild heart attack.

There was no lift in 17 Eaton Square, so he and Daška moved into a more convenient flat in Barkston Gardens, off the Earl's Court Road. Here he had a large sunny study overlooking trees and lawns, where he soon felt perfectly at home: his books were arranged on shelves reaching to the ceiling; there were enough cabinets and cupboards for his ever-expanding archives; his silver ashtrays and other familiar objects resumed their role of lares et penates, and a painting to which he was deeply attached – a life-size portrait by Sickert of King Edward VIII wearing the full dress uniform of Colonel-in-Chief of the Welsh Guards – had pride of place on one wall.

This painting had a curious history. Sir James Dunn, the Canadian financier, had commissioned it in 1936. It was the only portrait of the monarch to be painted after his accession and, since he was too busy to sit for it, Sickert used a newspaper photograph as a model. Sir James was not pleased with the result; it looked too much like a magnified colour snapshot. 'Do me another,' he said. But this he turned down as well. Sickert managed to sell the first portrait to Sir James's close associate and fellow countryman Lord Beaverbrook, but he was left with a second one on his hands. It was still in his studio when Billy's mother, who was a friend of his, called on him one afternoon. She fell in love with it on sight and was lavish in her praise. 'Well, you can have it,' Sickert told her, only too pleased to be rid of it, 'for the cost of the canvas and the paints.'

In 1967 Billy's mother left it to the Welsh Guards for the duration of her life and, when she died two years later, the commanding officer wrote to Billy as her son and heir, telling him that it hung in the officers' mess at regimental headquarters, Wellington Barracks, and offering to hand it back to him. Not wishing to deprive them of it so abruptly, Billy let them keep it until further notice.

In November 1981 Daška and Tessa saw it on display in an exhibition at the Hayward Gallery, 'by courtesy of the Welsh Guards', according to the accompanying label, 'who had acquired it by auction in 1963', according to the catalogue. It was only a silly muddle, of course, but this faulty attribution of ownership was the last straw. Billy felt it was high time to retrieve his painting; he wrote to the regiment and asked for it back; they returned it at once with apologies.

For a year or so after his return from Pakistan Billy did nothing too strenuous. He would get up fairly early, but did not have his bath or shave until he had finished reading *The Times* and the *Daily Telegraph*, sitting in his study in pyjamas and dressing-gown. No longer occupied with politics and public life, he turned his attention to more personal concerns and more private pursuits. Shopping for antiques became a favourite pastime, and he would often come back from a stroll with an object that had seemed to beckon – 'just as though it had rung an electric bell as he walked past' was how Daška described it.

Then there was the Chinese Gourmet Club. It had been started nine years before by Ken Lo, the grandson of Sir Lo Feng-lu, imperial China's ambassador to the Court of St James, who was knighted by Queen Victoria. His father, Sir Lo's son, had carried on the diplomatic tradition by serving as consul-general in London. Ken himself was born and brought up in England, but pursued a very different career. He started to write about Chinese cooking just as Chinese food was beginning to enjoy a great vogue, then went on to arrange dinners for selected paying guests in Chinese restaurants all over London. Billy and Daška formed part of his loyal following and when he started a restaurant of his own – Memories of China, in Ebury Street – they joined him on the board of directors. This gave Billy a perfect excuse for eating there as often as possible – it wasn't just greed: the more he patronised the place, the better it was for business.

There was also the Queen's Bodyguard for Scotland, the Royal Company of Archers. This august body was founded in 1676 as an archery club for Edinburgh gentlemen and became increasingly exclusive (one black ball excluding a candidate for life) until George IV, on a visit to Scotland in 1822, invited its members to attend him as his official bodyguard. From then on it was a royal company, with duties similar to those of the Honourable Corps of Gentlemen in London and, though it was still concerned with archery and maintained butts and organised competitions, its *raison d'être* was to attend the Sovereign at such functions as the Installation of Thistle Knights or any like event occurring in the course of a royal visit. It was the sort of anachronistic outfit that appealed to Billy's love of ceremonial – and also to his sense

of humour, for he had to admit there was something laughable about it
– and he was the sort of romantic yet ostensibly 'Establishment' figure
that befitted the company's ranks. He was duly elected.

It was now thirty years since he had first donned the uniform
designed by Sir Walter Scott – Border-green long-skirted tunic and
trews trimmed in black braid showing crimson lights, and Kilmarnock
bonnet ornamented with eagle's tail feather – and gone on parade
'armed' with the prescribed bow and three arrows. This is how a
fellow archer captured the atmosphere of one such occasion:

> Between the Palace and the Hill
> Behold the ranks of Archers stand.
> They are not standing straight or still
> And yet the spectacle is grand.
>
> Upon their bosoms, row on row,
> Medals acquired in warfare shine.
> Look! There's a lad who fought the foe
> (Six clasps) in 1889.
>
> And there are other medals too,
> Won from the battle's strife afar;
> This man's a Fellow of the Zoo,
> And that's an OBE (and bar).
>
> The Adjutant has shouted ' 'Shun!'
> What do they care – 'It's only Cis!'
> And through the serried ranks there run
> Fragments of dialogue like this:
>
> 'Have you got heather-beatle still?'
> 'This year the plover's eggs were late.'
> 'What do you think of Herbert's Bill?'
> 'My God! I've dropped my dental plate!'
>
> But yet the Monarch proudly knows
> In gazing on this noble Corps
> That he is guarded by those bows
> Which few can hold, and fewer draw.

Billy certainly never drew his. A parade, for him, was an opportunity
to have a good time with his Edinburgh friends and to stay with John
Warrender, the closest friend of all, fellow archer, fellow old Etonian,
and one-time fellow officer in the Greys. It also gave him an excuse
for getting away on his own. 'I have to be on duty,' he would say, in

a tone that suggested compulsion. Who was to know that service with the company was voluntary?

There was another institution which gave Billy particular pleasure. It was called Le Cercle, and outside the circle nothing was known about it but the name. Its origins and membership were (and still are) as deeply cocooned in mystery as those of the most exclusive Masonic lodge. It appears to have been founded by the French statesman, Antoine Pinay, and when he retired Julian Amery took over the chairmanship. It seems to have been a small assembly of European and American Conservatives meeting on an *ad hoc* basis once or twice a year, for two or three days at a time, to exchange views on world affairs. Because of his knowledge and understanding of the Middle East and North Africa, Billy was a most acceptable candidate for membership, which in due course he acquired. He had already attended several meetings – in Bonn, Munich, Washington and elsewhere – and looked forward to attending more.

During the first half of 1986 Billy's health deteriorated steadily. His respiration grew worse and so did the diabetes; the pills he had been taking for it no longer worked and he had to give himself insulin injections. In July he began to suffer from an infected toe and, since infections in a diabetic are notoriously difficult to control, he went to hospital for a course of penicillin. The danger of gangrene was averted and Daška, who had gone to Majorca, flew back and took him off to convalesce at La Guarda.

The toe that had been infected dried up and dropped off, and his general condition improved. But his voluntarily staying much of the time in bed showed that he was not yet by any means his old self. From his room he could see the last beams of the sun reflected in the Bay of Pollensa as it sank behind the hills at the head of the promontory of Formentor. 'If one has to be ill,' he said more than once, as he watched the colour of the sea change from orange and gold to silver and midnight-blue, 'this is the place to be.'

His room gave directly on to the patio, in summertime the heart of the house, so that he was able to take part in, or at least overhear, the activities of the household. Daška's children came to stay one after another, bringing with them their own children. There were other visitors too. But family life prevailed throughout the summer. Had he been in the best of health he might have dodged it – he had done so before – but convalescence seemed to make him more amenable and benign.

His recovery was slow but constant. The children knew he was getting better when he started cracking jokes again at their expense and reminding them of incidents in which they had not appeared at their best. These now formed part of a private decameron which he never tired of relating. There was the time, for instance, when Marina, newly married, rang up her mother and asked how much it cost to have curtains made. 'It depends on the size of the window,' said Daška. 'My man charged me so much per yard, but that was just for the work, without the material.' There was a moment's silence at the end of the line before Marina piped up: 'But how *does* one make curtains without material?' Then there was the time when Alexander – like his father, a consultant engineer – nearly blinded himself mending a ceiling light. Somehow he let two wires touch; there was a flash and a drop of molten metal fell towards his upturned face. Luckily it landed on his glasses. 'Just imagine!' Billy would chortle, as he came to the end of the story. 'The great electrical expert had forgotten to remove the fuse!' A moment later he would be launched on yet another chapter of the family saga: 'Do you remember when . . . ?'

When the holidays were over, he and Daška flew back to London. He was still under doctor's orders, still injecting himself with insulin, but felt well enough at the end of October to attend a meeting of Le Cercle in the Hôtel Negresco at Nice. He rang up from there and told Daška he would be back in time for dinner three days hence. That evening she had to go out for a while, knowing that Billy would most likely arrive before she returned. Still, he had his key with him and would be able to let himself in; and she looked forward to his welcoming her home instead of the other way about. So she was rather disappointed when she did get back and saw no light in his study windows – he could not have arrived after all. But when she went upstairs she found the door no longer locked – so he must have arrived.

He had indeed. She found him lying on his bed in the dark, in pain and shuddering with fever. He had fallen ill during the flight back and was feeling dreadful. She took his temperature – 104°. She gave him some soup and dosed him with aspirin, but in the morning his temperature was the same and he felt no better. She called the doctor; he was unable to diagnose on the spot and arranged for Billy to be admitted to King Edward VII hospital for blood samples and other tests. The results were not reassuring. Another toe was septic and the infection was travelling up to the heart. The kidneys were also affected and the murmur in the heart had intensified. . . .

Daška knew that the end was near when his fingers felt more swollen each time she held his hand. She wanted the comfort of a

Catholic priest, knowing that if Billy had belonged to any Church it would have been the Roman, but none was immediately available. Tessa, herself a Catholic, applied to Farm Street, but the Company of Jesus had no one to spare for several days. She then got in touch with a personal friend of hers, the Catholic priest at Eton (a recent appointment and the first in the history of the College since before the Reformation) but he too was unable to come at once. She finally secured the services of one of the Holy Ghost Fathers, a mission working mainly in Africa, and he came and said a Mass in the ward next door.

Billy died on 17 November 1986.

His funeral service, in the Little Oratory in the Brompton Road, was attended by the family, who occupied most of one half of the small church, and by close friends, who occupied the other. His coffin was draped in the McLean tartan, and his body was laid to rest in the cemetery near the Hogarth roundabout. A later memorial service at St Margaret's Westminster enabled hundreds of others to pay tribute. Among them were Crown Prince Alexander and Crown Princess Katherine of Yugoslavia, and representatives of the King of Jordan, King Leka of the Albanians, the Imam of the Yemen, the Crown Prince of Ethiopia, the Speaker of the House of Commons, and the Colonel of the Royal Scots Dragoon Guards, the regiment formed in 1971 by the amalgamation of the Greys with the 3rd Carabiniers Princess of Wales's Dragoon Guards. Colin Mackenzie and Alan Hare read the lessons. David Smiley gave a reading from Canon Henry Scott Holland: 'Death is nothing at all. . . . I have only slipped away into the next room. . . . ' Asfa-Wossen Asserate read a prayer and quoted from Juliet's memorable invocation to 'loving, black-brow'd night':

> . . . when he shall die,
> Take him and cut him out in little stars,
> And he will make the face of heaven so fine
> That all the world will be in love with night,
> And pay no worship to the garish sun.

and, as a final emphasis on the ecumenical nature of the service, Julian Amery gave the address and Father Gabriel of the Holy Orthodox Church of Ethiopia pronounced the blessing.

A tribute from the younger generation came from Billy's own step-grandson, Cassian Elwes, who wrote a poem for the occasion:

In my dreams, you stopped and knelt.
As if by God, your hand was filled with the desert.
Though the Sun of David beat upon your head,
The sand was as cool as the waters of Wadi Rum.
The night was falling.
The shifting sand whispered the hearts
Of your friends beneath it:
Never forgotten.
Never forgotten.
You rose, the sand of time still falling
Through your fingers.
Behind a thousand gleaming swords
Of our Jihad twinkled, stars in
The Heaven of Aden.
Like Gordon and the Lionheart before him,
We were Crusaders in a holy Land.

The last of the three hymns, 'I vow to thee, my country . . . the service of my love', illustrated Billy's patriotism and the sense of dedication that had informed his life and moulded his career. He had put his ideals into practice but, modesty apart, the very nature of many of his exploits precluded their being universally recognised. As Harold Macmillan wrote to him in March 1979, 'You are one of those people whose services to our dear country are known only to a few . . . '

The many, meanwhile, will remember him as the last of the paladins, and an inspiration to the *beaux sabreurs* of the future.

References

Preface

xi	'Life at Tara . . . ': Amery, 329.
xii	Billy's 'intelligent blue eyes': Hoxha, 34 and 61.
xii	Billy's maddening expression: information from John Warrender.
xiii	Billy's reaction to probing questions: Patrick Leigh Fermor, 'Billy McLean', *Spectator*, 22 November 1986.

1 The Making of thc Man

1	Billy's ancestry: Sinclair, 36–58; Moncreiffe, 166–8.
1	Sir Harry Maclean: *Dictionary of National Biography, 1912–1921*, OUP, 1927.
2	Billy's father: information from Callum McLean.
3	Antecedents of Billy's mother: information from Patrick Pollock.
5	Billy's mother in Hungary: information from Boriska Karolyi.
7	Billy collecting old silver: Amery, 53.
7	Billy at Boulestin's: information from Hugh Henderson.

2 The Born Leader

11	Wingate's taste for Biblical allusions: Allen, 41.
12	The Abyssinian character: Allen, 33.
14	The Emperor's camp likened to Bonnie Prince Charlie's: Allen, 65.
20	The 'little rains': Allen, 114.
21	Older colleague's description of Billy: Allen, 124.

3 The Student of Intrigue

25	Billy's Abyssinian decoration: information from John Warrender.
27	Cairo, the Clapham Junction of the war: Amery, 285.
27	Exiled kings, etc. in Cairo: Foot, 158.

28   'It was widely known . . .': Amery, 306.
28   MI9 escape route: Foot, 38.
31   Pan-Turanism: Kinross, 46.

4 The Irregular Warrior

32   Julian's childhood: Amery, 26, 34.
36   Description of Abas Kupi: Amery, 164.
39   Description of ambush: Kemp, 108–10.
42   'None of that Wingate stuff . . .': Kemp, 152.

For the whole of this chapter in general: Smiley (1984), *passim*.

5 The Oriental Traveller

53   Description of the Colombo camp: Sweet-Escott, 231.
55–6   Journey across the Himalayas: Gordon Etherington-Smith, an
        unpublished diary.
63–4   Journey from Delhi to Tehran: Charles Rankin, an unpublished
        account.
63   'felt the presence of the river . . .': Byron, 236.
66   Hanging of Kurdish ringleaders: Eagleton, 121.
66   Estimation of Kurdish population: Schmidt (1964), 8*n*.

6 The Neophyte Civilian

70   Billy's large overdraft: information from Colin Mackenzie.
73   Daška's antecedents: Ivanović, 69.
75–6   Conditions in Albania: Bethell, 30–1.
76   'The position of the Albanian state . . .': Amery, 'The Case
        for Retaliation', *Time & Tide*, 22 January 1949.
78   Meeting with King Zog in Alexandria: Bethell, 65–6; Robyns,
        151.
81   Treachery at a high level: Philby, *passim*.

7 The Parliamentary Candidate

87   Independence of Indonesia: Dahm, 143; Brackman, 43.
87   Westerling's activity: Dahm, 147–8.

All personal information about Billy in this and every subsequent
chapter comes from Daška.

8 The Honourable Member

97	British policy in the Middle East: Epstein, 30.
97	Suez Group: Epstein, 41.
97	British troops in Middle East: Thomas, 11.
98	Baghdad pact: Trevelyan, 56–9.
102	Rioting in Amman: Trevelyan, 60.
102	Rioting in Bahrain: Trevelyan, 60.
103	Nationalisation of the Suez Canal: Epstein, 32.
105	Billy's activity in the Suez Group: information from Julian Amery and Katharine Macmillan.
105–6	French attitude to the nationalisation: Thomas, 48.
106	Anglo-French ultimatum: Epstein, 35–6.
106	Suez Group hails the operation: Epstein, 48.
106	Gaitskell furious: Thomas, 126.
106	Ceasefire resolution: Thomas, 134–7.
112–13	Dominick's report to Billy: information from Tessa Kennedy and Caroline Cabrera.
113	Natural for Cyprus to belong to Greece: Foley, 12; Hill, IV, 515–16; Stephens, 108–9.
114	Greekness of Cypriots: Storrs, 469–70.
114	Hopkinson's statement: Stephens, 136.
114	Cyprus a clear-cut case of imperialism: Stephens, 139.
116	Effect of the Iraqi *coup d'état* on Cyprus: Stephens, 139.
117	Events in Iraq after the *coup d'état*: Trevelyan, 139, 143.
118	Patrice Lumumba: Hyland, 86, 190.
120–1	Situation in the Congo when Billy arrived: Hempstone, 104–9.
122	Conference of Congolese leaders: Hempstone, 118–20.
123	Deterioration of the situation: Hempstone, 127–9.
123	Tshombe declares 'total war': Hempstone, 129.
124	Hammarskjöld's death: Hempstone, 134; Dayal, 178–9.
124	Shift in world opinion against Tshombe: Hempstone, 134.
127	Raid on central post office of Oran: Horne, 130.
127	Independence of Morocco and Tunisia: Horne, 130.

9 McLean of the Yemen

130	Sallal's coup: Holden and Johns, 224–5; el-Shoureki, 33; Loring, 14; Schmidt (1968), 20–35.
133	Importance of Billy's telegram: Holden and Johns, 228; Schmidt (1968), 191.
140	West Germany's recognition of Sallal: el-Shoureki, 38.
140	Arms secretly flown out from England: Holden and Johns, 229.

143–4	Disengagement treaty broken by both sides: Holden and Johns, 234.
146	David's view on mercenaries: Smiley (1975), 155.
147	Parachute drops from 'somewhere in Africa': Halliday, 140.
148	Emergence of Third Force: Bidwell, 209.
148	Erkwit meeting: Holden and Johns, 243; O'Ballance, 131; Schmidt (1968), 205.
150	Nasser's 'Vietnam': Bidwell, 209.
152	Sallal's downfall: O'Ballance, 183; Bidwell, 216.
153	Mohammed Hussein hesitates: Smiley (1975), 236.
154	Strenuous conditions in the Yemen: Thesiger, 271.
154	Billy's cigars: Thesiger, 274.
154	Siege of Sana: O'Ballance, 196; Schmidt (1968), 295–6; Bidwell, 217.
154	Mohammed Hussein 'Deputy Imam': O'Ballance, 201.
155	End of war: Bidwell, 217–18; Stookey, 254; Smiley (1975), 237.

10 The Scarlet Pimpernel

156	Russian delegation to the Highlands: information from Julian Amery and Daška.
160	FLN split into rival groups: Horne, 540; Gordon, 67.
161	For the Algerian adventure, I have relied on information from the principal participants. King Leka gave me his account of it in a long letter; Simon Courtauld made available the diary he kept at the time; and Peter Winter let me have a tape recording, from which I have quoted at length.

11 The Unofficial Under-Secretary

170	Billy's clarity of mind and purpose: Ivanović, 70.
171	'Though anything but a cynic . . . ': these words, written about Julian Amery (by Jonathan Guinness in the foreword to a Monday Club publication) apply equally well to Billy.
173	Creation of Israel and its consequences: Becker, 29.
174	Palestinians deliberately kept separate: Becker, 2–3.
174	Creation of PLO and *fedayeen*: Becker, 37–8.
175	The Six-Day War and its aftermath: Becker, 54–67.
175	Hussein's action against the *fedayeen*: Becker, 76–7.
177	Billy's boxes of cartridges: information from Hugh Henderson.
177	Billy's health: information from David Hay.
177	Discontent and unrest in Ethiopia: Thomson, 22–5, 42.
178	Creation of the Dergue: Thomson, 103.

185   Carter's opinion of the Shah: Shawcross, 21.

186   Anti-Shah demonstrations: Rubin, 256; Shawcross, 21.

186   Situation in Tehran in October: Shawcross, 27, 38, 110.

187   Shah's cancer: Rubin, 204.

187   Khomeini's move to France: Rubin, 220–2; Shawcross, 10.

190   Nasser's remark to Julian: Amery, *Daily Telegraph*, 26 November 1979.

192   Threat of Soviet imperialism: Amery, *Daily Telegraph*, 27 November 1979.

12 The Unrepentant Patriot

196   International terrorism: I have paraphrased *The Times* leader of 24 January 1985, which faithfully echoes Billy's views.

202   The Sickert painting: information from Daška and Tessa Kennedy.

203   The Royal Company of Archers: information from John Warrender.

206   Billy's private decameron: information from Marina Cobbold and Alexander Kennedy.

Bibliography

W. E. D. Allen, *Guerrilla War in Abyssinia*, Penguin, 1943.

Julian Amery, *Approach March*, Hutchinson, 1973.

Jillian Becker, *The PLO*, Weidenfeld & Nicolson, 1984.

Nicholas Bethell, *The Great Betrayal*, Hodder & Stoughton, 1984.

Robin Bidwell, *The Two Yemens*, Longman, 1983.

Arnold C. Brackman, *Indonesian Communism*, New York, 1963.

Robert Byron, *The Road to Oxiana*, Macmillan, 1937.

Bernhard Dahm, *History of Indonesia in the Twentieth Century*, Pall Mall Press, 1971.

Rajeshwar Dayal, *Mission for Hammarskjöld*, Oxford University Press, 1976.

William Eagleton Jr, *The Kurdish Republic of 1946*, Oxford University Press, 1963.

Leon D. Epstein, *British Politics in the Suez Crisis*, Pall Mall Press, 1964.

Charles Foley, *Legacy of Strife*, Penguin, 1964.

M. R. D. Foot, *Resistance*, Methuen, 1976.

David C. Gordon, *The Passing of French Algeria*, Oxford University Press, 1966.

Fred Halliday, *Arabia Without Sultans*, Penguin, 1974.

Smith Hempstone, *Katanga Report*, Faber, 1962.

Sir George Hill, *History of Cyprus*, 4 volumes, Cambridge University Press, 1940–52.

David Holden and Richard Johns, *The House of Saud*, Sidgwick & Jackson, 1981.

Alistair Horne, *A Savage War of Peace*, Macmillan, 1977.

Enver Hoxha, *The Anglo-American Threat to Albania*, Tirana, 1982.

Paul Hyland, *The Black Heart*, Gollancz, 1988.

Vane Ivanović, *LX. Memoirs of a Jugoslav*, Weidenfeld & Nicolson, 1977.

Peter Kemp, *No Colours or Crest*, Cassell, 1958.

Lord Kinross, *Atatürk*, Weidenfeld & Nicolson, 1964.

Ulick Loring, *The Yemeni Monarchy*, Monarchist Press Association, no date.

Ministry of Information, *The Abyssinian Campaign*, HMSO, 1942.
Sir Iain Moncreiffe of that Ilk, *The Highland Clans*, Barrie & Jackson, 1967.
Jawaharlal Nehru, *Toward Freedom*, New York, 1941.
Edgar O'Ballance, *The War in the Yemen*, Faber, 1971.
Mohammed Reza Pahlavi, *The Shah's Story*, Michael Joseph, 1980.
Kim Philby, *My Secret War*, Macgibbon & Kee, 1968.
Gwen Robyns, *Geraldine of the Albanians*, Mühler, Blond & White, 1987.
Barry M. Rubin, *Paved with Good Intentions*, Oxford University Press, 1980.
Dana Adams Schmidt, *Yemen: the Unknown War*, Bodley Head, 1968.
——, *Journey Among Brave Men*, Atlantic Monthly Press, 1964.
William Shawcross, *The Shah's Last Ride*, Chatto & Windus, 1989.
Ibrahim el-Shoureki, *The Bloody Strife in Yemen*, Ettela'at, 1965.
Rev. A. Maclean Sinclair, *The Clan Gillean*, Haszard & Moore, 1899.
David Smiley, *Albanian Assignment*, Chatto & Windus, 1984.
——, *Arabian Assignment*, Cooper, 1975.
Robert Stephens, *Cyprus: A Place of Arms*, Pall Mall Press, 1966.
Robert W. Stookey, *Yemen. The Politics of the Yemen Arab Republic*, Colorado, 1973.
Ronald Storrs, *Orientations*, Nicholson & Watson, 1949.
Bickham Sweet-Escott, *Baker Street Irregular*, Methuen, 1965.
Wilfred Thesiger, *Desert, Marsh and Mountain*, Collins, 1980.
Hugh Thomas, *The Suez Affair*, Weidenfeld & Nicolson, 1967.
Blair Thomson, *Ethiopia*, Robson, 1975.
Humphrey Trevelyan, *The Middle East in Revolution*, Macmillan, 1970.

Index

Abdullah, Crown Prince (Iraq), 114
Abdullah, King (Jordan), 101, 102, 173
Abdurrahman, Prince (Yemen), 132, 134, 141, 149
Abid, Maati ben, Moroccan prime minister, 191
Abyssinia, 11, 12–24; see also Ethiopia
Aden: British withdrawal from 151; consequences of, 153, 169, 178
Afghanistan, 62, 63, 88–9, 125, 193–4
Ahmed, Imam (Yemen), 130, 132
Ahmed, Hocine Ait, Algerian leader, 127, 129, 160–1, 168
Albania, 32, 33–51, 75–80, 198
Alexander, Crown Prince (Yugoslavia), 207
Algeria, 127–9, 160–1, 165–8
Alpetkin, Joseph, Central Asian refugee, 198–9
Amery, Catherine, née Macmillan, 72, 157
Amery, Julian, 32, 33, 36, 44, 45, 47, 49, 50, 51, 54, 71, 76, 77, 97, 104–7, 140, 156, 157, 181, 182, 190, 192, 193, 194, 200, 205, 207
Amery, Leo, Julian's father, 32, 71–2
Amery, Leo, Julian's son, 181
Anglo-Jordan Treaty, 102
Antibolshevik Bloc of Nations, 85–6
Arab Legion, 101, 102
Arafat, Yasser, 175
Arif, Abdul Salam, Iraqi president, 114, 117, 159
Armed Forces Co-ordinating Committee (Ethiopia) see Dergue, the

Asserate, Asfa-Wossen, 182, 207
Asserate Kasa, Ras, 169, 178, 180
Astor, Hugh, 155
Avars, Caucasian-speaking, 155

Badr, Imam Mohammed al- (Yemen), 130, 131, 132, 133, 141, 149, 154–5, 207
Baghdad Pact, 98, 101n, 108, 114
Baidani, Abdurrahman al-, Chairman of Free Yemenis, 134 and n, 135–6
Balfour, Arthur, British Foreign Secretary, 8n
Balfour Declaration, 8
Balkars, Turkic-speaking, 86
Balli Kombëtar, Albanian National Front, 36, 51; see also Zogists
Banac, Božo, Daška's stepfather, 73
Banac, Milica, née Popović, Daška's mother, 73, 79, 112, 161
Bannerman, John, 96
Barre, Challe Siad, Somali president, 184
Barzani, Mullah Mustafa, Kurdish leader, 67, 158–60, 173
Beaverbrook, Lord, 202
Bella, Ahmed Ben, Algerian leader, 127, 129, 160–1
Ben Sugen, Indochinese sect, 92
Biçi, Stiljan, Albanian interpreter, 39
Birrou, Fitaurari, Abyssinian leader, 16, 20, 22
Boumédienne, Houari, Algerian leader, 161
Brown, George, British foreign secretary, 152n
Butler, R. A., Lord Privy Seal, 105

'C' Section, 32n; *see also* Secret
   Intelligence Service
Cabrera, Caroline, *née* Kennedy, Billy's
   stepdaughter, 83
Cairo, the Clapham Junction of the
   war, 27
Cao-Daists, Indochinese sect, 92
Carter, President, 185, 187
Castro, Fidel, 184
Caxton Hall Register Office, 80
Cercle, Le, 205, 206
Chechens, 86
Chiang Kai-shek, 53
Churchill, Winston, 95, 98
Cobbold, Marina, *née* Kennedy,
   Billy's stepdaughter, 83, 111, 206
Condé, Abdurrahman, 139, 143
Congo, Belgian, 118–21, 122–4, 126
Convention of Defensive Alliance,
   113
Corfu Channel incident, 76
Courtauld, Simon, 161, 165, 166, 167
Cuduilig, Abbot of Lismore, 1
Curzon, Lord, 30
Cyprus, 107–8, 113–14, 116

da Gama, Christian, 122
da Gama, Vasco, 122
Daghestani, Ghazi, Iraqi major-
   general, 127
Dargins, 86
Danyo, Dedjaz, Abyssinian leader,
   16, 17, 18, 19, 20, 21, 22
David I, King (Scotland), 1
Davies, Brigadier 'Trotsky', 41, 42,
   43, 44, 45
Debra Tabor, 17, 19, 20, 21, 22
de Gaulle, Charles, 128
Dementyev, Pietr, Soviet minister of
   aviation, 156
Derbyshire, Norman, 64, 65
Dergue, the, 178, 182, 183, 184
Dibra League of Bajraktars, 36, 38
Douglas Force, Abyssinia, 22, 23, 24
Douglas-Hamilton, Lord Malcolm,
   93
Duffy, Lt Garry, 33
Dugald of Scone, Old, 1
Dulles, John Foster, 106
Dunn, Sir James, 202

EAM, Greek National Liberation
   Front, 34, 35, 36

Eden, Anthony, 43, 46, 51, 72, 98,
   106
EDES, National Republican Greek
   League, 34
EDU, Ethiopian Democratic Union,
   182, 183
Eisenhower, Dwight, 156
ELAS, Greek Popular Liberation
   Army, 35
ELF, Eritrean Liberation Front, 182
Elwes, Cassian, Billy's step-
   grandson, 207
Elwes, Damian, Billy's step-
   grandson, 181
Elwes, Dominick, 111–13
Elwes, Simon, 112
Elwes, Tessa *see* Kennedy, Tessa
EOKA, Cypriot Liberation
   Organisation, 107, 108, 114
Ermenye, Abas, Albanian leader, 50
Etherington-Smith, Gordon, 55–8
Ethiopia, 35n, 94–5, 121–2, 168–9,
   177–8, 182–4, 193; *see also* Abyssinia
Evian Treaty, 127, 128

Farouk, King (Egypt), 97, 101
Federation of South Arabia, later the
   People's Democratic Republic
   of Yemen, 132, 153
Feisal I, King (Iraq), 32
Feisal II, King (Iraq), 114
Feisal, Crown Prince, later King
   (Saudi Arabia), 135, 141, 147, 148,
   149, 150, 151
FLN, Algerian National Liberation
   Front, 127, 129, 161
Force Publique (Congo), 120
Foreign Legion, French, 91–3
Fraser, Hugh, 72
Freemasons, Billy's fear of, 100

Gaitskill, Hugh, 106
George II, King (Greece), 27, 46n
Geraldine, Queen (Albania), 32, 43
Gideon Force, Abyssinia, 11, 13, 25
Gillean of the Battle-Axe, 1
Glencalvie, McLean seat in
   Ross-shire, 3, 4, 74, 79
Glubb, General Sir John Bagot,
   101–2

Guarda, La, Daška's house in
Majorca, 172, 181, 202, 205–6

Haile Selassie, Emperor of
Abyssinia, 11, 14, 26, 121, 168
Hamid, General Shahid, 200–1
Hammarskjöld, Dag, 124, 126
Hanky, Lord, 97
Haq, Zia ul-, Pakistani premier,
193–4, 200
Harding, Field-Marshal Sir John,
107, 108
Hare, Alan, 41, 45, 48, 50, 72, 77,
80, 108
Hassan, King (Morocco), 191
Hassan, Prince Abdullah al-
(Yemen), 132, 133, 138–9, 141,
143, 155
Hassan, Crown Prince (Jordan), 176
Hassan, Crown Prince (Yemen), 132,
133, 137, 147–8
Hassan, Prince Hassan al- (Yemen),
132
Hector of the Battles, Red, 1
Hay, Dr David, 179–80
Hedin, Sven, 7
Hopkinson, Henry, 114
Hoxha, Enver, 37, 46, 48, 49, 53,
75, 81
Hua Hua, Indochinese sect, 92
Huang Hua, Chinese foreign minister,
182
Hunza, Mir of, 56, 200
Hussein, King (Jordan), 101–2, 107,
116, 126, 131, 135, 140–1, 152, 153,
177, 207
Hussein, Prince Abdullah (Yemen),
137–8, 141
Hussein, Prince Mohammed
(Yemen), 137, 147–8, 153, 154–5
Hussein, Sherif (Beihan), 132, 150

Ilyushin, S. V., 157
Indochina, 91–3
Indonesia, 87–8, 90
Ingushes, 86
Inverness, 93, 94, 95, 96, 99, 106,
108–9, 148
Iran, 64, 65, 83, 158–9, 172–3,
185–7
Iran, Shah of *see* Mohammed Reza
Shah Pahlavi

Iraq, 114–16, 117
Irvine of Drum, Sir Alexander, 1
Ismail, Prince Mohammed (Yemen),
133
Istanbul, centre of espionage, 30
Ivanović, Vane, Billy's brother-in-
law, 75, 171

James I, King (Scotland), 1
Jerusalem, Mufti of, 8, 101
Jordan, 101–2, 116, 126, 131, 173–7

Kalmucks, 60, 86
Karachays, 86
Karolyi, Countess Francesca,
('Fanny'), 5–6
Kasavubu, Joseph, Congolese
president, 118, 120, 122
Kashgar, 54, 56, 58, 59, 60
Kassem, Abdul Karim, Iraqi leader,
114, 115, 117, 159
Katanga, 118–21, 122–4, 126
Katherine, Crown Princess
(Yugoslavia), 207
Kazaks, 50, 54, 59, 62, 86
Kearns, Audrey *see* McLean, Audrey
Kearns, Grace, *née* Kelly, Billy's
maternal grandmother, 3
Kearns, Patrick, 3
Kemp, Peter, 38, 39–40, 161, 163
Kennedy, Alexander, Billy's stepson,
83, 111, 206
Kennedy, Caroline *see* Cabrera,
Caroline
Kennedy, Daška *see* McLean, Daška
Kennedy, Geoffrey, Daška's first
husband, 74
Kennedy, Marina *see* Cobbold,
Marina
Kennedy, President, 140
Kennedy, Tessa, Billy's
stepdaughter, 83, 111, 113, 202–3, 206
Khider, Mohammed, Algerian leader,
160–1, 168n
Khomeini, Ayatollah, 186, 187
Kibsy, Ibrahim al-, 137, 146
Killearn, Lord, 97
Kirghiz, 54, 58, 59, 62, 86
Kryeziu, Gani, Albanian tribal chief, 47
Kupi, Agha Abas, Zogist leader, 36,
38, 44, 45, 46, 47, 49–50, 51, 53

Kurds, 65, 66, 67, 126, 127, 158–9, 160, 173
Krushchev, Sergei, 157

Lachlan the Big-Bellied, 1
Lachlan the Crafty, 1
Lawrence, T. E., lessons to be learnt from, 12, 25
Lebanon, 124–5
Leka, Prince, later King (Albania), 32, 162, 163–5, 167, 197–8, 207
Lezgians, 86
Listowel, Lord, 72
Lloyd George, David, 32
LNC, Albanian National Liberation Movement, 36, 37, 43; *see also* Partisans
Lo, Ken, 203
Louis XVIII, King (France), 72n
Lovat, Lord, 72, 95, 156
Low, Robert, 78
Lumumba, Patrice, Congolese prime minister, 118, 120, 122

Mackenzie, Colin, 70, 207
Maclaine, Gillean, 2
Maclean, Sir Fitzroy, 97
Maclean, Sir Harry Aubrey de Vere, 1–2
McLean, Audrey, *née* Kearns, Billy's mother, 2, 3, 4, 5, 79, 146, 160, 170
McLean, Daška, *née* Ivanović, Billy's wife, 73, 79, 80, 81, 82, 83, 93, 100, 110, 111, 161, 171, 179, 202, 203, 205, 206
McLean, Gillian, Billy's brother, 3, 9
McLean, Godfrey, Billy's paternal uncle, 4
McLean, Neil, Billy's paternal grandfather, 2
McLean, Neil Gillean, Billy's father, 2, 3, 4, 7, 79, 146
McLean, Neil Loudon Desmond (Billy): ancestry, 1; parentage, 2; birth, 3; Eton, 6–7; Sandhurst, 7; joins Scots Greys, 7; in Palestine, 8–10; in Abyssinia, 10–25; joins SOE, 26; Yugoslav section, 28; joins MI9, 28; in Turkey, 29–31; rejoins SOE, 31; first mission to Albania, 33–43; wins DSO, 43; second mission to Albania, 44–52; in Ceylon, 53; journey from Delhi to Kashgar, 54–8; Kashgar, 59–61; back in Delhi, 61–2; journey from Delhi to Cairo, 63–8; resigns commission and stands for Parliament, 70; meets Daška, 73; adopted as candidate for Preston South, 75; engagement, 75; Albanian operation, 75–81; marriage in London, 80; wedding in Rome, 81; loses at Preston, 83; moodiness, 85; in Indonesia, 87–8; loses again at Preston, 89; Far East tour, 90–3; adopted as candidate for Inverness, 93; elected, 96; joins Suez Group, 97; nervous breakdown, 99–100; maiden speech, 101–3; Suez crisis, 103–7; in Middle East, 108; constituency work, 109–13; Iraq crisis, 114–16; in Jordan, 116; African tour, 118; in Congo, 120–1; return to Ethiopia, 121–2; criticises UN interference in Katanga, 123–4; in Lebanon and Afghanistan 124–5; plan for overthrowing Kassem in Iraq, 126–7; in Algeria, 127–9; in the Yemen 131–55; loses Inverness seat, 148, 157; in Iran to meet Barzani, 158–60; Algerian adventure, 161–8; in Ethiopia again, 169; mother dies, 170; in Iran again, 172–3; in Jordan, 175–7; illness, 177–9; in China, 182; in Mengistu's Ethiopia, 182–4; in Somalia, 184–5; in Iran in revolt, 185–8; in Egypt, 190; in Western Sahara, 191–2; in Pakistan, 193–4; in Egypt again, 194–5; in South Africa, 197–8; in Istanbul, 198–9; in Sinkiang on guided tour 199–200; in Pakistan with General Hamid, 200–1; Chinese Gourmet Club, 203; Royal Company of Archers, 203–4; Le Cercle, 205; final illness, 205–6; death, 207; funeral, 207–8
McLean of Ross, Neil, 1
McLean's 79th Foot, 22
Macmillan, Alexander, 105
Macmillan, Catherine, *see* Amery, Catherine
Macmillan, Harold, 51, 72, 117, 208
Macmillan, Katharine, *née* Ormsby-Gore, 72

Macmillan, Maurice, 72
Mao Tse-tung, 53
Margadale, Lord *see* Morrison, John
Mauritania, 191
Menant, Guy, 76
Menelik I, Emperor (Abyssinia), 122
Mengistu Haile Mariam, 182–3, 193
MI9, escape organisation, 28–9, 30
Mihajlović, Draža, 46n
Mikoyan, Arten, 157
Mobutu, Joseph, Congolese chief-of-
staff, 120, 122
Mohammed Reza Shah Pahlavi, 172,
185–7, 188, 189
Moncreiffe of that Ilk, Sir Iain, 177
Morocco, 127, 172, 191–2
Mubarak, Hosni, 194–5
Mulay Hassan, Sultan, 1–2

Nahas Pasha, 105
Nasser, Colonel Gamel, 97, 103, 104,
115, 130, 135, 136, 150, 151, 173–4,
190
National Liberation Front (PDRY), 153
Neil of the Thumbs, 1
Norodom, King (Cambodia), 93
Northern Force, Abyssinia, 15–16, 18,
20
Nuri Said, Iraqi premier, 114, 116

O'Brien, Conor Cruise, 123
Organisation Armée Secrète (OAS),
Algeria, 128 and n, 129
Ormsby-Gore, David, 72
Ormsby-Gore, Katharine, *see*
Macmillan, Katharine
Ossetians, Iranian-speaking, 86

Paget, General, 44
Pakhtunistan, 88–9
Pakistan, 88, 193–4, 200–1
Palestine, 8–9, 173
Palestine Liberation Organisation
(PLO), 173–4, 175, 192, 194
Pan-Turanism, 31
Papagos, Field-Marshal, 77
Partisans, 35, 37, 38, 47
Paterson, W., 96
People's Democratic Republic of
Yemen (PDRY), 153
Persian Gulf, British withdrawal from,
172, 193

Peter, King (Yugoslavia), 27
Philby, Kim, 81
Popular Front for the Liberation of
the Occupied Arab Gulf, 189
Popular Front for the Liberation of
Saguia el Hamra and Rio de Oro
(Polisario), 191, 192, 193
Powell, Enoch, 97

Rainier, Prince (Monaco), 3, 161
Raisuli, Sherif, 2
Rankin, Charles, 63, 64
Reza Shah Pahlavi (Iran), 188
Rommel, Field-Marshal, 28, 31
Rothschild, Lord, 8n
Royal Company of Archers, 203–4
Royal Scots Greys, 7, 9, 10, 25–6,
42, 94, 204

Sadat, Anwar, 190–1, 194
Sahara, Western, 190–2
Saharan Arab Democratic Republic,
191
St Oswald, Lord, 72
SS Luca e Martina al Foro Romano,
Church of, 81
Salisbury, Lord, 200
Sallal, Abdullah, Yemeni rebel, 130,
131, 152, 153
Sandford, Brigadier Dan, 25
Sandys, Duncan, 153, 155
Saud, King (Saudi Arabia), 131, 133,
140, 141
Saudi Arabia, 131, 133, 140
SAVAK, Iranian secret police, 158–9,
186, 187
Sayaghi, Ahmed al-, 132, 141
Seale, Patrick, 139
Secret Intelligence Service (SIS), 32
Selbourne, Lord, 53
Shamy, Ahmed al-, 141, 147
Shishakli, Colonel, 101
Sickert, Walter, 202
Sinkiang, 54, 55, 60, 61, 62, 198–9
Six-Days War, 102n, 152
Sjahir, Sjutan, Indonesian leader, 90
Smiley, David, 9, 33, 34, 36 and n,
38, 43, 44, 45, 47, 49, 50, 51, 77,
145, 146, 152, 158, 207
Smith, Major Victor, 48
Somalia, 183, 184–5
Somaliland, British, 9

Somaliland Camel Corps, 9, 33
Spahiu, Bedri, partisan leader,
    35, 36
Special Operations Executive (SOE),
    cover names for, 26n
Stein, Aurel, 7
Storrs, Sir Ronald, 114
Suez Canal, 98, 103–4, 106
Suez Group, 97, 104–5, 106

Talal, King (Jordan), 101
Tajiks, 50, 62, 86
Tartars, 54, 103
Thatcher, Margaret, 189, 192, 194, 195
Thesiger, Wilfred, 154
Tito, Marshal, 76
Toptani, Ihsan, 49, 51
Tshombe, Moise, 119, 121, 122,
    124, 126
Tungans, 55
Turkestan, 62, 86, 88
Turkis, 54, 57, 60
Turkish cuisine, 30, 58
Turkomans, 50, 63

Union for the Defence of Christianity
    (UMDC), Indochina, 92
United Nations: troops in Egypt, 106;

in the Congo and Katanga, 119–20,
    123–4
Universal Suez Maritime Canal
    Company, 104
Uzbeks, 50, 54, 62, 86

Wahba, Sheikh Hafiz, 140
Warrender, John, 204
Waterhouse, Captain Charles, 97
Watson, Edward, 2
Wavell, Field-Marshal Lord, 61
Westerling 'Turk', 87 and n
Whakhis, 62
Williamson, Corporal, 33, 37, 38, 42
Wilson, General, 51
Wingate, Lt. Col. Orde, 11, 15, 16n,
    23, 25
Winn, Rowland *see* St Oswald, Lord
Winter, Peter, 162–5

Yahya, Imam (Yemen), 147
Yemen Arab Republic, 155
Yemen Imamate, 130–3, 134–9,
    140–6, 155

Zog, King (Albania), 32, 36, 43, 45,
    46 and n, 78
Zogists, 36, 38, 47